Year in London

year ahead – there are festivals, cultural events and fairs to look
porting calendar culminating with the Athletics World Championships.
2 all over again, with sports fever gripping the capital. From left: Chinese New
ea Flower Show (p10); St Patrick's Day Parade (p8); Notting Hill Carnival (p13)

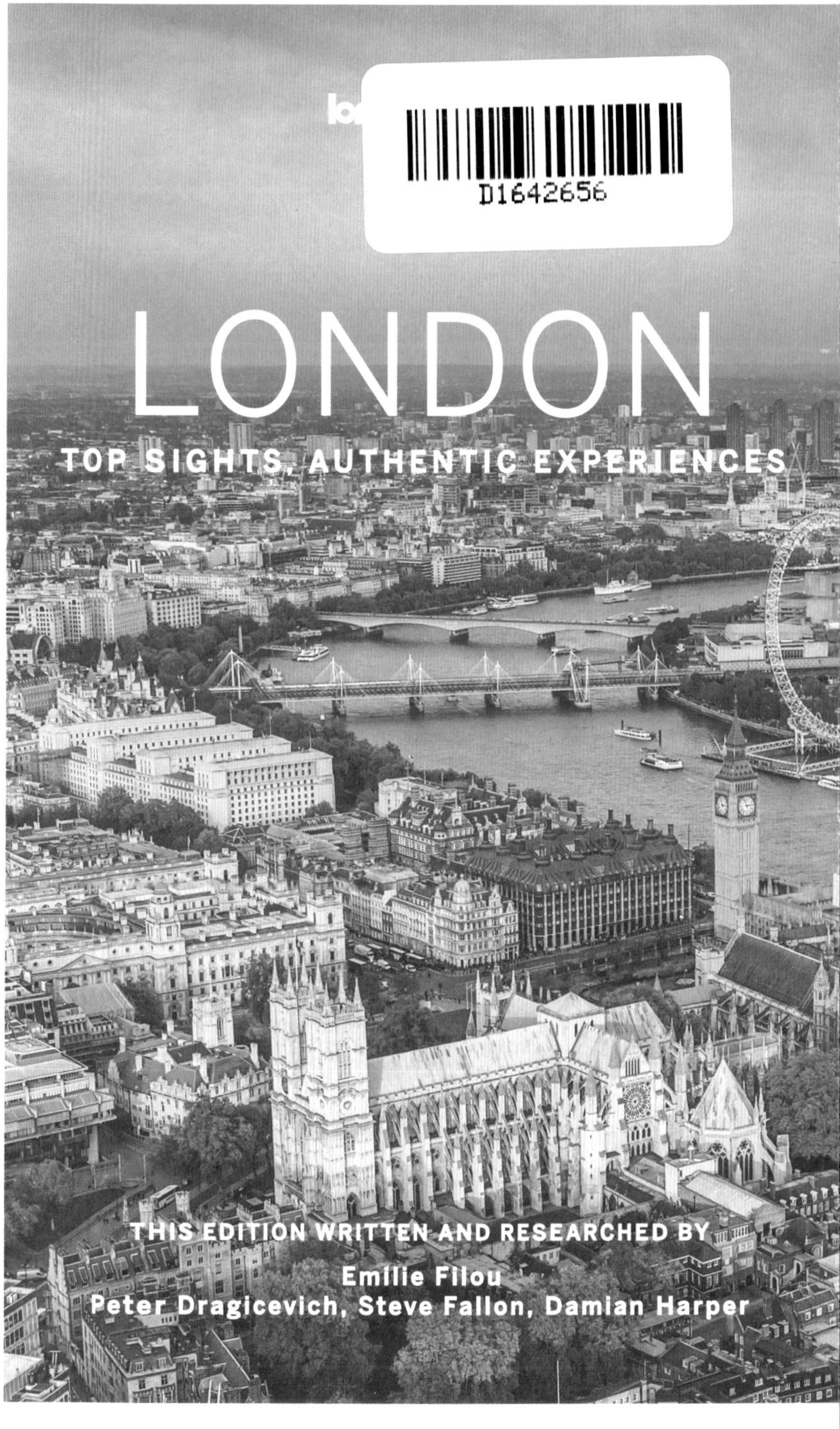

LONDON

TOP SIGHTS, AUTHENTIC EXPERIENCES

THIS EDITION WRITTEN AND RESEARCHED BY

Emilie Filou

Peter Dragicevich, Steve Fallon, Damian Harper

Camden & North London
Parks, markets and Camden and Islington after dark guarantee a glorious day and night out. *(Map p256)*

Clerkenwell, Shoreditch & Spitalfields
Good food and a great night out in one of London's trendiest areas. *(Map p255)*

The West End
The beating heart of London, with iconic sights, shopping and nightlife. *(Map p252)*

Kensington & Hyde Park
Three world-class museums and the largest of the royal parks in a well-heeled district. *(Map p249)*

King's Cross & Euston
Euston
British Museum
SOHO
National Portrait Gallery
National Gallery
Trafalgar Square
Hyde Park
Churchill War Rooms
Buckingham Palace
Natural History Museum
Victoria & Albert Museum
Victoria

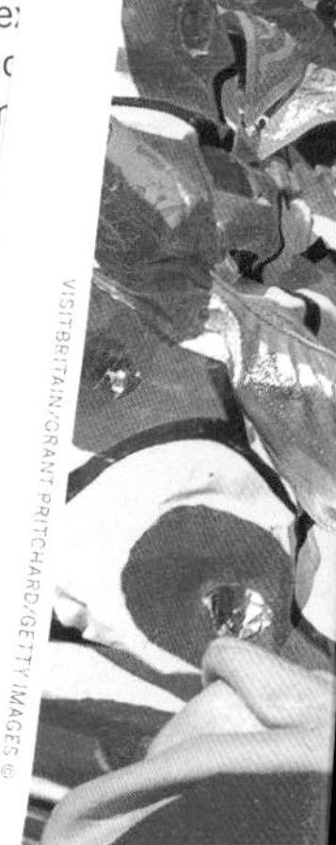

JUSTIN TALLIS/AFP/GETTY IMAGES ©

Top Festivals & Events

Wimbledon Lawn Tennis Championships – July (p12)

Notting Hill Carnival – August (p13)

World Athletics Championships – August (p13)

Guy Fawkes Night – November (p16)

New Year's Celebrations – December (p17)

LEFT: PETER MACDIARMID/GETTY IMAGES ©; RIGHT: NEIL EMMERSON/GETTY IMAGES ©

Plan Your Trip
This Year in London

January

January in London kicks off with a big bang at midnight. London is in the throes of winter, with short days: light appears at 8am and is all but gone by 4pm.

18–22 January

London Art Fair

Over 100 major galleries participate in this contemporary art fair (www.londonartfair.co.uk), now one of the largest in Europe, with thematic exhibitions, special events and the best emerging artists.

Late January

☆ London International Mime Festival

Held in the last two weeks of January, this festival (www.mimefest.co.uk) is a must for lovers of originality, playfulness, physical talent and the unexpected.

28 January

Chinese New Year

Chinatown fizzes, crackles and pops during this colourful street festival, which includes a Golden Dragon parade, eating and partying.

January

Tate Modern Extension

Opened in June 2016, the new Tate Modern extension makes an already fabulous museum even more compelling. Check out the permanent collection in its new home and dwell in those wonderful South Bank views.

Above: Performers from the London International Mime Festival; Right: Chinese New Year parade

February

February is usually chilly, wet and even snow-encrusted. Schools break off for a week mid-month when museums and parks swell with children on holidays.

12 February

☆ BAFTAs

The British Academy of Film and Television Arts (BAFTA; www.bafta.org) rolls out the red carpet on Leicester Sq to hand out its annual cinema awards, the BAFTAs (the British Oscars, if you will). Expect plenty of celebrity glamour.

14 February

☆ Valentine's Day

Whether you're single or part of a loved-up couple, you'll be able to choose from themed and alternative parties, special movie nights and dedicated menus. Book ahead as it's a popular night.

February

☆ A Night at the Opera

The nights are long and cold so what better way to cosy up than inside the stunning Royal Opera House (p192) to revel in world-class opera or ballet? (Plus it's a great chance to dress up.)

MICHAELPUCHE/SHUTTERSTOCK ©

28 February

Pancake Races

On Shrove Tuesday, you can catch pancake races and associated silliness at various venues around town (Spitalfields Market, in particular).

Plan Your Trip

This Year in London

March

March sees spring in the air and trees beginning to flower, most colourfully in parks and gardens. London is getting in the mood to head outdoors again.

19 March

St Patrick's Day & Parade

This is the top festival for the Irish in London, held on the Sunday closest to 17 March, with a colourful parade through central London and other festivities in and around Trafalgar Sq.

March

Flare

This LGBT film festival, organised by the British Film Institute (www.bfi.org.uk/flare), runs a packed program of film screenings, along with parties, talks and events for schools and families.

25 March

Head of the River Race

Some 400 crews take part in this colourful annual boat race (www.horr.co.uk) held over a 7km course on the Thames, from Mortlake to Putney.

March

Spring Watch

Spring is in the air – the days are getting longer, it's mild, the daffodils carpet the capital's lawns, the squirrels are out in force – head to Hyde Park or St James's Park for a giddy walk in the spring air.

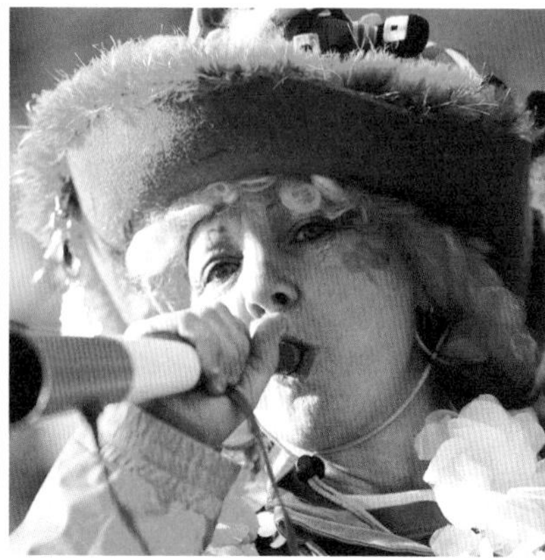

Above: Spring in Hyde Park; Right: St Patrick's Day festivities

April

April sees London in bloom, with warmer days and a spring in everyone's step. British summer time starts late March, so it's now light until 7pm. Some sights previously shut for winter reopen.

2 April

Oxford & Cambridge Boat Race

Crowds line the banks of the Thames to witness the country's two most famous universities going oar-to-oar from Putney to Mortlake (www.theboatraces.org).

April–July

☆ Udderbelly Festival

Housed in a temporary venue in the shape of a purple upside-down cow on the South Bank, this festival (www.udderbelly.co.uk) of comedy, circus and general family fun has become a spring favourite. Events run from April to July.

April

☆ London Coffee Festival

From robusta to arabica and barista, Londoners have become obsessed with coffee. This festival (www.londoncoffeefestival.com) notably hosts the UK Barista Championship.

April to mid-October

☆ Shakespeare's Globe Theatre

Watch the works of the world's most famous playwright in a faithful reproduction of a 17th-century theatre (p195). The theatre is outdoors and most of the audience is standing.

SAMIR HUSSEIN/WIREIMAGE/GETTYIMAGES ©

23 April

London Marathon

Some 35,000 runners – most running for charity – pound through London in one of the world's biggest road races (www.virginmoneylondonmarathon.com), heading from Greenwich Park to the Mall.

Plan Your Trip

This Year in London

May

A delightful time to be in London: days are warming up and Londoners begin to start lounging around in parks, particularly over the month's two bank holiday weekends (the first and the last).

17–20 May

⊙ Museums at Night

Numerous museums across London open after-hours (www.museumsatnight.org.uk), with candlelit tours, spooky atmospheres, sleepovers and special events such as talks and concerts.

23–27 May

⊙ Chelsea Flower Show

The world's most renowned horticultural event (www.rhs.org.uk/chelsea) attracts the cream of London's green-fingered and flower-mad gardeners.

May–September

☆ London Wonderground

Where else would you get a festival devoted to the art of circus and cabaret? There are dedicated family and children's shows, as well as mainstream performances (www.londonwonderground.co.uk).

London Wonderground

2017

June

The peak season begins with long, warm days (it's light until 10pm), pavement drinking and lots of alfresco events.

1–30 June

London Festival of Architecture

This month-long celebration of London's built environment (www.londonfestivalofarchitecture.org) explores the significance of architecture and design and how London has become a centre for innovation in these fields.

17 June

Trooping the Colour

The Queen's official birthday (www.trooping-the-colour.co.uk) is celebrated with plenty of flag-waving, parades, pageantry and noisy flyovers.

June

Open Garden Squares Weekend

Over one weekend, more than 200 gardens in London that are usually inaccessible to the public fling open their gates for exploration (www.opensquares.org).

June–August

Royal Academy Summer Exhibition

Beginning in June and running through to August, this exhibition at the Royal Academy of Arts (p49) showcases works submitted by artists from all over Britain, distilled to a thousand or so pieces.

ROB STOTHARD/GETTY IMAGES ©

June

Pride in London

The gay community paints the town pink in this annual extravaganza (www.prideinlondon.org), featuring a smorgasbord of experiences, from talks to live events, and culminating in a huge parade across London.

Year in London

July

This is the time to eat strawberries, drink in beer gardens and join in outdoor activities. Summer events (especially music festivals) are very popular and sell out months in advance, so plan ahead.

July

☆ Wireless

One of London's top music festivals, with an emphasis on dance and R&B, Wireless (www.wirelessfestival.co.uk) takes place in Finsbury Park in northeast London.

BOB THOMAS/GETTY IMAGES ©

3–16 July

Wimbledon Lawn Tennis Championships

For two weeks a year, the quiet South London village of Wimbledon falls under a sporting spotlight as the world's best tennis players gather to battle for the championships.

Mid-July to Mid-September

☆ BBC Promenade Concert (The Proms)

The Proms offer two months of outstanding classical concerts (www.bbc.co.uk/proms) at various prestigious venues, centred on the Royal Albert Hall. Every concert has standing tickets available on the day.

July

☆ Lovebox

This two-day music celebration (www.loveboxfestival.com) in Victoria Park in East London was created by dance duo Groove Armada in 2002. Although its raison d'être is dance music, there are plenty of other genres featured, including indie, pop and hip-hop.

July

☆ Greenwich Comedy Festival

This week-long laugh fest – London's largest comedy festival (www.greenwichcomedyfestival.co.uk) – brings big names and emerging acts to the National Maritime Museum.

August

Schools have broken up for summer, families are holidaying and the hugely popular annual Caribbean carnival dances into Notting Hill.

August

☆ Summer Screen at Somerset House

For a fortnight, Somerset House turns its stunning courtyard into an open-air cinema (www.somersethouse.org.uk/film) screening an eclectic mix of film premieres, cult classics and popular requests.

August

Great British Beer Festival

Organised by CAMRA (Campaign for Real Ale), this boozy festival (www.gbbf.org.uk) cheerfully cracks open casks of ale from the UK and abroad at the Olympia exhibition centre.

5–13 August

World Athletics Championships

London is hosting the 2017 World Athletics Championships (www.london2017athletics.com) at the Olympics Stadium in east London. Expect Londoners to rekindle their 2012 Olympic fever. The championships for Para-athletics take place 15 to 23 July.

26–28 August

Notting Hill Carnival

Europe's biggest – and London's most vibrant – outdoor carnival is a celebration of Caribbean London, featuring music, dancing and costumes over the summer bank-holiday weekend.

Great British Beer Festival

Plan Your Trip

This Year in London

September

The end of summer is a lovely time to be in town; the weather is usually good, the kids have gone back to school, and properties normally shut to the public open their doors for one weekend.

1–30 September

Totally Thames

Celebrating the River Thames, this cosmopolitan festival (www.totallythames.org) sees fairs, street theatre, music, food stalls, fireworks and river races.

15–19 September

London Fashion Week

If you love fashion, don't miss out on this ultimate fashion experience. Highlights include exclusive access to catwalk shows, curated talks, designer shopping and trend presentations.

16–17 September

Open House London

For one weekend only, the public is invited in to see over 700 heritage buildings throughout the capital that are normally off-limits (www.openhouselondon.org.uk). Expect queues at the most high-profile sites.

September

Picnic in Hyde Park

Before the autumnal air settles in, get some picnic supplies in town, find a sunny spot, hire a deck chair and enjoy an alfresco meal in the royal park.

…: Tall Ships Festival at

…ARMID/

October

The weather is getting colder, but London's parklands are splashed with gorgeous autumnal colours. Clocks go back to winter time on the last weekend of the month.

October

Autumn Walks

London's parks look truly glorious on a sunny day when the trees have turned a riot of yellows and reds. Hyde Park and Greenwich Park are beautiful at this time of year and offer great views of London's landmarks, too.

October

☆ Dance Umbrella

London's annual festival of contemporary dance (www.danceumbrella.co.uk) features three weeks of performances by British and international dance companies at venues across London.

October

Affordable Art Fair

For four days, Battersea Park turns into a giant art fair (www.affordableartfair.com/battersea), where more than 100 galleries offer works of art from just £100. There are plenty of talks and workshops, too.

JOHN PHILLIPS/GETTY IMAGES © for BFI

October

☆ London Film Festival

The city's premier film event (www.bfi.org.uk/lff) attracts big overseas names and you can catch over 100 British and international films before their cinema release. Masterclasses are given by world-famous directors.

Plan Your Trip

This Year in London

November

London nights are getting longer, but they crackle with fireworks in the first week of November. Schools usually break for holidays the first week of the month.

5 November

Guy Fawkes Night (Bonfire Night)

Bonfire Night commemorates Guy Fawkes' foiled attempt to blow up Parliament in 1605. Bonfires and fireworks light up the night, with Primrose Hill, Highbury Fields, Alexandra Palace, Clapham Common and Blackheath hosting some of the best firework displays.

11 November

Lord Mayor's Show

In accordance with the Magna Carta of 1215, the newly elected Lord Mayor of the City of London travels in a state coach from Mansion House to the Royal Courts of Justice to take an oath of allegiance to the Crown. The floats, bands and fireworks that accompany the Mayor (www.lordmayors show.london) were added later.

Mid-November

Lighting of the Christmas Lights

A celebrity is normally carted in to switch on all the festive lights that line Oxford, Regent and Bond streets, and a towering Norwegian spruce is set up in Trafalgar Sq.

Mid-November

London Jazz Festival

Musicians from around the world swing into town for 10 days of jazz (www.efg londonjazzfestival.org.uk). World influences are well represented, as are more conventional strands.

Above: Christmas lights on Regent Street; Right: Lord Mayor's Show

PAWEL LIBERA/LIGHTROCKET/GETTY IMAGES ©; THOMAS OWEN JENKINS/LIGHTROCKET/SHUTTERSTOCK ©

December

London may see snow and a festive mood reigns as Christmas approaches and the city's streets don lights and decorations. London shuts down on Christmas Day, with virtually no public transport.

December

☆ Catch a Musical

Just like Broadway, London has an embarrassment of riches when it comes to musicals: from classics *(Phantom of the Opera)* to more recent additions *(Matilda)*, kids' favourites *(Lion King)* to grown-up treats *(Book of Mormon)*.

December

Ice Skating

From mid-November until January, open-air ice rinks pop up across the city, including one in the exquisite courtyard of Somerset House (p69) and another one in the grounds of the Natural History Museum (p112).

December

Christmas Shopping

London has everything you could possibly want – and more. Hamleys (p160) and its five storeys of toys will mesmerise children, Harrods (p164) will wow with its sheer extravagance, and the Christmas decorations everywhere will put a spring in your step.

GARY YEOWELL/GETTY IMAGES ©

31 December

New Year's Celebrations

The famous countdown to midnight with Big Ben is met with terrific fireworks from the London Eye and massive crowds. The best spots to watch are now ticketed (www.london.gov.uk).

Plan Your Trip
Need to Know

Daily Costs

Budget
Less than £85

- Dorm bed: £10–32
- Market-stall lunch £5, supermarket sandwich £3.50–4.50
- Many museums: free
- Standby theatre tickets: £5–25
- Santander Cycles daily rental fee: £2

Midrange
£85–185

- Double room in a midrange hotel: £100–200
- Two-course dinner with a glass of wine: £35
- Theatre ticket: £15–60

Top End
More than £185

- Four-star/boutique hotel room: £200
- Three-course dinner in a top restaurant with wine: £60–90
- Black-cab trip: £30
- Top theatre ticket: £65

Advance Planning

- **Three months before** Book weekend performances of top shows; make dinner reservations for renowned restaurants with celebrity chefs; snatch up tickets for must-see temporary exhibitions; book accommodation at boutique properties.
- **One month before** Check listings for fringe theatre, live music and festivals on entertainment sites such as Time Out, and book tickets.
- **A few days before** Check the weather on the Met Office website (www.metoffice.gov.uk).

Useful Websites

- **Lonely Planet** (www.lonelyplanet.com/london) Bookings, traveller forum and more.
- **Time Out London** (www.timeout.com/london) Up-to-date and comprehensive listings.
- **Londonist** (www.londonist.com) A website about London and everything that happens in it.
- **Transport for London** (www.tfl.gov.uk) Essential tool for staying mobile in the capital.

Currency
Pound sterling (£)

Language
English

Visas
Not required for US, Canadian, Australian, New Zealand or South African visitors for stays of up to six months. EU nationals can stay indefinitely.

Money
ATMs are widespread. Major credit cards are accepted everywhere. The best place to change money is in post office branches, which do not charge a commission.

Mobile Phones
Buy local SIM cards for European and Australian phones, or a pay-as-you-go phone. Set other phones to international roaming.

Time
London is on GMT; during British Summer Time (BST; late March to late October), London clocks are one hour ahead of GMT.

Tourist Information
Visit London (www.visitlondon.com) can fill you in on everything you need to know.

When to Go

Summer is peak season: days are long and festivals are afoot, but expect crowds. Spring and autumn are cooler, but delightful. Winter is cold, but quiet.

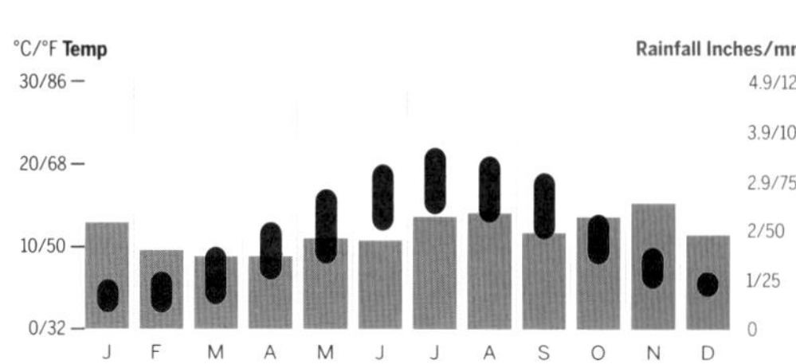

Arriving in London

- **Heathrow Airport** Trains, London Underground (tube) and buses to central London from just after 5am to before midnight (night buses run later) £5.70 to £21.50; taxi £45 to £85.
- **Gatwick Airport** Trains to central London from 4.30am to 1.35am, £10 to £20; hourly buses to central London around the clock from £5; taxi £100.
- **Stansted Airport** Trains to central London from 5.30am to 1.30am, £23.40; round-the-clock buses to central London from £12; taxi from £130.
- **Luton Airport** Trains to central London from 7am to 10pm from £14; round-the-clock buses to central London £10; taxi £110.
- **London City Airport** DLR trains to central London from 5.30am to 12.30am Monday to Saturday, 7am to 11.15pm Sunday from £2.80; taxi around £30.

Digital London

There are scores of cool apps for travellers. Here are some of our favourite free ones – from inspirational to downright practical. Many museums and attractions also have their own.

- **Streetmuseum** Historical images (photographs, paintings, drawings etc) superimposed on modern-day locations.
- **Street Art Tours London** Hand-picked graffiti and other street-art locations.
- **Soho Stories** Social history of London's most Bohemian neighbourhood, told through poems and extracts from novels and newspapers.
- **Uber** A taxi, private car or rideshare at competitive prices.
- **Hailo** Summons the nearest black cab right to the curb.
- **London Bus Live** Real-time route finder and bus arrivals for a stop of your choice.
- **Santander Cycles** Find a bike, a route and a place to return it.
- **ToiletFinder** Where to find one when you need it most.

Sleeping

Hanging your hat (and anything else you care to remove) in London can be painfully expensive, and you'll almost always need to book your room well in advance. Decent, central hostels are easy enough to find and also offer reasonably priced double rooms. Bed and breakfasts are a dependable and inexpensive, if rather simple, option. Hotels range from cheap, no-frills chains through boutique choices to luxury five-star historic hotels.

For more information, see the **Survival Guide** (p232)

Top Days in London

The West End & the South Bank

Plunge into the heart of the West End for some of London's top sights. This itinerary also spans the River Thames to the South Bank, taking in Westminster Abbey, Buckingham Palace, Trafalgar Square, the Houses of Parliament and the London Eye.

Day 01

❶ Westminster Abbey (p36)

Begin at Westminster Abbey to steep yourself in British history back to 1066.

➡ Westminster Abbey to Buckingham Palace

🚶 Cross the road to Storey's Gate and walk west along Birdcage Walk.

❷ Buckingham Palace (p46)

Peer through the gates, go on a tour of the interior (summer only) or catch the Changing of the Guard at 11.30am.

➡ Buckingham Palace to Inn the Park

🚶 Stroll through lovely St James's Park to the northeast corner.

❸ Lunch at Inn the Park (p138)

Set on the lake in St James's Park, this lovely cafe-restaurant is a particularly fine place in the warmer months.

➡ Inn the Park to Trafalgar Sq

🚶 Walk along the Mall and under Admiralty Arch to Trafalgar Sq.

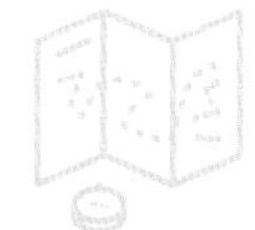

SYLVAIN SONNET/GETTY IMAGES ©

❹ Trafalgar Square (p58)

Visit London's epicentre (all distances are measured from here), and explore the National Gallery (p54).

➡ Trafalgar Sq to Houses of Parliament

🚶 Walk down Whitehall.

❺ Houses of Parliament (p50)

Dominating the east side of Parliament Sq is the Palace of Westminster, with one of London's ultimate sights, Big Ben.

➡ Houses of Parliament to London Eye

🚶 Cross Westminster Bridge.

❻ London Eye (p102)

Hop on a 'flight' on the London Eye. Pre-book tickets online or grab a fast-track ticket to shorten wait times.

➡ London Eye to Skylon

🚶 Walk 100m north to the Royal Festival Hall.

❼ Dinner at Skylon (p143)

Just steps away from the Eye, atop the Royal Festival Hall, is this fine restaurant, grill and bar. To tie up the day, consider a concert or a play at the National Theatre (p194) next door.

From left: Exterior of Westminster Abbey (p36); Big Ben and the Houses of Parliament (p50)

Top Days in London

History, Views & a Spot of Shakespeare

Get set for more of London's top sights – once again on either side of the Thames. Visit the British Museum in Bloomsbury, climb the dome of St Paul's Cathedral, explore the Tower of London and soak up some Shakespeare.

Day 02

❶ British Museum (p42)

Begin with a visit to the British Museum and ensure you tick off the highlights, including the Rosetta Stone, the Egyptian mummies and the Parthenon Marbles.

British Museum to St Paul's Cathedral

Take the Central Line from Holborn or Tottenham Court Rd to St Paul's.

❷ St Paul's Cathedral (p80)

Enjoy a light lunch (and scrumptious desserts) at Bea's of Bloomsbury (p141) before exploring the cathedral across the way. Don't miss climbing the dome for its astounding views of London, and save plenty of time for visiting the fascinating crypt.

St Paul's Cathedral to Tower of London

Hop on bus 15 from the cathedral to the Tower of London.

PETER ADAMS/GETTY IMAGES ©

❸ Tower of London (p74)

The millennium of history contained within the Tower of London, including the Crown Jewels, Traitors' Gate, the White Tower and its armour collection, and the all-important resident ravens, deserves at least a couple of hours to fully explore.

➔ Tower of London to Tower Bridge

Walk along Tower Bridge Approach from the Tower of London to Tower Bridge.

❹ Tower Bridge (p86)

Cross the Thames via elegant Tower Bridge, popping into the exhibition en route. Check the website for bridge lift times if you want to see it open and close.

➔ Tower Bridge to Oblix at the Shard

Stroll west along the river to the Shard; the entrance is on St Thomas St.

❺ Drinks at Oblix (p179)

Round off the day with drinks, live music and fabulous views of London from the 32nd floor of the Shard, London's most spectacular skyscraper.

➔ Oblix at the Shard to Shakespeare's Globe

Walk through Borough Market and then follow the Thames west to Shakespeare's Globe.

❻ A Play at Shakespeare's Globe (p195)

Watch one of Shakespeare's famous plays in a theatre as it would have been in Shakespeare's day: outdoors in summer months in the Globe, or by candlelight in the Playhouse.

From left: Tower Bridge (p86); The dome at St Paul's Cathedral (p82)

Plan Your Trip

Top Days in London

STUART BLACK/GETTY IMAGES ©

Kensington Museums, Knightsbridge Shopping & the West End

Passing through some of London's most attractive and well-heeled neighbourhoods, this route takes in three of the city's best museums and a world-famous department store before delivering you to the bright lights of the West End.

Day

❶ Victoria & Albert Museum (p108)

Start your day in South Kensington, home to several of the best museums in the city. Cross off some of the Victoria & Albert's 146 galleries, but leave a little time for the huge Natural History Museum (p112) and the interactive Science Museum (p115).

Victoria & Albert Museum to Kensington Gardens & Hyde Park

Walk north along Exhibition Rd to Kensington Gardens.

❷ Kensington Gardens & Hyde Park

Follow the museums with an exploration of Kensington Gardens (p107) and Hyde Park (p104). Make sure you take a look at the Albert Memorial (p107) and the Royal Albert Hall (p196), take a peek inside Kensington Palace (p106) and stroll along the Serpentine.

Kensington Gardens & Hyde Park to Magazine

Stroll through Hyde Park to Magazine, in the middle of the park by the Serpentine Sackler Gallery.

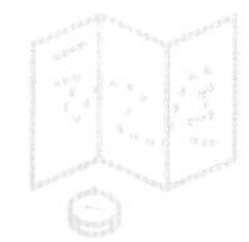

BRENT WINEBRENNER/GETTY IMAGES ©

❸ Lunch at Magazine (p145)

Dine on lovely modern European food in the other-wordly undulating building designed by prize-winning architect Zaha Hadid. Afternoon tea is another great option.

Magazine to Harrods

Walk down West Carriage Drive and then across Knightsbridge to reach Harrods.

❹ Harrods (p164)

A visit to Harrods is both fun and fascinating, even if you don't plan to buy anything. The food court is a great place for edible souvenirs.

Harrods to Piccadilly Circus

Walk to Knightsbridge station, then take the Piccadilly Line three stops to Piccadilly Circus.

❺ Piccadilly Circus (p73)

Jump off the tube at this busy roundabout to have a look at the famous statue (Eros' brother) and enjoy a night out in Soho.

Piccadilly Circus to Yauatcha

Walk up Shaftesbury Ave and turn left onto Rupert St, which becomes Berwick St, then left into Broadwick St.

❻ Dinner at Yauatcha (p71)

For the most sophisticated and exquisite dim sum, Yauatcha is unrivalled. The selection of tea is second to none. Bookings are essential.

Yauatcha to Experimental Cocktail Club

Head back down to take a left on Shaftesbury Ave, then right on Wardour St down to Gerrard St. Look for the shabby door next to the Four Seasons restaurant.

❼ Drinks at Experimental Cocktail Club (p176)

Ease further into the evening with drinks at this super stylish Chinatown speakeasy with a stunning cocktail menu.

From left: Autumn in Hyde Park (p104); Lunching at Harrods (p164)

Top Days in London

Greenwich to Camden

You don't want to neglect sights further afield, and this itinerary makes a big dent in what's on offer. Lovely Greenwich has a whole raft of stately sights, while a visit to the East End and Camden will help to develop a feel for Londoners' London.

Day 04

❶ Royal Observatory & Greenwich Park (p116)

Start the day in riverside Greenwich and make sure you visit Greenwich Park and the Royal Observatory, checking out the renovated Cutty Sark (p119) clipper ship. A browse through Greenwich Market (p169) always turns up surprises.

Royal Observatory & Greenwich Park to Tayyabs

& Take the DLR from Cutty Sark station to Bow Church and change for the District or Hammersmith & City underground lines to Whitechapel.

❷ Lunch at Tayyabs (p149)

Dip into the multicultural East End with lunch at this classic Punjabi restaurant. After your meal, wander around Whitechapel, soaking up its atmosphere and visiting the ground-breaking Whitechapel Gallery (p126).

Tayyabs to Spitalfields Market

Walk north from Whitechapel Rd up Osborn St and Brick Lane to Spitalfields Market.

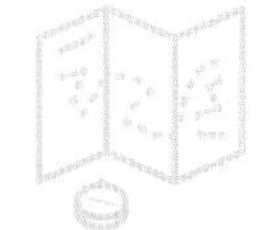

JON ARNOLD/GETTY IMAGES ©

❸ Spitalfields Market (p125)

Wander along Brick Lane and explore absorbing Georgian Spitalfields before browsing through Spitalfields Market. The best days for the market are Thursday, Friday and Sunday.

➜ Spitalfields Market to Worship St Whistling Shop

Walk west from the market along Spital Sq, then north up Bishopgate to Worship St.

❹ Worship St Whistling Shop (p180)

Sample the edgy, creative and offbeat Shoreditch atmosphere by dropping in on this basement drinking den to try one of its curious cocktails (Undyed Bloodshed, anyone?).

➜ Worship St Whistling Shop to Market

Stroll to Old St station, then jump on a Northern Line tube to Camden Town.

❺ Dinner at Market (p152)

End the day in North London by browsing the stalls of Camden Market (p169) – if still open – and dining on modern British cuisine at the excellent Market before turning to the riveting choice of local bars, pubs and live-music venues in this invigorating neighbourhood.

From left: Stone figure adorning the exterior of the Royal Observatory (p116); Food stalls at Camden Lock Market (p169)

Hotspots For...

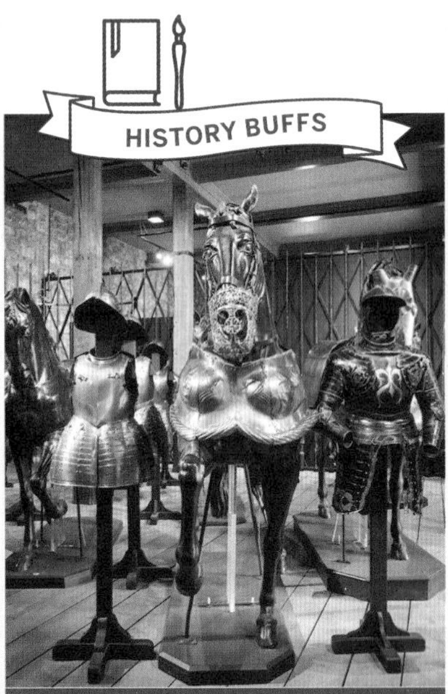

Tower of London From executions to the dazzling Crown Jewels, the Tower has seen it all. (Pictured above; p74)

Westminster Abbey Virtually every monarch has been crowned here since 1066, and many are also buried here. (p36)

Princess Louise A Victorian stunner of fine tiles, etched mirrors and a horseshoe bar. (p177)

Guide London Hire a Blue Badge guide for a tailor-made historical tour of the capital. (p206)

Ye Olde Mitre One of the city's oldest pubs, with no music to spoil the drinking and chatting. (p180)

V&A Fashion, sculpture, jewellery, photography – there isn't a decorative art the V&A doesn't cover. (p108)

Royal Observatory Learn how 18th-century luminaries solved the longitude problem and how GMT came to be. (Pictured below; p116)

Thames River Services Hop on a boat for a scenic and informative cruise about London's highlights. (p204)

Dinner by Heston Blumenthal Splendid gastronomy blending traditional and experimental techniques. (p145)

Rake Forget about Carling or Heineken: this is your chance to go on a beer discovery journey. (p180)

GLITZ & GLAMOUR

Buckingham Palace Pomp, pageantry and a lot of gilded ceilings in the Queen's main residence. (p46)

Dukes Bar Drink where Ian Fleming of James Bond fame drank. (p183)

Royal Opera House Ballet or opera in the glittering surroundings of London's premier opera house. (p192)

Ronnie Scott's Legendary jazz venue where all the big names have played. (p72)

Harrods Egyptian-themed elevator, stratospheric prices and opulent displays – it's London's most extravagant department store. (p164)

CRAFTY CREATIVES

Jensen Small, independent gin distillery making signature London Dry gin as well as flavoured varieties. (p183)

Duke's Brew & Que Smoky American-style ribs, decadent brunch and beers from a Hackney brewery – very hip indeed. (p150)

Sunday UpMarket Garments from young designers, quirky crafts and a fabulous array of food stalls. (Pictured above; p125)

Drink, Shop & Do Lego robots, quizzes, *Thriller* choreography classes – this is no ordinary night out. (p184)

Cecil Sharp House Forget bopping up and down in hip clubs, here it's all about English folk dancing. (p198)

BARGAIN HUNTERS

Tate Modern Most galleries of this standing charge admission fees, but not the Tate. Enjoy! (p94)

Borough Market All the free samples will easily make a starter – you can the buy the mains from your favourite stall. (p88)

Oblix Coffee with stunning panoramas for a fraction of the price of the viewing platform. (p179)

Burberry Outlet Store Genuine Burberry, just 30% cheaper. (p168)

Camden Market One of London's most iconic markets, with lots of cheap and cheerful goods. (Pictured above; p169)

Plan Your Trip
What's New

Round-the-Clock Tube

We didn't think we'd live to see the day, but 24-hour service at the weekend (only) has begun on five of the London Underground's nine lines, with night-time departures averaging every 10 minutes.

Tasteful Views from on High

Two of the new additions to the London skyline – the Shard (p91) and the Walkie Talkie (p178) – now feature a number of restaurants and cafes from which to enjoy the city on high.

A New Park for London

The southern half of the 2012 Olympic site has opened as **Queen Elizabeth Olympic Park** (www.queenelizabetholympicpark.co.uk; E20; ⊖Stratford), with the Aquatics Centre (p207) now available for swimming, the Velodrome for cycling and the **ArcelorMittal Orbit** (www.arcelormittalorbit.com; E20; ⊖Stratford) for abseiling.

More Room at the British Museum

A long-awaited £135 million new extension called the World Conservation and Exhibitions Centre has opened at this august institution (p42).

All Change in Trafalgar Square

Hans Haacke's *Gift Horse*, a skeletal, riderless equine with live-stock-exchange ticker will make way for a new work on the Fourth Plinth (p61) during the second half of 2017. Watch this space.

Above: Sky Garden restaurant, Walkie Talkie (p178)

Plan Your Trip
For Free

PAWEL LIBERA/GETTY IMAGES ©

London for Free

London may be one of the world's most expensive cities, but it doesn't always cost the earth. Many sights and experiences are free, including many of the top museums.

Museums

The permanent collections of all state-funded museums and galleries are open to the public free of charge; temporary exhibitions cost extra.

Changing of the Guard

London's most famous open-air freebie, the Changing of the Guard in the forecourt of Buckingham Palace (p46) takes place at 11.30am from April to July (and alternate days, weather permitting, August to March). Alternatively, catch the changing of the mounted guard at Horse Guards Parade (p65) at 11am (10am on Sundays).

Houses of Parliament

When parliament (p50) is in session, it's free to attend and watch UK parliamentary democracy in action.

Concerts at St Martin-in-the-Fields

This magnificent church (p61) hosts free concerts at 1pm on Monday, Tuesday and Friday.

Walking in London

Walking around town is possibly the best way to get a sense of the city and its history. Try our walking tours: East End Eras (p98), and Northern Point of View (p130).

Architecture & Interiors

For one weekend in September, Open House London (p79) opens the doors to more than 700 buildings for free.

Best for Free

- National Gallery (p54)
- British Museum (p42)
- Victoria & Albert Museum (p108)
- Natural History Museum (p112)
- Tate Modern (p94)

Above: Changing of the Guard, Buckingham Palace (p46)

Family Travel

VISITBRITAIN/SIMON WINNALL/GETTY IMAGES ©

Need to Know

- **Babysitters** Find a babysitter or nanny at Greatcare (www.greatcare.co.uk).
- **Cots** Available in most hotels, but always request them in advance.
- **Public transport** Under-16s travel free on buses, under-11s travel free on the tube, and under-5s ride free on trains.

Museums

London's museums are particularly child friendly. You'll find storytelling at the National Gallery (p54) for children aged three years and over, arts-and-crafts workshops at the Victoria & Albert Museum (p108), train-making workshops at the London Transport Museum (p67), plenty of finger-painting opportunities at the Tate Modern (p94) and Tate Britain (p53), and performance and handicraft workshops at Somerset House (p69). And what's more, they're all free (check websites for details).

Other excellent activities for children include sleepovers at the British, Science and Natural History Museums, though you'll need to book months ahead. The last two are definitive children's museums, with interactive displays and play areas.

Other Attractions

Kids love the **London Zoo** (Map p256; www.londonzoo.co.uk; Outer Circle, Regent's Park, NW1; adult/child £26/18; 10am-5.30pm Mar-Oct, to 4pm Nov-Feb; 274), London Eye (p102), London Dungeon (p103) and **Madame Tussauds** (Map p256; 0870 400 3000; www.madame-tussauds.com/london; Marylebone Rd, NW1; adult/child £30/26; 9.30am-5.30pm; Baker St). Ice rinks glitter around London in winter at the Natural History Museum (p112), Somerset House, Hyde Park (p104) and the moat of the Tower of London (p74). There's also a seasonal rink further afield at Hampton Court Palace.

In addition there's the exciting climbs up the dome of St Paul's Cathedral (p80) or the Monument (p78), feeding the ducks in St James's Park (p49) and watching the performers in Trafalgar Square (p58) or

Covent Garden Piazza (p67). Many arts and cultural festivals aimed at adults also cater for children. London's parks burst with possibilities: open grass, playgrounds, wildlife, trees and, in the warmer weather, ice-cream trucks.

Most attractions offer family tickets and discounted entry for kids under 15 or 16 years (children under five usually go free).

Eating & Drinking with Kids

Most of London's restaurants and cafes are child-friendly and offer baby-changing facilities and high chairs. Note that high-end restaurants and small, quiet cafes may be less welcoming, particularly if you have toddlers or small babies.

The one place that isn't traditionally very welcoming for those with children is the pub. By law, minors aren't allowed into the main bar (though walking through is fine), but many pubs have areas where children are welcome, usually a garden or outdoor space. Things are more relaxed during the day on Sunday.

Top Spots for Kids

Natural History Museum (p112)
Changing of the Guard (p47)
Hamleys (p160)
Cutty Sark (p119)

Getting Transport with Kids

When it comes to getting around, buses are better for children than the tube, which is often very crowded and hot in summer. As well as being big, red and iconic, buses in London are usually the famous double-decker ones; kids love to sit on the top deck and get great views of the city. Another excellent way to get around is simply to walk.

From left: Tate Modern (p94) and Millennium Bridge (p85); Victoria & Albert Museum (p108)

TOP EXPERIENCES

The very best to see and do

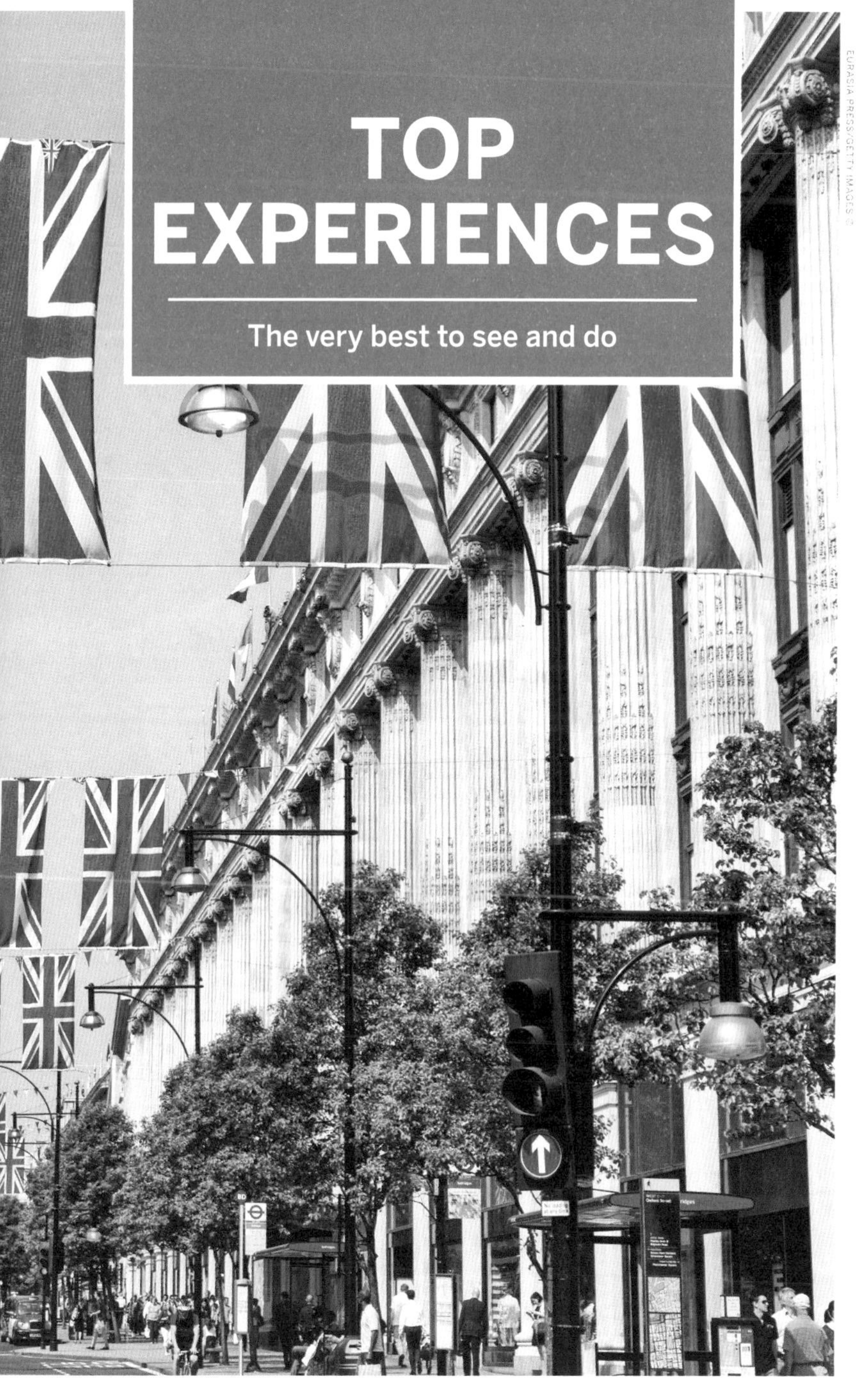

EURASIA PRESS/GETTY IMAGES ©

Westminster Abbey

Westminster Abbey is such an important commemoration site that it's hard to overstress its symbolic value or imagine its equivalent anywhere else in the world. With a couple of exceptions, every English sovereign has been crowned here since William the Conqueror in 1066, and most of the monarchs from Henry III (died 1272) to George II (died 1760) are buried here.

Great For...

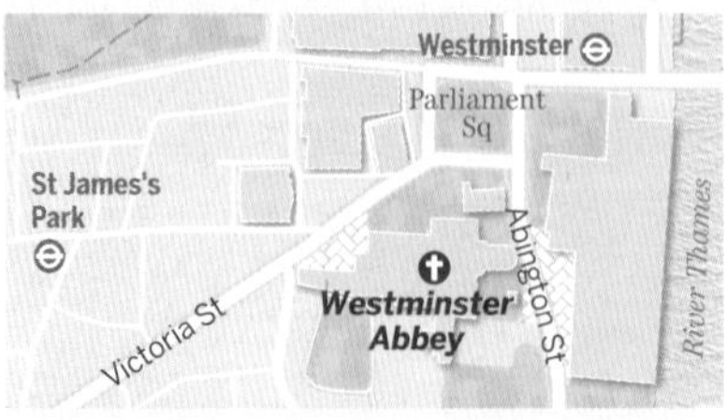

Need to Know

Map p252; 020-7222 5152; www.westminster-abbey.org; 20 Dean's Yard, SW1; adult/child £20/9, verger tours £5, cloister & gardens free; 9.30am-4.30pm Mon, Tue, Thu & Fri, to 7pm Wed, to 2.30pm Sat; Westminster

★ Top Tip

The Abbey gets incredibly busy, even at opening, so come armed with patience.

EURASIA PRESS/GETTY IMAGES ©

There is an extraordinary amount to see at the Abbey. The interior is chock-a-block with ornate chapels, elaborate tombs of monarchs and grandiose monuments to sundry luminaries throughout the ages. First and foremost, however, it is a sacred place of worship.

A Regal History

Though a mixture of architectural styles, the Abbey is considered the finest example of Early English Gothic (1190–1300). The original church was built in the 11th century by King (later St) Edward the Confessor, who is buried in the chapel behind the sanctuary and main altar. Henry III (r 1216–72) began work on the new building, but didn't complete it; the French Gothic nave was finished by Richard II in 1388. Henry VII's huge and magnificent Lady Chapel was added in 1519.

The Abbey was initially a monastery for Benedictine monks, and many of the building's features attest to this collegial past (the octagonal Chapter House, the Quire and four cloisters). In 1536, Henry VIII separated the Church of England from the Roman Catholic Church and dissolved the monastery. The king became head of the Church of England and the Abbey acquired its 'royal peculiar' status, meaning it is administered directly by the Crown and exempt from any ecclesiastical jurisdiction.

North Transept, Sanctuary & Quire

Entrance to the Abbey is via the Great North Door. The North Transept is often referred to as Statesmen's Aisle: politicians

Henry VII's Lady Chapel

and eminent public figures are commemorated by large marble statues and imposing marble plaques.

At the heart of the Abbey is the beautifully tiled **sanctuary** (or sacrarium), a stage for coronations, royal weddings and funerals. George Gilbert Scott designed the ornate **high altar** in 1873. In front of the altar is the **Cosmati marble pavement** dating back to 1268. It has intricate designs of small pieces of marble inlaid into plain marble, which predicts the end of the world in AD 19,693! At the entrance to the lovely **Chapel of St John the Baptist** is a sublime Virgin and Child bathed in candlelight.

The **Quire**, a magnificent structure of gold, blue and red Victorian Gothic by Edward Blore, dates back to the mid-19th century. It sits where the original choir for the monks' worship would have been, but bears no resemblance to the original. Nowadays, the Quire is still used for singing, but its regular occupants are the Westminster Choir – 22 boys and 12 'lay vicars' (men) who sing the daily services.

☑ **Don't Miss**

Part of the original 14th-century Benedictine monastery, Cellarium (Map p252; ☎020-7222 0516; www.cellariumcafe.com; Westminster Abbey, 20 Dean's Yard, SW1; mains £10.50-14.50; ⌚8am-6pm Mon-Fri, 9am-5pm Sat, 10am-4pm Sun). **It has stunning views of the Abbey's architectural details.**

HOBERMAN COLLECTION/UIG VIA GETTY IMAGES ©

Chapels & Chairs

The sanctuary is surrounded by chapels. **Henry VII's Lady Chapel**, in the easternmost part of the Abbey, is the most spectacular, with its fan vaulting on the ceiling, colourful banners of the Order of the Bath and dramatic oak stalls. Behind the chapel's altar is the elaborate sarcophagus of Henry VII and his queen, Elizabeth of York.

Beyond the chapel's altar is the **Royal Air Force Chapel**, with a stained-glass window commemorating the force's finest hour, the Battle of Britain (1940), and the 1500 RAF pilots who died. A stone plaque on the floor marks the spot where Oliver Cromwell's body lay for two years (died 1658) until the Restoration, when it was disinterred, hanged and beheaded. Two bodies, believed to be those of the child princes allegedly murdered in the Tower of London in 1483, were buried here almost two centuries later in 1674.

There are two small chapels either side of Lady Chapel with the tombs of famous monarchs: on the left (north) is where **Elizabeth I** and her half-sister **Mary I** (aka Bloody Mary) rest. On the right (south) is the tomb of **Mary Queen of Scots**, beheaded on the orders of her cousin Elizabeth.

The vestibule of the Lady Chapel is the usual place for the rather ordinary-looking **Coronation Chair**, upon which every monarch since the early 14th century has been crowned.

Shrine of St Edward the Confessor

The most sacred spot in the Abbey lies behind the high altar; access is generally restricted to protect the 13th-century flooring. St Edward was the founder of the Abbey and the original building was consecrated a few weeks before his death. His tomb was slightly altered after the original was destroyed during the Reformation, but still contains Edward's remains – the only complete saint's body in Britain. Ninety-minute **verger-led tours** of the Abbey include a visit to the shrine.

Outer Buildings & Gardens

The oldest part of the cloister is the East Cloister (or East Walk), dating to the 13th century. Off the cloister are three museums. The octagonal **Chapter House** has one of Europe's best-preserved medieval tile floors and retains traces of religious murals on the walls. It was used as a meeting place by the House of Commons in the second half of the 14th century. To the right of the entrance to Chapter House is what is claimed to be the **oldest door** in Britain – it's been there for 950 years.

The adjacent **Pyx Chamber** is one of the few remaining relics of the original Abbey and holds the Abbey's treasures and liturgical objects. It contains the pyx, a chest with standard gold and silver pieces for testing coinage weights in a ceremony called the Trial of the Pyx.

Next door in the vaulted undercroft, the **Westminster Abbey Museum** (Map p252; 10.30am-4pm) exhibits the death masks of generations of royalty, wax effigies representing Charles II and William III (who is on a stool to make him as tall as his wife, Mary II), armour and stained glass. Highlights include the graffiti-inscribed **Mary Chair** (used for the coronation of Mary II) and the **Westminster Retable**, England's oldest altarpiece, from the 13th century.

To reach the 900-year-old **College Garden** (Map p252; 10am-6pm Tue-Thu Apr-Sep, to 4pm Tue-Thu Oct-Mar), enter Dean's Yard and the Little Cloisters off Great College St.

South Transept & Nave

The south transept contains **Poets' Corner**, where many of England's finest writers are buried and/or commemorated by monuments or memorials.

In the nave's north aisle is **Scientists' Corner**, where you will find **Sir Isaac Newton's tomb** (note the putto holding a prism to the sky while another feeds material into a smelting oven). Just ahead of it is the north aisle of the Quire, known as **Musicians' Aisle**, where baroque composers Henry Purcell and John Blow are buried, as well as more modern music-makers such as Benjamin Britten and Edward Elgar.

Poets' Corner memorials

The two towers above the west door are the ones through which you exit. These were designed by Nicholas Hawksmoor and completed in 1745. Just above the door, perched in 15th-century niches, are the additions to the Abbey unveiled in 1998: 10 stone statues of international 20th-century martyrs who died for their Christian faith. These include American pacifist Dr Martin Luther King, the Polish priest St Maximilian Kolbe, who was murdered by the Nazis at Auschwitz, and Wang Zhiming, publicly executed during the Chinese Cultural Revolution.

Did You Know?

On 29 April 2011, Prince William married his fiancée Catherine Middleton at Westminster Abbey. The couple had chosen the Abbey for the relatively intimate setting of the sanctuary. Unusually, the couple decided to decorate the Abbey with trees; less controversial was the bride's decision to opt for a gown by a British designer, Sarah Burton (of Alexander McQueen). And, in a tradition started by the future Queen Mother in 1923, Kate left her bridal bouquet on the Tomb of the Unknown Warrior.

☑ Don't Miss

The oldest door in Britain, Poet's Corner, the Coronation Chair, the Lady Chapel, a 900-year old garden, royal sarcophagi and much more.

TRAVELIB EUROPE/ALAMY STOCK PHOTO ©

Great Court

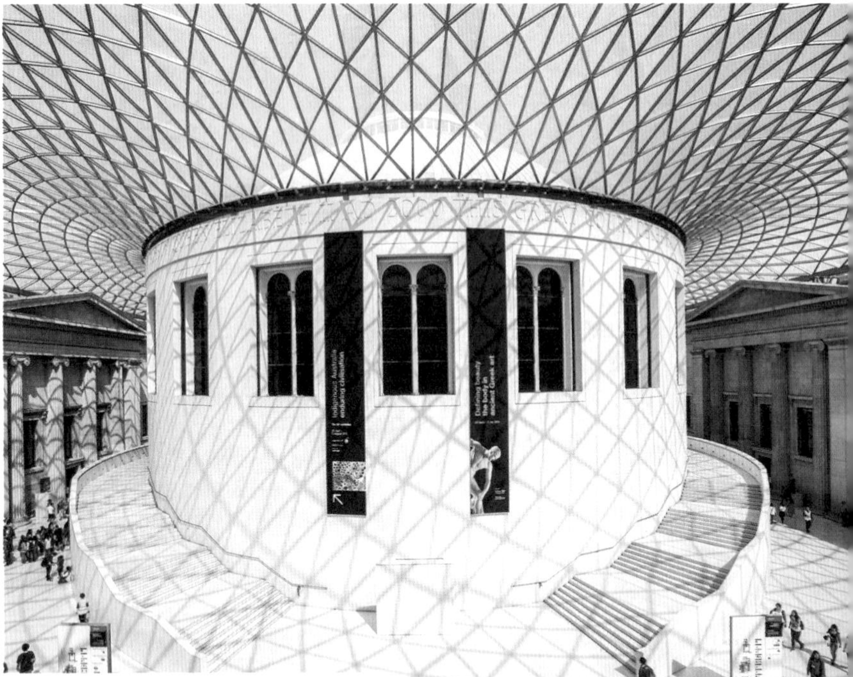

British Museum

Britain's most visited attraction – founded in 1753 when royal physician Hans Sloane sold his 'cabinet of curiosities'– is an exhaustive and exhilarating stampede through 7000 years of human civilisation.

Great For...

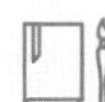

☑ Don't Miss

The Rosetta Stone, the Mummy of Katebet and the marble Parthenon sculptures.

The British Museum offers a stupendous selection of tours, many of them free. There are 15 free 30- to 40-minute eyeOpener tours of individual galleries per day. The museum also has free daily gallery talks, a highlights tour (adult/child £12/free, 11.30am and 2pm Friday, Saturday and Sunday) and excellent multimedia iPad tours (adult/child £5/3.50), offering six themed one-hour tours, and a choice of 35-minute children's trails.

Great Court

Covered with a spectacular glass-and-steel roof designed by Norman Foster in 2000, the Great Court is the largest covered public square in Europe. In its centre is the world-famous **Reading Room**, formerly the British Library, which has been frequented by all the big brains of history, from

Sculpted relief

Mahatma Gandhi to Karl Marx. It is currently used for temporary exhibits.

Ancient Egypt, Middle East & Greece

The star of the show here is the Ancient Egypt collection. It comprises sculptures, fine jewellery, papyrus texts, coffins and mummies, including the beautiful and intriguing **Mummy of Katebet** (room 63). The most prized item in the collection (and the most popular postcard in the shop) is the **Rosetta Stone** (room 4), the key to deciphering Egyptian hieroglyphics. In the same gallery is the enormous bust of the pharaoh **Ramesses the Great** (room 4).

Assyrian treasures from ancient Mesopotamia include the 16-tonne **Winged Bulls from Khorsabad** (room 10), the heaviest object in the museum. Behind it are the exquisite **Lion Hunt Reliefs from Nineveh** (room 10) from the 7th century BC, which influenced Greek sculpture. Such antiquities are all the more significant after the Islamic State's bulldozing of Nimrud in 2015.

A major highlight of the museum is the **Parthenon sculptures** (room 18). The marble frieze is thought to be the Great Panathenaea, a blow-out version of an annual festival in honour of Athena.

Roman & Medieval Britain

Upstairs are finds from Britain and the rest of Europe (rooms 40 to 51). Many items go back to Roman times (when the Empire spread across much of the continent), such as the **Mildenhall Treasure** (room 49), a collection of pieces of 4th-century Roman silverware from Suffolk with both pagan and early-Christian motifs.

Lindow Man (room 50) is the well-preserved remains of a 1st-century man

Need to Know

Map p256; 020-7323 8000; www.britishmuseum.org; Great Russell St, WC1; 10am-5.30pm Sat-Thu, to 8.30pm Fri; Russell Sq or Tottenham Court Rd; FREE

Take a Break

Just around the corner from the museum down a quiet back street, **Abeno** (Map p252; 020-7405 3211; www.abeno.co.uk; 47 Museum St, WC1; mains £7.95-25.80; noon-10pm; Tottenham Court Rd) has savoury pancakes and other tasty dishes.

★ Top Tip

The museum is huge, so pick your interests and consider the free tours.

(comically dubbed Pete Marsh) discovered in a bog near Manchester in northern England in 1984. Equally fascinating are artefacts from the **Sutton Hoo Ship-Burial** (room 41), an elaborate Anglo-Saxon burial site from Suffolk dating back to the 7th century.

Perennial favourites are the lovely **Lewis Chessmen** (room 40), 12th-century game pieces carved from walrus tusk and whale teeth that were found on a remote Scottish island in the early 19th century. They served as models for the game of Wizard Chess in the first Harry Potter film.

Enlightenment Galleries

Formerly known as the King's Library, this stunning neoclassical space (room 1) was built between 1823 and 1827 and was the first part of the new museum building as it is seen today. The collection traces how disciplines such as biology, archaeology, linguistics and geography emerged during the Enlightenment of the 18th century.

What's Nearby?

Sir John Soane's Museum — Museum

(Map p250; www.soane.org; 13 Lincoln's Inn Fields, WC2; 10am-5pm Tue-Sat & 6-9pm 1st Tue of month; Holborn) FREE This little museum is one of the most atmospheric and fascinating in London. The building is the beautiful, bewitching home of architect Sir John Soane (1753–1837), which he left brimming with surprising personal effects and curiosities, and the museum represents his exquisite and eccentric taste.

Soane was a country bricklayer's son, most famous for designing the Bank of England.

Parthenon sculptures

The heritage-listed house is largely as it was when Soane died and is itself a main part of the attraction. It has a canopy dome that brings light right down to the crypt, a colonnade filled with statuary and a picture gallery where paintings are stowed behind each other on folding wooden panes. This is where Soane's choicest artwork is displayed, including *Riva degli Schiavoni, looking West*, by Canaletto, architectural drawings by Christopher Wren and Robert Adam, and the original *Rake's Progress*, William Hogarth's set of satirical cartoons of late-8th-century London lowlife. Among Soane's more unusual acquisitions are an Egyptian hieroglyphic sarcophagus, a mock-up of a monk's cell and slaves' chains.

★ Top Tip

Check out the outstanding 'A History of the World in 100 Objects' radio series (www.bbc.co.uk/podcasts/series/ahow), which retraces two million years of history through 100 objects from the museum's collections.

FOX PHOTOS/HULTON ARCHIVE/GETTY IMAGES ©

Squares of Bloomsbury Square

The Bloomsbury Group, they used to say, lived in squares, moved in circles and loved in triangles. **Russell Square** (Map p256; ⊖Russell Sq) sits at the very heart of the district. Originally laid out in 1800, a striking facelift a decade ago spruced it up and gave the square a 10m-high fountain. The centre of literary Bloomsbury was **Gordon Square** (Map p256; ⊖Russell Sq or Euston Sq), where some of the buildings are marked with blue plaques. Lovely **Bedford Square** (Map p256; ⊖Tottenham Court Rd) is the only completely Georgian square still surviving in Bloomsbury.

At various times, Gordon Sq was occupied by Bertrand Russell (No 57), Lytton Strachey (No 51) and Vanessa and Clive Bell, Maynard Keynes and the Woolf family (No 46), while Strachey, Dora Carrington and Lydia Lopokova (the future wife of Maynard Keynes) all took turns living at No 41.

Charles Dickens Museum Museum

(Map p256; www.dickensmuseum.com; 48 Doughty St, WC1; adult/child £8/4; ⏲10am-5pm, last admission 4pm; ⊖Chancery Lane or Russell Sq) A £3.5-million renovation made this museum, located in a handsome four-storey house that was the great Victorian novelist's sole surviving residence in London, bigger and better than ever. The museum showcases the family drawing room (restored to its original condition), a period kitchen and a dozen rooms containing various memorabilia.

The prolific writer didn't stay here long – a mere 2½ years (1837–39) – but this is where his work really flourished: he dashed off *The Pickwick Papers*, *Nicholas Nickleby* and *Oliver Twist*, despite anxiety over debts, the death of his beloved sister-in-law, Mary Hogarth, and his ever-growing family.

Changing of the Guard

PETER PHIPP/GETTY IMAGES ©

Buckingham Palace

Built in 1705 as Buckingham House for the duke of the same name and then purchased by George III, the palace has been the Royal Family's London lodgings since 1837. St James's Palace was judged too old-fashioned and insufficiently impressive, although Buckingham Palace underwent a number of modifications until it was deemed fit.

Great For...

☑ Don't Miss

Peering through the gates, going on a tour of the interior (summer only) or catching the Changing of the Guard.

The State Rooms are only open in August and September, when Her Majesty is holidaying in Scotland. The Queen's Gallery, however, is open year-round, and the Royal Mews from April to December.

State Rooms

The **tour** starts in the **Grand Hall** at the foot of the monumental **Grand Staircase**, commissioned by George IV in 1828. It takes in John Nash's Italianate **Green Drawing Room**, the **State Dining Room** (all red damask and Regency furnishings), the **Blue Drawing Room** (which has a gorgeous fluted ceiling by Nash) and the **White Drawing Room**, where foreign ambassadors are received.

The **Ballroom**, where official receptions and state banquets are held, was built between 1853 and 1855 and opened with

Victoria Memorial

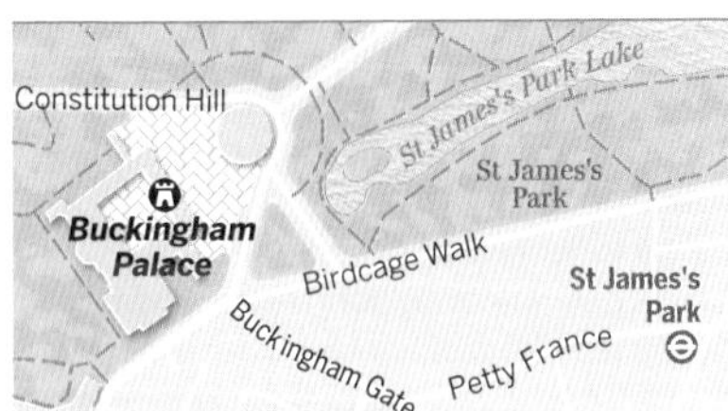

Need to Know

Map p252; 020-7766 7300; www.royalcollection.org.uk; Buckingham Palace Rd, SW1; adult/child £20.50/11.80; 9.30am-7.30pm late Jul-Aug, to 6.30pm Sep; St James's Park, Victoria or Green Park

Take a Break

During the summer months, you can enjoy light refreshments in the **Garden Café** on the Palace's West Terrace.

★ Top Tip

Come early for front-row views of the Changing of the Guard.

a ball a year later to celebrate the end of the Crimean War. The **Throne Room** is rather anticlimactic, with his-and-hers pink chairs initialled 'ER' and 'P', sitting under a curtained theatre arch.

Picture Gallery & Garden

The most interesting part of the tour is the 47m-long Picture Gallery, featuring splendid works by such artists as Van Dyck, Rembrandt, Canaletto, Poussin, Claude Lorrain, Rubens, Canova and Vermeer.

Wandering the 18 hectares of gardens is another highlight – as well as admiring some of the 350 or so species of flowers and plants and listening to the many birds, you'll get beautiful views of the palace and a peek of its famous lake.

Changing of the Guard

At 11.30am daily from April to July, and on alternate days, weather permitting, from August to March, the old guard (Foot Guards of the Household Regiment) comes off duty to be replaced by the new guard on the forecourt of Buckingham Palace.

Crowds come to watch the carefully choreographed marching and shouting of the guards in their bright-red uniforms and bearskin hats. It lasts about 40 minutes and is very popular, so arrive early if you want to get a good spot.

Queen's Gallery

Since the reign of Charles I, the Royal Family has amassed a priceless collection of paintings, sculpture, ceramics, furniture and jewellery. The splendid **Queen's Gallery** (Map p252; www.royalcollection.org.uk; southern wing, Buckingham Palace, Buckingham Gate, SW1; adult/child £10/5.20, with Royal Mews

£17.10/9.60; 10am-5.30pm; St James's Park, Victoria or Green Park) showcases some of the palace's treasures on a rotating basis.

The gallery was originally designed as a conservatory by John Nash. It was converted into a chapel for Queen Victoria in 1843, destroyed in a 1940 air raid and reopened as a gallery in 1962. A £20-million renovation for Elizabeth II's Golden Jubilee in 2002 added three times as much display space.

Royal Mews

Southwest of the palace, the **Royal Mews** (Map p252; www.royalcollection.org.uk; Buckingham Palace Rd, SW1; adult/child £9/5.40, with Queen's Gallery £17.10/9.60; 10am-5pm daily Apr-Oct, to 4pm Mon-Sat Nov & Dec; Victoria) started life as a falconry, but is now a working stable looking after the royals' three dozen immaculately groomed horses, along with the opulent vehicles – motorised and horse-driven – the monarch uses for transport. The Queen is well known for her passion for horses; she names every horse that resides at the mews and still rides every weekend. Nash's 1820 stables are stunning.

Highlights for visitors include the enormous and opulent Gold State Coach of 1762, which has been used for every coronation since that of George III; the 1911 Glass Coach used for royal weddings and the Diamond Jubilee in 2012; Queen Alexandra's State Coach (1893), used to transport the Imperial State Crown to the official opening of Parliament; and a Rolls-Royce Phantom VI from the royal fleet.

Royal Mews

What's Nearby?

St James's Park Park

(Map p252; www.royalparks.org.uk; The Mall, SW1; deckchairs per hour/day £1.50/7; 5am-midnight, deckchairs daylight hours Mar-Oct; St James's Park or Green Park) At just 23 hectares, St James's is one of the smallest but best-groomed of London's royal parks. It has brilliant views of the London Eye, Westminster, St James's Palace, Carlton Tce and the Horse Guards Parade; the sight of Buckingham Palace from the footbridge spanning the central lake is photo-perfect and the best you'll find.

The lake brims with different types of ducks, geese, swans and general fowl, and the rocks on its southern side serve as a rest stop for a half-dozen pelicans (fed at 2.30pm daily).

Did You Know?

The State Rooms represent a mere 19 of the palace's 775 rooms.

TIM GRAHAM/GETTY IMAGES ©

Royal Academy of Arts Gallery

(Map p252; www.royalacademy.org.uk; Burlington House, Piccadilly, W1; adult/child £10/6, prices vary for exhibitions; 10am-6pm Sat-Thu, to 10pm Fri; Green Park) Britain's oldest society devoted to fine arts was founded in 1768, moving to Burlington House exactly a century later. The collection contains drawings, paintings, architectural designs, photographs and sculptures by past and present Academicians such as Joshua Reynolds, John Constable, Thomas Gainsborough, JMW Turner, David Hockney and Norman Foster.

The famous **Summer Exhibition** (Jun–mid-Aug), which has showcased contemporary art for sale by unknown as well as established artists for nearly 250 years, is the Academy's biggest annual event.

Green Park Park

(Map p252; www.royalparks.gov.uk; 24hr; Green Park) Less manicured than adjoining St James's, 19-hectare Green Park has huge oaks and hilly meadows, and it's never as crowded as its neighbour. It was once a duelling ground and, like Hyde Park, served as a vegetable garden during WWII.

It famously has no flowers beds as they were banned by Queen Catherine of Braganza after she learned her philandering husband Charles II had been picking posies for his mistresses. Or so the story goes (others blame diseased soil from a plague pit beneath the park).

Local Knowledge

At the centre of Royal Family life is the Music Room, where four royal babies have been christened: the Prince of Wales (Prince Charles), the Princess Royal (Princess Anne), the Duke of York (Prince Andrew) and the Duke of Cambridge (Prince William).

Big Ben and the Houses of Parliament

Houses of Parliament

Both the House of Commons and the House of Lords sit in the sumptuous Palace of Westminster, a neo-Gothic confection dating from the mid-19th century.

Great For...

☑ Don't Miss

Westminster Hall's hammer-beam roof, the Palace's Gothic Revival interior and Big Ben striking the hours.

Towers

The most famous feature of the Houses of Parliament is the Clock Tower, officially named Elizabeth Tower to mark the Queen's Diamond Jubilee in 2012, but commonly known as **Big Ben** (Map p252). Ben is actually the bell hanging inside and is named after Benjamin Hall, the over-6ft-tall commissioner of works when the tower was completed in 1858. Ben has rung in the New Year since 1924.

At the base of the taller **Victoria Tower** at the southern end is the **Sovereign's Entrance**, which is used by the Queen.

Westminster Hall

One of the most stunning elements of the Palace of Westminster, seat of the English monarchy from the 11th to the early 16th centuries, is Westminster Hall. Originally

Top of Big Ben (Elizabeth Tower)

TONY MARGIOCCHI/BARCROFT MEDIA/BARCROFT MEDIA VIA GETTY IMAGES ©

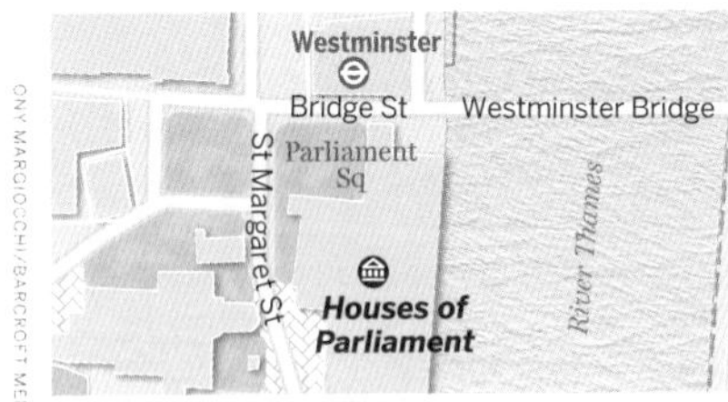

Need to Know

Map p252; www.parliament.uk; Parliament Sq, SW1; Westminster; FREE

Take a Break

The **Jubilee Café** (10am-5:30pm Mon-Fri, to 6pm Sat) near the north door of Westminster Hall serves hot drinks and snacks.

★ Top Tip

To find out what's being debated on a particular day, check the notice board beside the entrance, or check online at www.parliament.uk.

built in 1099, it is the oldest surviving part of the complex; the awesome **hammer-beam roof** was added around 1400. It has been described as 'the greatest surviving achievement of medieval English carpentry'. The only other part of the original palace to survive a devastating 1834 fire is the **Jewel Tower** (Map p252; 020-7222 2219; www.english-heritage.org.uk/daysout/properties/jewel-tower; Abingdon St, St James's Park, SW1; adult/child £4/2.40; 10am-5pm daily Apr-Oct, 10am-4pm Sat & Sun Nov-Mar; Westminster), built in 1365 and used to store the monarch's valuables.

Westminster Hall was used for coronation banquets in medieval times, and also served as a courthouse until the 19th century. The trials of William Wallace (1305), Thomas More (1535), Guy Fawkes (1606) and Charles I (1649) all took place here. In the 20th century, monarchs and Sir Winston Churchill lay in state here after their deaths.

House of Commons

The **House of Commons** (Map p252; http://www.parliament.uk/business/commons; Parliament Sq, SW1; 2.30-10pm Mon & Tue, 11.30am-7.30pm Wed, 10.30am-6.30pm Thu, 9.30am-3pm Fri; Westminster) is where Members of Parliament (MPs) meet to propose and discuss new legislation and to grill the prime minister and other ministers.

The layout of the **Commons Chamber** is based on St Stephen's Chapel in the original Palace of Westminster. The chamber, designed by Giles Gilbert Scott, replaced the one destroyed by a 1941 bomb.

Although the Commons is a national assembly of 650 MPs, the chamber has seating for only 437. Government members sit to the right of the Speaker and Opposition members to the left.

House of Lords

The **House of Lords** (Map p252; www.parliament.uk/business/lords; Parliament Sq, SW1; 2.30-10pm Mon & Tue, 3-10pm Wed, 11am-7.30pm Thu, 10am-close of session Fri; Westminster) is visited via the amusingly named Strangers' Gallery. The intricate **'Tudor Gothic' interior** led its poor architect, Augustus Pugin (1812–52), to an early death from overwork and nervous strain.

Most of the 780-odd members of the House of Lords are life peers (appointed for their lifetime by the monarch); there is also a small number – 92 at the time of writing – of hereditary peers and a group of 'crossbench' members (numbering 179, not affiliated to the main political parties), and 26 bishops.

Tours

On Saturdays year-round and on most weekdays during Parliamentary recesses including Easter, summer and Christmas, visitors can join a 90-minute **guided tour** (Map p252; 020-7219 4114; www.parliament.uk/guided-tours; Parliament Sq, SW1; adult/child £25/10), conducted by qualified Blue Badge Tourist Guides in seven languages, of both chambers, Westminster Hall and other historic buildings.

Afternoon tea in the Terrace Pavilion overlooking the River Thames is a popular add-on to the tours. Tour schedules change with every recess and are occasionally subject to variation or cancellation due to the State Opening of Parliament and other Parliamentary business, so check ahead and book.

Commons Chamber

What's Nearby?

Tate Britain — Gallery

(www.tate.org.uk; Millbank, SW1; ⏲10am-6pm, to 10pm 1st Fri of month; ⊖Pimlico) FREE Splendidly refurbished with a stunning new art deco–inspired staircase and a rehung collection, the more elderly and venerable of the two Tate siblings celebrates paintings from 1500 to the present, with works from Blake, Hogarth, Gainsborough, Barbara Hepworth, Whistler, Constable and Turner, as well as vibrant modern and contemporary pieces from Lucian Freud, Francis Bacon, Henry Moore and Tracey Emin. Join free 45-minute **thematic tours** (⏲11am, noon, 2pm & 3pm) and 15-minute **Art in Focus talks** (⏲1.15pm Tue, Thu & Sat).

The star of the show at Tate Britain is, undoubtedly, the light infused visions of JMW Turner. After he died in 1851, his estate was settled by a decree declaring that whatever had been found in his studio – 300 oil paintings and about 30,000 sketches and drawings – would be bequeathed to the nation. The collection at the Tate Britain constitutes a grand and sweeping display of his work, including classics like *The Scarlet Sunset* and *Norham Castle, Sunrise*.

Tate Britain hosts the prestigious and often controversial Turner Prize for contemporary art from October to early December every year. Audioguides (£3.50) are also available.

Did You Know?

The House of Lords contains Lords Spiritual, linked with the established church, and Lords Temporal, who are both appointed and hereditary.

JUSTIN TALLIS/AFP/GETTY IMAGES ©

Supreme Court — Landmark

(Map p252; ☎020-7960 1900/1500; www.supremecourt.uk; Parliament Sq, SW1; ⏲9.30am-4.30pm Mon-Fri; ⊖Westminster) FREE The Supreme Court, the highest court in the UK, was the Appellate Committee of the House of Lords until 2009. It is now housed in the neo-Gothic Middlesex Guildhall (1913), and members of the public are welcome to observe cases when the court is sitting (Monday to Thursday).

For who or what's on trial, ask for a list at reception, or go to the Current Cases page of the court's website. On the lower ground floor there's a permanent exhibition looking at the work and history of the UK's highest court as well as the building's history. The self-guided tour booklet is £1; tours are also available on Fridays (£5; 11am, 2pm and 3pm).

★ Top Tip

When Parliament is in session, visitors are welcome to attend the debates in both houses. Enter via Cromwell Green Entrance. Expect queues.

Fountain on Trafalgar Square and the National Gallery

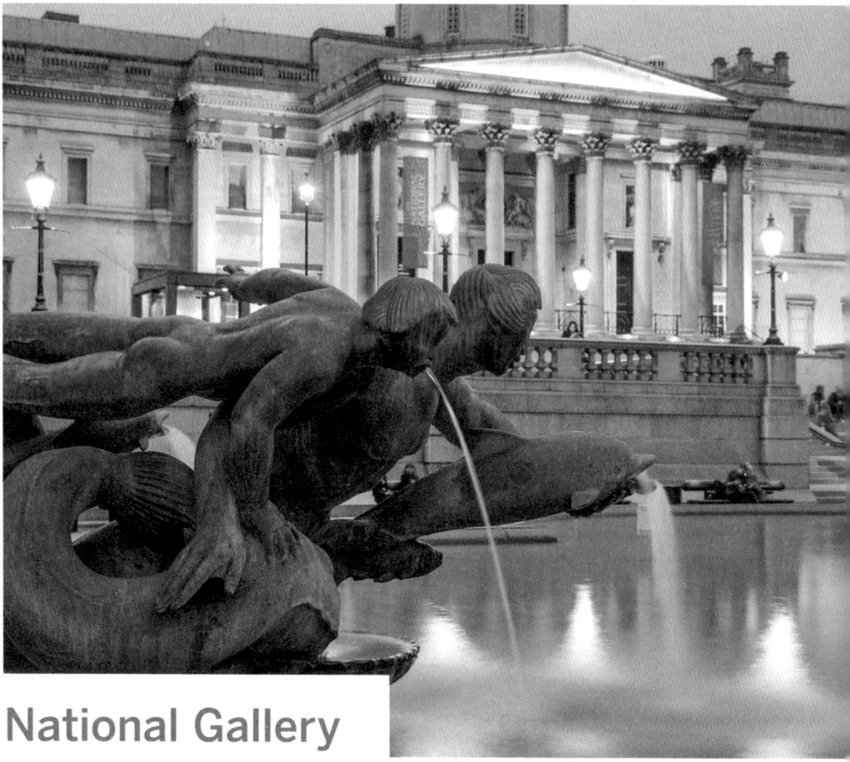

NEIL EMMERSON/GETTY IMAGES ©

National Gallery

With some 2300 European paintings on display, this is one of the world's richest art collections, including works by Leonardo da Vinci, Michelangelo, Titian, Van Gogh and Renoir.

Great For...

☑ Don't Miss

Venus & Mars by Botticelli, *Sunflowers* by Van Gogh and *Rokeby Venus* by Velázquez.

The National Gallery's collection spans seven centuries of European painting displayed in sumptuous, airy galleries. All are masterpieces, but some stand out for their iconic beauty and brilliance. Don't overlook the astonishing floor mosaics in the main vestibule inside the entrance to the gallery.

The gallery overlooks Trafalgar Square (p58) and adjoins the equally brilliant National Portrait Gallery (p56).

Sainsbury Wing

The modern Sainsbury Wing on the gallery's western side houses paintings from 1250 to 1500. Here you will find largely religious paintings commissioned for private devotion, such as the *Wilton Diptych*, as well more unusual masterpieces, such as Botticelli's *Venus & Mars* and Van Eyck's

Bronze sculpture of James II

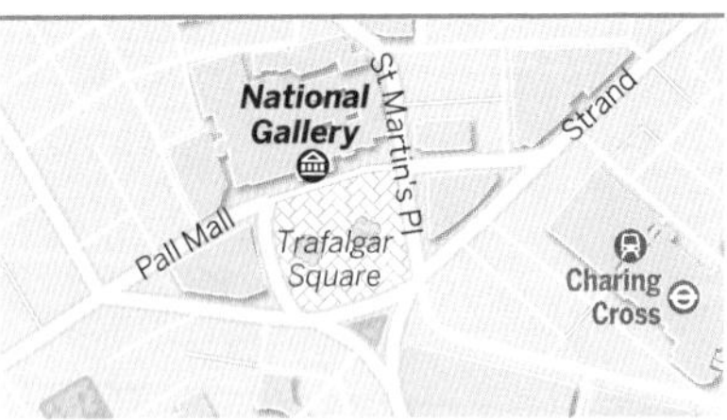

Need to Know

Map p252; www.nationalgallery.org.uk; Trafalgar Sq, WC2; 10am-6pm Sat-Thu, to 9pm Fri; Charing Cross; FREE

Take a Break

The National Dining Rooms (p150) have high-quality British food and splendid afternoon teas.

Top Tip

Take a free tour to learn the stories behind the gallery's most iconic works.

Arnolfini Portrait. Leonardo da Vinci's *Virgin of the Rocks*, in room 57, is a stunning masterpiece.

West Wing & North Wing

Works from the High Renaissance (1500–1600) embellish the West Wing where Michelangelo, Titian, Raphael, Correggio, El Greco and Bronzino hold court; Rubens, Rembrandt and Caravaggio grace the North Wing (1600–1700). Notable are two self-portraits of Rembrandt (age 34 and 63) and the beautiful *Rokeby Venus* by Velázquez.

East Wing

Many visitors flock to the East Wing (1700–1900), where works by 18th-century British artists such as Gainsborough, Constable and Turner, and seminal Impressionist and post-Impressionist masterpieces by Van Gogh (such as *Sunflowers*), Renoir and Monet await.

Visiting

The comprehensive audioguides (£4) are highly recommended, as are the free one-hour taster tours that leave from the information desk in the Sainsbury Wing daily at 11.30am and 2.30pm, and at 7pm Friday. There are also special trails and activity sheets for children. The gallery also runs popular storytelling sessions for children aged two to five on Sunday morning.

National Portrait Gallery

The National Portrait Gallery celebrates famous British faces through a staggering collection of 4000 paintings, sculptures and photographs from the 16th century to the present day.

Great For...

☑ Don't Miss

Self by Mark Quinn, the Shakespeare 'Chandos portrait' attributed to John Taylor and *Jane Austen* by Cassandra Austen.

What makes the National Portrait Gallery – the only such museum in Europe – so compelling is its familiarity; in many cases you'll have heard of the subject (royals, scientists, politicians, celebrities) or the artist (Andy Warhol, Annie Leibovitz, Sam Taylor-Wood).

The collection is organised chronologically (starting with the early Tudors on the 2nd floor), and then by theme. A highlight is the famous 'Chandos portrait' of William Shakespeare, the first artwork the gallery acquired (in 1856); believed to be the only one to have been painted during the playwright's lifetime. Other highlights include the 'Ditchley' portrait of Queen Elizabeth I displaying her might by standing on a map of England, and a touching sketch of novelist Jane Austen by her sister.

NEIL SETCHFIELD/GETTY IMAGES ©

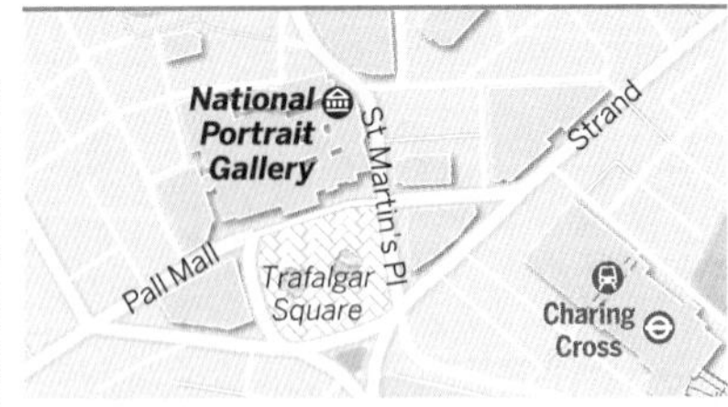

Need to Know

Map p252; www.npg.org.uk; St Martin's Pl, WC2; 10am-6pm Sat-Wed, to 9pm Thu & Fri; Charing Cross or Leicester Sq; FREE

Take a Break

The Portrait (p150) restaurant has superb views towards Westminster and does wonderful food.

★ Top Tip

The gallery runs excellent temporary exhibitions (admission fees apply).

First Floor

The 1st-floor portraits illustrate the rise and fall of the British Empire through the Victorian era and the 20th century. Don't miss the high-kitsch statue of Victoria and Albert in Anglo-Saxon dress in room 21.

Ground Floor

The ground floor is dedicated to modern figures and celebrities, employing various media, including sculpture, photography and video. Among the most popular are the iconic Blur portraits by Julian Opie, and Sam Taylor-Wood's *David*, a (low-res by today's standards) video-portrait of David Beckham asleep after football training. Don't miss *Self* by Mark Quinn, a frozen, refrigerated sculpture of the artist's head, made from 4.5L of his own blood and recast every five years.

Audioguides

The excellent audioguide (£3; ID required) highlights 200 portraits and allows you to hear the voices of some of the subjects.

Nelson's Column (p60)

Trafalgar Square

In many ways Trafalgar Sq is the centre of London, where tens of thousands congregate for anything from Christmas celebrations to political protests. The great square was neglected over many years, until a scheme was launched in 2000 to pedestrianise it and transform it into the kind of space John Nash had intended when he designed it in the 19th century.

Great For...

Need to Know

Map p252; Charing Cross

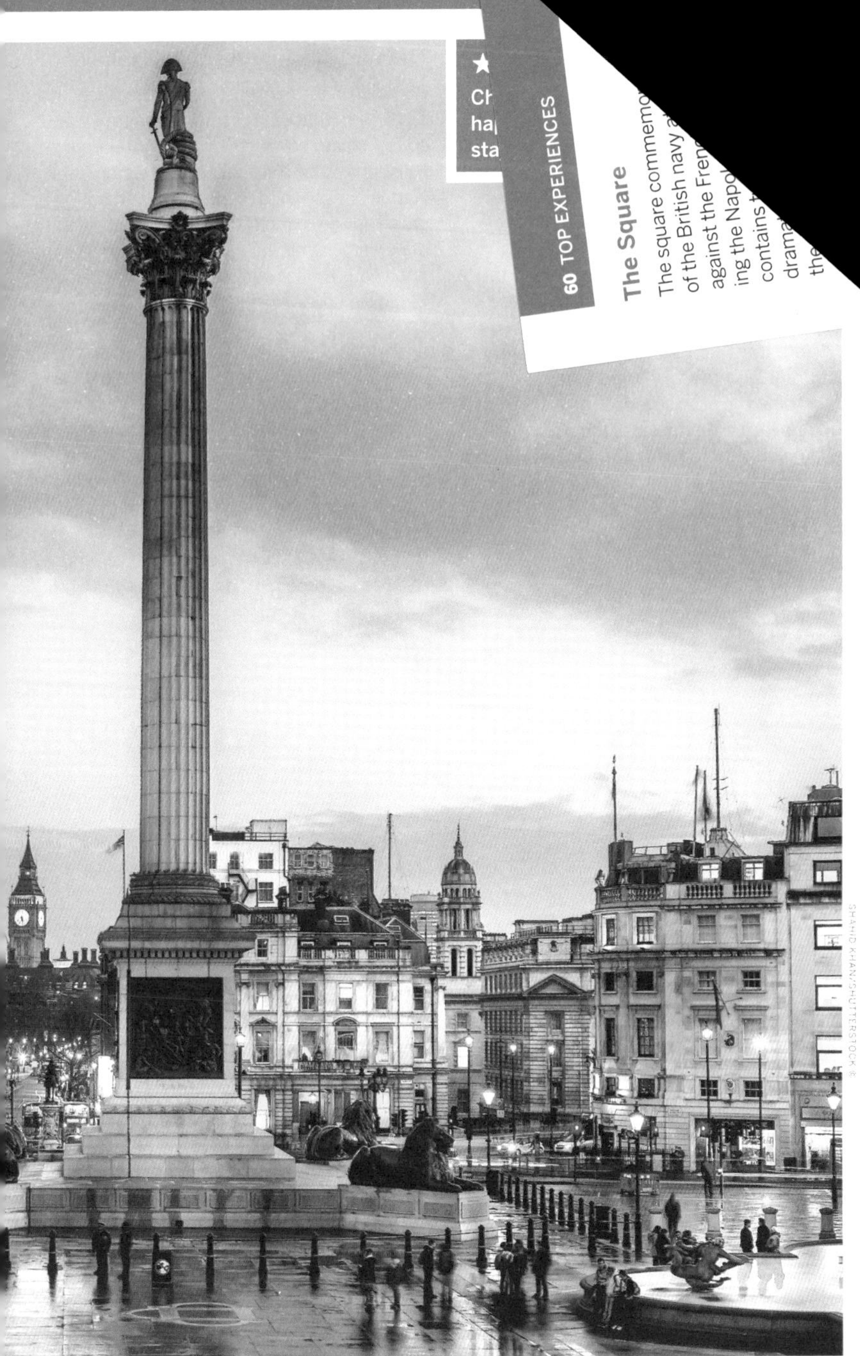

SHAHID KHAN/SHUTTERSTOCK ©

rates the 1805 victory t the Battle of Trafalgar ch and Spanish navies dur- eonic wars. The main square wo beautiful fountains, which are tically lit at night. At each corner of square is a plinth, three topped with statues of military leaders and the fourth, in the northeast corner, now an art space called the Fourth Plinth.

Note the much overlooked, if not entirely ignored, 19th-century brass plaques recording the precise length of imperial units – including the yard, the perch, pole, chain and link – set into the stonework and steps below the National Gallery (p54).

Nelson's Column

Standing in the centre of the square since 1843, the 52m-high Dartmoor granite *Nelson's Column* honours Admiral Lord Horatio Nelson, who led the fleet's heroic victory over Napoleon. The good (sandstone) admiral gazes down Whitehall towards the Houses of Parliament, his column flanked by four enormous bronze statues of lions sculpted by Sir Edwin Landseer and only added in 1867.

The Fourth Plinth

Three of the four plinths at Trafalgar Sq's corners are occupied by notables: King George IV on horseback, and military men General Sir Charles Napier and Major General Sir Henry Havelock. The fourth, originally intended for a statue of William IV, has largely remained vacant for the past 150 years (although some say it is reserved for an effigy of Queen Elizabeth II, on her death).

Trafalgar Square and the National Gallery (p54)

The Royal Society of Arts conceived the unimaginatively titled **Fourth Plinth Project** (Map p252; www.london.gov.uk/fourthplinth) in 1999, deciding to use the empty space for works by contemporary artists. They commissioned three works: *Ecce Homo* by Mark Wallinger (1999), a life-size statue of Jesus, which appeared tiny in contrast to the enormous plinth; Bill Woodrow's *Regardless of History* (2000); and Rachel Whiteread's *Monument* (2001), a resin copy of the plinth, turned upside down.

The mayor's office has since taken over what's now called the Fourth Plinth Commission, continuing with the contemporary-art theme. From March 2015 to late 2016, the plinth was occupied by Hans Haacke's *Gift Horse* depicting a skeletal, riderless horse. Each artwork is exhibited for 18 months.

☑ Don't Miss

The huge Christmas tree Norway gives London each year, which is displayed on Trafalgar Sq, to commemorate Britain's help during WWII.

KIMBERLEY COOLE/GETTY IMAGES ©

Buildings Around Trafalgar Square

The splendid buildings ringing the square are, clockwise from 12 o'clock (north): the National Gallery, with the National Portrait Gallery (p56) behind it; St Martin-in-the-Fields; and three commissions – South Africa House, Malaysia House and Canada House, designed by Robert Smirke in 1827. If you look southwest down Whitehall, past the equestrian statue of Charles I (which gazes to the point where he was beheaded at Banqueting House in Whitehall), you'll also get a glimpse of Big Ben at the Houses of Parliament.

Admiralty Arch

To the southwest of Trafalgar Sq stands Admiralty Arch, from where the ceremonial Mall leads to Buckingham Palace. It is a grand Edwardian monument, a triple-arched stone entrance designed by Aston Webb in honour of Queen Victoria in 1910 and earmarked for transformation into a five-star hotel. The large central gate is opened only for royal processions and state visits.

What's Nearby?

St Martin-in-the-Fields Church

(Map p252; ☎020-7766 1100; www.stmartin-in-the-fields.org; Trafalgar Sq, WC2; ⏰8.30am-6pm Mon, Tue, Thu & Fri, 8.30am-5pm Wed, 9.30am-6pm Sat, 3.30-5pm Sun; Ⓤ Charing Cross) The 'royal parish church' is a delightful fusion of classical and baroque styles. It was completed by James Gibbs in 1726 and serves as a model for many churches in New England.

✕ Take a Break

Mint Leaf (Map p252; ☎020-7930 9020; www.mintleafrestaurant.com), just up from Trafalgar Sq, has a highly inventive menu.

Churchill War Rooms

Winston Churchill coordinated the Allied resistance against Nazi Germany from this underground military HQ during WWII. The Cabinet War Rooms remain much as they were when the lights were flicked off in 1945, capturing the drama and dogged spirit of the time, while the multimedia Churchill Museum affords intriguing insights into the resolute, cigar-smoking wartime leader.

Great For...

Need to Know

Map p252; www.iwm.org.uk; Clive Steps, King Charles St, SW1; adult/child £18/9; 9.30am-6pm, last entry 5pm; Westminster

★ **Top Tip**

The audioguide is well worth a listen, especially the anecdotes from former staff.

WAR ROOMS

MUSEUM

EFFREY BLACKLER/ALAMY STOCK PHOTO ©

In late August 1939, with war seemingly imminent, the British cabinet and chiefs of the armed forces decided to move underground into a converted basement below what is now the Treasury. On 3 September Britain was at war.

The bunker served as the nerve centre of the war cabinet until the end of WWII in 1945; here, chiefs of staff ate, slept and plotted Hitler's downfall, believing they were protected from Luftwaffe bombs (it turns out the 3m slab of cement above them would have crumpled had the area taken a direct hit).

Cabinet War Rooms

The Cabinet War Rooms have been left much as they were on 15 August 1945. Many rooms have been preserved, including the room where the War Cabinet met 115 times; the **Transatlantic Telegraph Room**, with a hotline to President Roosevelt; the converted broom cupboard that was **Churchill's office-bedroom** (though he slept here only three times); and the all-important **Map Room**, which was the operational centre.

The free audioguide is very informative and entertaining and features plenty of anecdotes, including some from people who worked here in the war.

Churchill Museum

This superb multimedia museum doesn't shy away from its hero's foibles – it portrays the heavy-drinking Churchill as having a legendary temper, being a bit of a maverick and, on the whole, a pretty lousy peace-time politician. It does focus on his strongest suit: his stirring speeches.

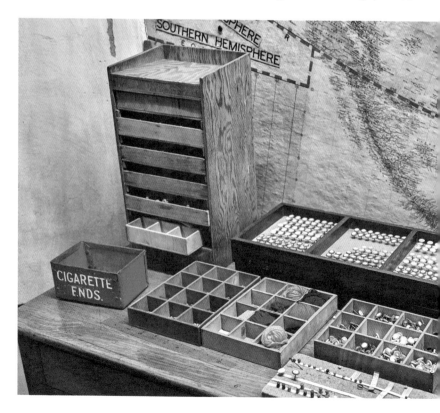

Churchill's orations are replayed for each goose-bumped visitor who steps in front of the interactive displays.

What's Nearby?

No 10 Downing Street Historic Building

(Map p252; www.number10.gov.uk; 10 Downing St, SW1; ⊖Westminster) The official office of British leaders since 1732, when George II presented No 10 to Robert Walpole, this has also been the Prime Minister's London residence since refurbishment in 1902. For such a famous address, No 10 is a small-looking building on a plain-looking street, hardly warranting comparison with the White House, for example. Yet it is actually three houses joined into one and boasts roughly 100 rooms plus a garden covering 2000 sq metres.

The street was cordoned off with a rather large iron gate during Margaret Thatcher's time, so you won't see much. After an IRA mortar attack in 1991, the stout wooden door was replaced with a blast-proof steel version (which cannot be opened from the outside).

RIK HAMILTON/ALAMY STOCK PHOTO ©

Horse Guards Parade Historic Site

(Map p252; www.changing-the-guard.com/london-programme.html; Horse Guards Parade, off Whitehall, W1; ⏲11am Mon-Sat, 10am Sun; ⊖Westminster or St James's Park) In a more accessible version of Buckingham Palace's Changing of the Guard, the mounted troops of the Household Cavalry change guard here daily, at the official vehicular entrance to the royal palaces. A slightly less pompous version takes place at 4pm when the dismounted guards are changed. On the Queen's official birthday in June, the Trooping of the Colour is staged here.

The parade ground and its buildings were built in 1745 to house the Queen's so-called Life Guards. During the reigns of Henry VIII and his daughter Elizabeth, jousting tournaments were staged here.

Banqueting House Palace

(Map p252; ☎020-3166 6155; www.hrp.org.uk/banquetinghouse; Whitehall, SW1; adult/child £6.60/free; ⏲10am-5pm; ⊖Westminster) After the Holbein Gate was demolished in 1759, this is the sole surviving part of the Tudor Whitehall Palace (1532) that once stretched most of the way down Whitehall before going skywards in a 1698 conflagration. Designed by Inigo Jones in 1622 and controversially refaced in Portland stone in the 19th century, Banqueting House was England's first purely Renaissance building and resembled no other structure in the country at the time. The English apparently loathed it for over a century.

Take a Break

Inn the Park (p138), in nearby St James's Park, combines lovely food with a great setting.

Covent Garden Piazza

Covent Garden

London's first planned square is now mostly the preserve of visitors, who flock here to shop among the quaint old arcades or visit some of the excellent nearby sights.

Great For...

☑ Don't Miss

Clambering over old tramways at the London Transport Museum.

History

Covent Garden was originally pastureland that belonged to a 'convent' associated with Westminster Abbey in the 13th century. The site became the property of John Russell, the first Earl of Bedford, in 1552. His descendants employed the architect Inigo Jones to convert a vegetable field into a square in the 17th century. He built the elegant Italian-style piazza, and its tall terraced houses soon started to draw rich socialites who coveted the central living quarters. The bustling fruit and veg market – immortalised in *My Fair Lady* where it was a flower market – dominated the piazza. London society, including such writers as Pepys, Fielding and Boswell, gathered here in the evenings, looking for some action among the coffee houses, theatres, gambling dens and brothels.

MAREMAGNUM/GETTY IMAGES ©

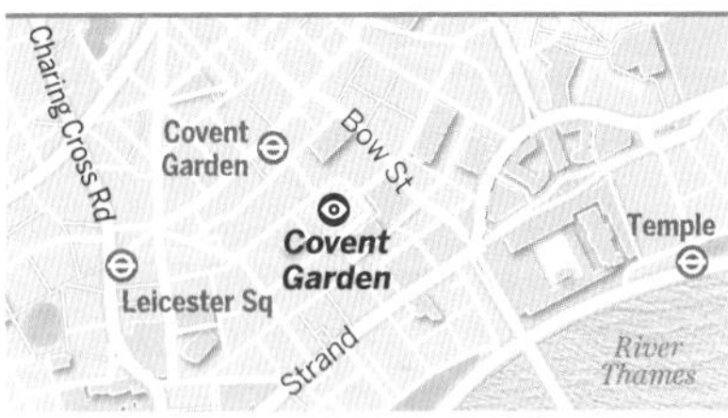

Need to Know

Map p252; Covent Garden

Take a Break

Head to Bombay diner Dishoom (p141) for authentic Indian fare.

★ Top Tip

The many ice-cream parlours and street artists are perfect for families with small children.

Lawlessness became commonplace, leading to the formation of a volunteer police force known as the Bow Street Runners. In 1897, Oscar Wilde was charged with gross indecency in the now-closed Bow St Magistracy. A flower market designed by Charles Fowler was added at the spot where London's Transport Museum now stands.

During the 1970s, the city traffic made it increasingly difficult to maintain the fruit and veg market so it was moved to Nine Elms in South London in 1974. Property developers loomed over the space and there was even talk of the market being demolished for a road but, thanks to the area's dedicated residential community who demonstrated and picketed for weeks, the piazza was saved.

The Piazza

Covent Garden seems to heave whatever the time of day or night. The arcades are chock-a-block with boutiques, market stalls, cafes, ice-cream parlours and restaurants (the quality is usually good, but prices are high).

The **piazza** (Map p252) is a magnet for street artists: there are human statues, classical-music concerts, magicians, stand-up comics and more.

The streets around the piazza are full of top-end boutiques, including famous British designers. Covent Garden is also home to the Royal Opera House and a number of theatres, so even at night, the area buzzes with excitement.

Sights

London Transport Museum — Museum

(Map p252; www.ltmuseum.co.uk; Covent Garden Piazza, WC2; adult/child £16/free; 10am-6pm Sat-Thu, 11am-6pm Fri; Covent Garden) This

entertaining and informative museum looks at how London developed as a result of better transport. It contains everything from horse-drawn omnibuses and early taxis to underground trains you can drive yourself and a forward look at Crossrail (a high-frequency rail service linking Reading with east London, southeast London and Essex, due to open in 2018), plus everything in between. Check out the museum shop for imaginative souvenirs, including historical tube posters and 'Mind the Gap' socks.

London Film Museum Museum
(Map p252; www.londonfilmmuseum.com; 45 Wellington St, WC2; adult/child £14.50/9.50; 10am-5pm; Covent Garden) Recently moved from County Hall south of the Thames, this museum's star attraction is its signature Bond in Motion exhibition. Get shaken and stirred at the largest official collection of 007 vehicles, including Bond's submersible Lotus Esprit (*The Spy Who Loved Me*), the iconic Aston Martin DB5, Goldfinger's Rolls Royce Phantom III and Timothy Dalton's Aston Martin V8 (*The Living Daylights*).

Royal Opera House Historic Building
(Map 252; 020-7304 4000; www.roh.org.uk; Bow St, WC2; adult/child general tours £9.50/7.50, backstage tours £12/8.50; general tour 4pm daily, backstage tour 10.30am, 12.30pm & 2.30pm Mon-Fri, 10.30am, 11.30am, 12.30pm & 1.30pm Sat; Covent Garden) On the north-eastern flank of Covent Garden piazza is the gleaming Royal Opera House. The 'Velvet, Gilt & Glamour Tour' is a general 45-minute turn around the auditorium; more distinctive

London Transport Museum

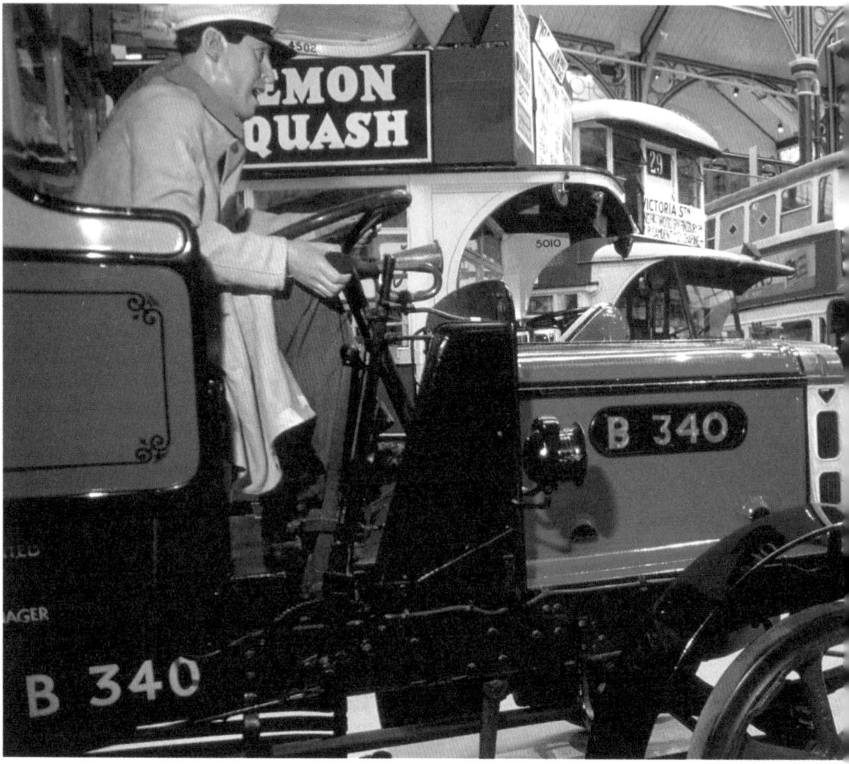

are the 1¼-hour backstage tours taking you through the venue – a much better way to experience the preparation, excitement and histrionics before a performance.

What's Nearby?

Somerset House — Historic Building

(Map p250; www.somersethouse.org.uk; The Strand, WC2; galleries 10am-6pm, Safra Courtyard 7.30am-11pm; Charing Cross, Embankment or Temple) Designed by William Chambers in 1775 for royal societies, Somerset House now contains two fabulous galleries. Near the Strand entrance, the **Courtauld Gallery** (Map p250; www.courtauld.ac.uk; Somerset House, The Strand, WC2; adult/child Tue-Sun £7/free, temporary exhibitions an additional £1.50; 10am-6pm; Charing Cross, Embankment or Temple) displays a wealth of 14th- to 20th-century art, including masterpieces by Rubens, Botticelli, Cézanne, Degas, Renoir, Seurat, Manet, Monet, Léger and others. Downstairs, the Embankment Galleries are devoted to temporary (mostly photographic) exhibitions; prices and hours vary.

Somerset House hosts a number of open-air events in the grand Safra Fountain Court, such as concerts and film screenings in summer and ice skating in winter. The riverside terrace is a popular spot for coffee with a view of the Thames.

☑ Don't Miss

The much beloved Shakespeare Fountain (1874) in Leicester Sq.

VISITBRITAIN/BRITAIN ON VIEW/GETTY IMAGES ©

Leicester Square — Square

(Map p252; Leicester Sq) Although Leicester Sq was very fashionable in the 19th century, more recent decades won it associations with antisocial behaviour, rampant pickpocketing and outrageous cinema ticket prices. The square received an extensive facelift in 2012 and is now a sleek, open-plan plaza. It retains its many cinemas and nightclubs, and as a glamorous premiere venue it still attracts celebrities and their spotters.

St Paul's Church — Church

(Map p252; www.actorschurch.org; Bedford St, WC2; 8.30am-5pm Mon-Fri, varies Sat, 9am-1pm Sun; Covent Garden) The Earl of Bedford, the man who had commissioned Inigo Jones to design Convent Garden Piazza, asked for the simplest possible church, basically no more than a barn. The architect responded by producing 'the handsomest barn in England'. It has long been regarded as the actors' church for its associations with the theatre, and contains memorials to the likes of Charlie Chaplin and Vivien Leigh. The first Punch and Judy show took place in front of it in 1662.

✕ Take a Break

Join the tons of noodle diners at Shoryu (p140) and try the *tonkotsu* ramen.

Lively Soho

A Night Out in Soho

The centre of London nightlife may have shifted east, but Soho remains a perennial favourite for a night out, honouring timeless and classic establishments over the more trendy and fickle. It definitely comes into its own in the evenings, and Soho's reputation as a proud gay neighbourhood is legendary and well deserved.

Great For...

☑ Don't Miss

Old Compton St, Soho's gay village. It's a street loved by all, gay or other, for its great bars, risqué shops and general good vibes.

Pre-Dinner Drinks

French House Bar

(Map p252; www.frenchhousesoho.com; 49 Dean St, W1; noon-11pm Mon-Sat, to 10.30pm Sun; Leicester Sq) French House is Soho's legendary boho boozer with a history to match: this was the meeting place of the Free French Forces during WWII, and De Gaulle is said to have drunk here often, while Dylan Thomas, Peter O'Toole and Francis Bacon all ended up on the wooden floor at least once.

Come to sip on Ricard, French wine or Kronenbourg and check out the quirky locals. Be warned: beer is served by the half-pint only.

LAB Cocktail Bar

(Map p252; 020-7437 7820; www.labbaruk.com; 12 Old Compton St, W1; 4pm-midnight

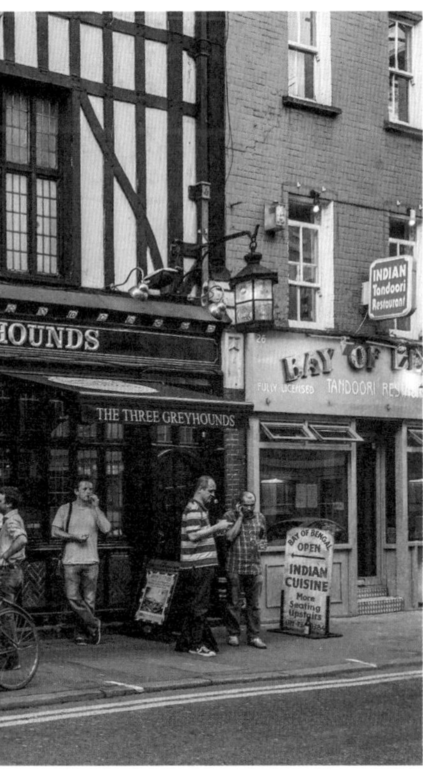

Mon-Sat, to 10.30pm Sun; ⊖Leicester Sq or Tottenham Court Rd) A long-standing Soho favourite for almost two decades, the London Academy of Bartenders (to give it its full name) has some of the best cocktails in town. The list is the size of a small book but, fear not, if you can't make your way through it, just tell the bartenders what you feel like and they'll concoct something divine.

Dinner

Courtesy of Chinatown, there is a wealth of excellent Chinese restaurants.

Yauatcha Chinese ££

(Map p252; ☎020-7494 8888; www.yauatcha.com; 15 Broadwick St, W1; dishes £4-30; ⊙noon-11.30pm Mon-Sat, to 10.30pm Sun; ⊖Piccadilly Circus or Oxford Circus) This most glamorous of dim sum restaurants has a Michelin star and is divided into two: the upstairs dining room offers a delightful blue-bathed oasis of calm from the chaos of Berwick St Market, while downstairs has a smarter, more atmospheric feel with constellations of 'star' lights. Both serve exquisite dim sum and have a fabulous range of teas.

Mildreds Vegetarian £

(Map p252; www.mildreds.co.uk; 45 Lexington St, W1; mains £8.20-10.50; ⊙noon-11pm Mon-Sat; 📶 🌶; ⊖Oxford Circus or Piccadilly Circus) Central London's most inventive vegetarian restaurant, Mildred's heaves at lunchtime so don't be shy about sharing a table in the sky lit dining room. Expect the likes of Sri Lankan sweet potato and cashew nut curry, pumpkin and ricotta ravioli, Middle Eastern meze, wonderfully exotic (and filling) salads and delicious stir-fries. There are also vegan and gluten-free options.

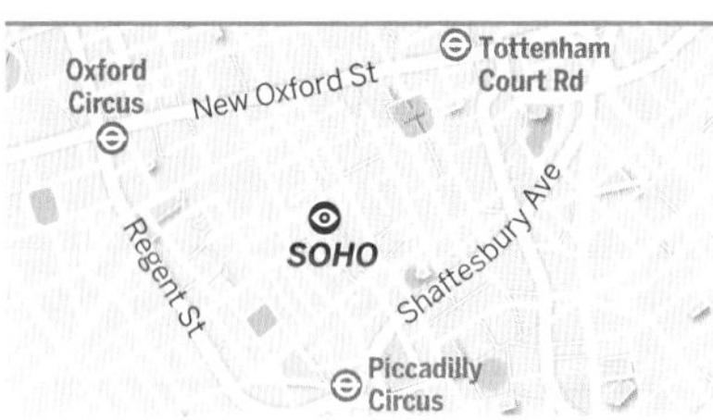

Need to Know

Map p252; ⊖Tottenham Court Rd or Leicester Sq

Take a Break

Nordic Bakery (p139) is a prime spot for an early-evening snack before hitting the late-night Soho sights.

★ Top Tip

Restaurant bookings are advisable for weekend nights.

Entertainment

Pizza Express Jazz Club Jazz

(Map p252; 0845 602 7017; www.pizzaexpresslive.com; 10 Dean St, W1; cover £10-35; Tottenham Court Rd) Pizza Express has been one of the best jazz venues in London since opening in 1969. It may be a bit of a strange arrangement, in a basement beneath the main chain restaurant, but it's highly popular. Lots of big names perform here, and promising artists such as Norah Jones, Jamie Cullum and the late Amy Winehouse played here in their early days.

Ronnie Scott's Jazz

(Map p252; 020-7439 0747; www.ronniescotts.co.uk; 47 Frith St, W1; 7pm-3am Mon-Sat, to midnight Sun; Leicester Sq or Tottenham Court Rd) Ronnie Scott originally opened his jazz club on Gerrard St in 1959 under a Chinese gambling den. The club moved to its current location six years later and became widely known as Britain's best jazz club. Gigs are at 8.15pm (8pm Sunday) with a second act at 11.15pm Friday and Saturday, and are followed by a late, late show until 2am. Expect to pay between £20 and £50.

Ronnie Scott's has hosted such luminaries as Miles Davis, Charlie Parker, Thelonious Monk, Ella Fitzgerald, Count Basie and Sarah Vaughan. The atmosphere is great, but talking during music is a big no-no.

Gay Soho

Village Gay

(Map p252; www.village-soho.co.uk; 81 Wardour St, W1; 4pm-1am Mon-Sat, to 11.30pm Sun; Piccadilly Circus) The Village is always up for a party, whatever the night of the week. There are karaoke nights, 'discolicious' nights,

Piccadilly Circus

go-go dancer nights – take your pick. And if you can't wait until the clubs open to strut your stuff, there is a dance floor downstairs, complete with pole, of course.

Yard Gay

(Map p252; ☎020-7437 2652; www.yardbar.co.uk; 57 Rupert St, W1; ⏰4-11.30pm Mon-Wed, 3-11.30pm Thu, 2pm-midnight Fri & Sat, 2-10.30pm Sun; ⊖Piccadilly Circus) This old Soho favourite attracts a cross section of the great and the good. It's fairly attitude-free, perfect for preclub drinks or just an evening out. There are DJs upstairs in the Loft most nights as well as a friendly crowd in the alfresco (heated in season) Courtyard Bar below.

☑ **Don't Miss**

Regent St's Christmas light displays, which get glowing with great pomp usually around mid-November.

IR STONE/SHUTTERSTOCK ©

She Soho Lesbian

(Map p252; ☎0207 437 4303; www.she-soho.com; 23a Old Compton St, W1D; ⏰4-11.30pm Mon-Thu, to 12.30am Fri & Sat, to 10.30pm Sun; ⊖Leicester Sq) Soho has lost a lesbian bar (Candy Bar) but gained another with this intimate and dimly lit place with DJs at weekends, comedy, live music and quiz nights.

What's Nearby?

Piccadilly Circus Square

(Map p252; ⊖Piccadilly Circus) John Nash had originally designed Regent St and Piccadilly in the 1820s to be the two most elegant streets in town but, curbed by city planners, couldn't realise his dream to the full. He may be disappointed, but suitably astonished, with Piccadilly Circus today: a traffic maelstrom, deluged with visitors and flanked by flashing advertisement panels. A seething hubbub, 'it's like Piccadilly Circus', as the expression goes, but it's certainly fun.

At the centre of the circus stands the famous aluminium statue of Anteros, brother of Eros the God of Love, dedicated to the philanthropist and child-labour abolitionist Lord Shaftesbury. Down the years, the angel has been mistaken for Eros and the misnomer has stuck (you'll even see signs for 'Eros' from the Underground).

Regent Street Street

(Map p252; ⊖Piccadilly Circus or Oxford St) The handsome border dividing the hoi polloi of Soho from the Gucci-two shoed of Mayfair, Regent St was designed by John Nash as a ceremonial route linking the Prince Regent's long-demolished city dwelling with the 'wilds' of **Regent's Park** (Map p256; www.royalparks.org.uk; ⏰5am-9.30pm; ⊖Regent's Park). Nash had to downscale his plan but Regent St is today a well-subscribed shopping street and a beautiful curve of listed architecture.

✕ **Take a Break**

Stop in at Koya (p139), a popular Japanese eatery serving authentic udon noodles.

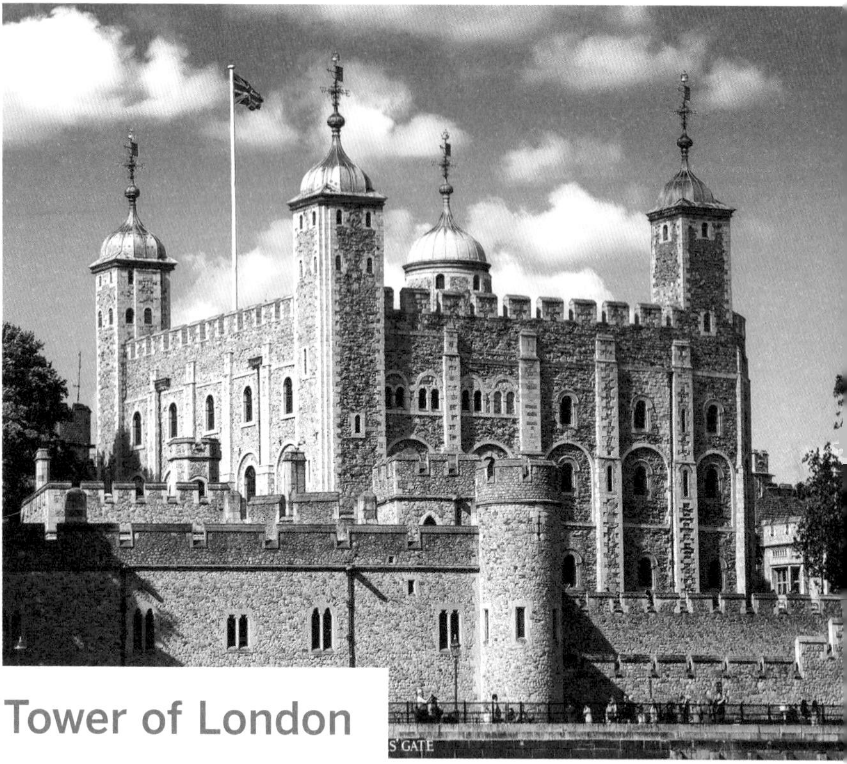

Tower of London

With a history as bleak as it is fascinating, the Tower of London is now one of the city's top attractions, thanks in part to the Crown Jewels.

Great For...

☑ Don't Miss

The colourful Yeoman Warders (or Beefeaters), the spectacular Crown Jewels, the soothsaying ravens and armour fit for a king.

Begun during the reign of William the Conqueror (1066–87), the Tower is in fact a castle containing 22 towers.

Tower Green

The buildings to the west and the south of this verdant patch have always accommodated Tower officials. Indeed, the current constable has a flat in Queen's House built in 1540. But what looks at first glance like a peaceful, almost village-like slice of the Tower's inner ward is actually one of its bloodiest.

Scaffold Site & Beauchamp Tower

Those 'lucky' enough to meet their fate here (rather than suffering the embarrassment of execution on Tower Hill, observed by tens of thousands of jeering and cheering onlookers) numbered but a handful and included two of Henry VIII's wives (and

Stained glass window in All Hallows by the Tower church

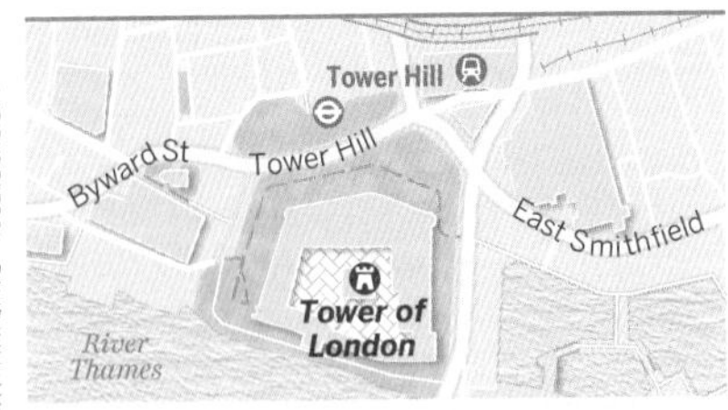

Need to Know

Map p250; 0844 482 7777; www.hrp.org.uk/toweroflondon; Tower Hill, EC3; adult/child £22/10, audioguide £4/3; 9am-5.30pm Tue-Sat, 10am-5.30pm Sun & Mon Mar-Oct, 9am-4.30pm Tue-Sat, 10am-4.30pm Sun & Mon Nov-Feb; Tower Hill

Take a Break

The **Wine Library** (Map p250; 020-7481 0415; www.winelibrary.co.uk; 43 Trinity Sq, EC3; set meal £18; 11.30am-3pm Mon, to 8pm Tue-Fri; Tower Hill) is a great place for a light lunch opposite the Tower.

★ Top Tip

The Tower is huge and will easily take half a day to explore.

alleged adulterers), Anne Boleyn and Catherine Howard; 16-year-old Lady Jane Grey, who fell foul of Henry's daughter Mary I by attempting to have herself crowned queen; and Robert Devereux, Earl of Essex, once a favourite of Elizabeth I.

Just west of the scaffold site is brick-faced Beauchamp Tower, where high-ranking prisoners left behind unhappy inscriptions and other graffiti.

Chapel Royal of St Peter ad Vincula

Just north of the scaffold site is the 16th-century Chapel Royal of St Peter ad Vincula (St Peter in Chains), a rare example of ecclesiastical Tudor architecture and the place where those beheaded on the scaffold outside – most notably Anne Boleyn, Catherine Howard and Lady Jane Grey – were reburied in the 19th century. The church can be visited on a Yeoman Warder tour, or during the first and last hour of normal opening times.

Crown Jewels

To the east of the chapel and north of the White Tower is **Waterloo Barracks**, the home of the Crown Jewels, said to be worth up to £20 billion, but in a very real sense priceless. Here, you file past film clips of the jewels and their role through history, and of Queen Elizabeth II's coronation in 1953, before you reach the vault itself.

Once inside you'll be greeted by lavishly bejewelled sceptres, church plate, orbs and, naturally, crowns. A moving walkway takes you past the dozen or so crowns and other coronation regalia, including the platinum crown of the late Queen Mother, Elizabeth, which is set with the 106-carat Koh-i-Noor (Mountain of Light) diamond, and the State Sceptre with Cross topped with the

530-carat First Star of Africa (or Cullinan I) diamond. A bit further on, exhibited on its own, is the centrepiece: the Imperial State Crown, set with 2868 diamonds (including the 317-carat Second Star of Africa, or Cullinan II), sapphires, emeralds, rubies and pearls. It's worn by the Queen at the State Opening of Parliament in May/June.

White Tower

Built in stone as a fortress in 1078, this was the original 'Tower' of London – its name arose after Henry III whitewashed it in the 13th century. Standing just 30m high, it's not exactly a skyscraper by modern standards, but in the Middle Ages it would have dwarfed the wooden huts surrounding the castle walls and intimidated the peasantry.

Most of its interior is given over to a **Royal Armouries** collection of cannons, guns, and suits of mail and armour for men and horses. Among the most remarkable exhibits on the entrance floor are Henry VIII's two suits of armour, one made for him when he was a dashing 24-year-old and the other when he was a bloated 50-year-old with a waist measuring 129cm. You won't miss the oversized codpiece.

Also here is the fabulous **Line of Kings**, a late 17th-century parade of carved wooden horses and heads of historic kings. On the 1st floor, check out the 2m suit of armour once thought to have been made for the giant-like John of Gaunt and, alongside it, a tiny child's suit of armour designed for James I's young son, the future Charles I. Up on the 2nd floor you'll find the block and axe used to execute Simon Fraser at the last public execution on Tower Hill in 1747.

Line of Kings

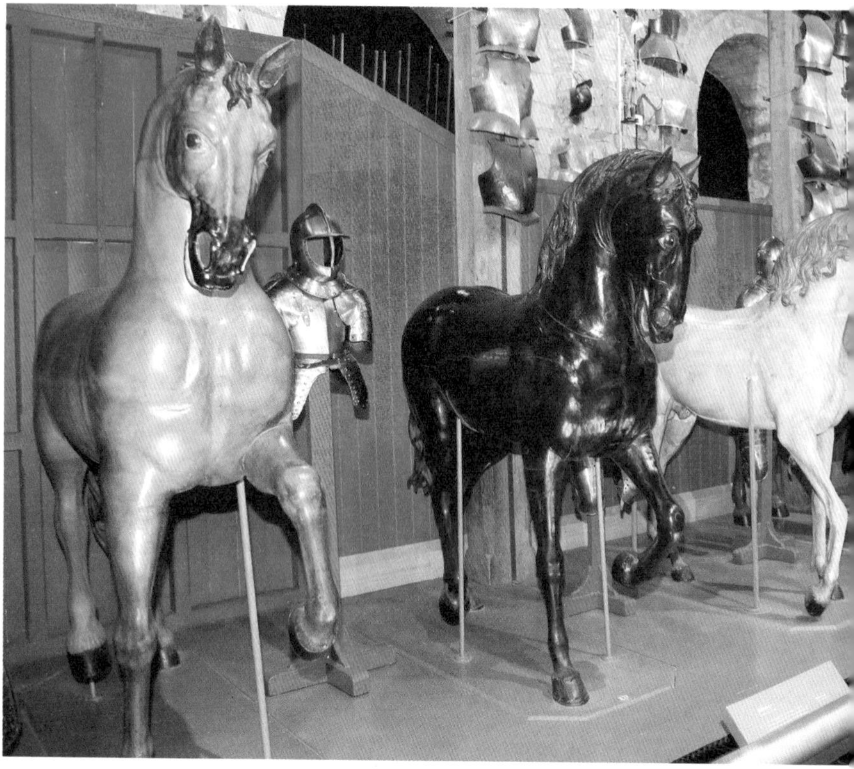

Medieval Palace & the Bloody Tower

The Medieval Palace is composed of three towers: St Thomas's, Wakefield and Langthorn. Inside **St Thomas's Tower** (1279) you can look at what the hall and bedchamber of Edward I might once have been like. Here, archaeologists have peeled back the layers of newer buildings to find what went before. Opposite St Thomas's Tower is **Wakefield Tower**, built by Edward's father, Henry III, between 1220 and 1240. Its upper floor is entered from St Thomas's Tower and has been even more enticingly furnished with a replica throne and other decor to give an impression of how, as an anteroom in a medieval palace, it might have looked. During the 15th-century Wars of the Roses between the Houses of York and Lancaster, King Henry VI was murdered as (it is said) he knelt in prayer in this tower. A plaque on the chapel floor commemorates this Lancastrian king. The **Langthorn Tower**, residence of medieval queens, is to the east.

Below St Thomas's Tower along Water Lane is the famous **Traitors' Gate**, the portal through which prisoners transported by boat entered the Tower. Opposite Traitors' Gate is the huge portcullis of the Bloody Tower, taking its nickname from the 'princes in the Tower' – Edward V and his younger brother, Richard – who were held here 'for their own safety' and later murdered to annul their claims to the throne. The blame is usually laid (notably by Shakespeare) at the feet of their uncle, Richard III, whose remains were unearthed beneath a car park in Leicester in late 2012, but that idea is now being re-examined. An exhibition inside looks at the life and times of Elizabethan adventurer Sir Walter Raleigh, who was imprisoned here three times by the capricious Elizabeth I and her successor James I.

Did You Know?

Over the years, the tower has served as a palace, observatory, armoury, mint and even a zoo.

DAVID GEE 3/ALAMY STOCK PHOTO ©

East Wall Walk

The huge inner wall of the Tower was added to the fortress in 1220 by Henry III to improve the castle's defences. It is 36m wide and is dotted with towers along its length. The East Wall Walk allows you to climb up and tour its eastern edge, beginning in the 13th-century **Salt Tower**, probably used to store saltpetre for gunpowder. The walk also takes in **Broad Arrow Tower** and **Constable Tower**, each containing small exhibits. It ends at the **Martin Tower**, which houses an exhibition about the original

Local Knowledge

Common ravens, which once feasted on the corpses of beheaded traitors, have been here for centuries. Nowadays, they feed on raw beef and biscuits.

coronation regalia. Here you can see some of the older crowns, with their precious stones removed. The oldest surviving crown (1715) is that of George I, which is topped with the ball and cross from the crown of James II. It was from this tower that Colonel Thomas Blood attempted to steal the Crown Jewels in 1671 disguised as a clergyman. He was caught but – surprisingly – Charles II gave him a full pardon.

Yeoman Warders

A true icon of the Tower, the Yeoman Warders have been guarding the fortress since at least the early 16th century. There can be up to 40 – they number 37 at present – and, in order to qualify for the job, they must have served a minimum of 22 years in any branch of the British Armed Forces. They all live within the Tower walls and are known affectionately as 'Beefeaters', a nickname they dislike.

There is currently just one female Yeoman Warder, Moira Cameron, who in 2007 became the first woman to be given the post. While officially they guard the Tower and Crown Jewels at night, their main role is as tour guides (and to pose for photographs with eager tourists). Free tours leave from the Middle Tower every 30 minutes from 10am to 3.30pm (2.30pm in winter).

What's Nearby?

All Hallows by the Tower Church

(Map p250; 020-7481 2928; www.ahbtt.org.uk; Byward St, EC3; 8am-5pm Mon, Tue, Thu & Fri, to 7pm Wed, 10am-5pm Sat & Sun; Tower Hill) All Hallows (meaning 'all saints'), which dates to AD 675, survived virtually unscathed by the Great Fire, only to be hit by German bombs in 1940. Come to see the church itself, by all means, but the best bits are in the atmospheric undercroft (crypt), where you'll the discover a pavement of 2nd-century Roman tiles and the walls of the 7th-century Saxon church.

Monument Tower

(Map p250; www.themonument.info; Fish St Hill, EC3; adult/child £4/2, incl Tower Bridge Exhibition £10.50/4.70; 9.30am-6pm Apr-Sep, to 5.30pm Oct-Mar; Monument) Sir Christopher Wren's 1677 column, known simply as the Monument, is a memorial to the Great Fire of London of 1666, whose impact on London's history cannot be overstated. An immense Doric column made of Portland stone, the Monument is 4.5m wide and 60.6m tall – the exact distance it stands from the bakery in Pudding Lane where the fire is thought to have started.

The Monument is topped with a gilded bronze urn of flames that some think looks like a big gold pincushion. Although Lilliputian by today's standards, the Monument would have been gigantic when built, towering over London.

Climbing up the column's 311 spiral steps rewards you with some of the best 360-degree views over London (due to its central location as much as to its height).

Leadenhall Market at Christmas

Leadenhall Market Market

(Map p250; www.leadenhallmarket.co.uk; Whittington Ave, EC3; 10am-6pm Mon-Fri; Bank or Monument) A visit to this covered mall off Gracechurch St is a step back in time. There's been a market on this site since the Roman era, but the architecture that survives is all cobblestones and late 19th-century Victorian ironwork. Leadenhall Market appears as Diagon Alley in *Harry Potter and the Philosopher's Stone*, and an optician's shop was used for the entrance to the Leaky Cauldron wizarding pub in *Harry Potter and the Goblet of Fire*.

30 St Mary Axe Notable Building

(Gherkin; Map p250; www.30stmaryaxe.info; 30 St Mary Axe, EC3; Aldgate) Nicknamed 'the Gherkin' for its unusual shape, 30 St Mary Axe is arguably the City's most distinctive skyscraper, dominating the skyline despite actually being slightly smaller than the neighbouring NatWest Tower. Built in 2003 by award-winning Norman Foster, the Gherkin's futuristic exterior has become an emblem of modern London – as recognisable as Big Ben and the London Eye.

The building is closed to the public, though in the past it has opened its doors over the **Open House London** (020-7383 2131; www.openhouselondon.org.uk) weekend in September.

Did You Know?

Yeoman Warders are nicknamed Beefeaters. It's thought to be due to the rations of beef – then a luxury food – given to them in the past.

ALLAN BAXTER/GETTY IMAGES ©

Looking toward the altar in St Paul's Cathedral

St Paul's Cathedral

St Paul's Cathedral is one of the most majestic buildings in London. Despite the far higher skyscrapers of the Square Mile, it still manages to gloriously dominate the skyline.

Great For...

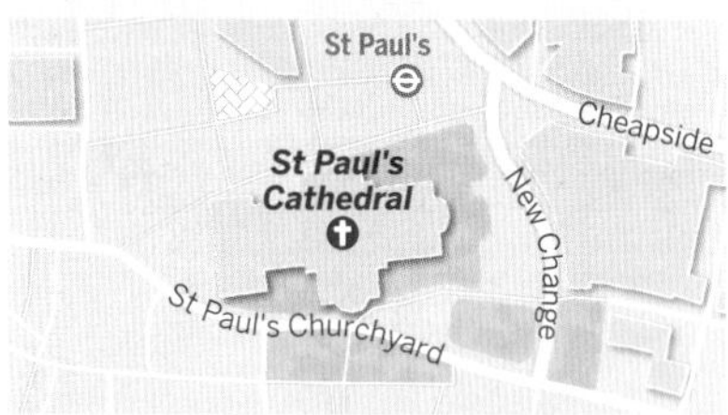

Need to Know

Map p250; 020-7246 8350; www.stpauls.co.uk; St Paul's Churchyard, EC4; adult/child £18/8; 8.30am-4.30pm Mon-Sat; St Paul's

ANDY WILLIAMSO/GETTY IMAGES ©

★ Top Tip

A visit to the church's hallowed ground must be made to fully appreciate its sublime architecture.

There has been a place of Christian worship on this site for over 1400 years. St Paul's Cathedral as we know it is the fifth Christian church to be erected here; it was completed in 1711 and sports the largest church dome in the capital.

Dome

Despite the cathedral's rich history and impressive (and uniform) English baroque interior, many visitors are more interested in climbing the dome for one of the best views of London. It actually consists of three parts: a plastered brick inner dome, a nonstructural lead outer dome visible on the skyline and a brick cone between them holding it all together, one inside the other. This unique structure, the first triple dome ever built and second only in size to St Peter's in the Vatican, made the cathedral Christopher Wren's tour de force. It all weighs 59,000 tonnes.

Some 528 stairs take you to the top, but it's a three-stage journey. Through a door on the western side of the southern transept, and some 30m and 257 steps above, you reach the interior walkway around the dome's base. This is the **Whispering Gallery**, so-called because if you talk close to the wall it carries your words around to the opposite side, 32m away. Climbing even more steps (another 119) you reach the **Stone Gallery**, an exterior viewing platform 53m above the ground, obscured by pillars and other suicide-preventing measures. The remaining 152 iron steps to the **Golden Gallery** are steeper and narrower than below, but are really worth the effort. From here, 85m above London, you can enjoy superb 360-degree views of the city.

View into the cathedral from the Whispering Gallery

Interior

Just beneath the dome is an **epitaph** written for Wren by his son: *Lector, si monumentum requiris, circumspice* (Reader, if you seek his monument, look around you). In the north aisle you'll find the grandiose **Duke of Wellington Memorial** (1912), which took 54 years to complete – the Iron Duke's horse Copenhagen originally faced the other way, but it was deemed unfitting that a horse's rear end should face the altar.

In the north transept chapel is William Holman Hunt's celebrated painting **The Light of the World**, which depicts Christ knocking at a weed-covered door that, symbolically, can only be opened from within. Beyond, in the cathedral's heart, you'll find the spectacular **quire** (or chancel) – its ceilings and arches dazzling with green, blue, red and gold mosaics telling the story of creation – and the **high altar**. The ornately carved choir stalls by Dutch-British sculptor Grinling Gibbons on either side of the quire are exquisite, as are the ornamental wrought-iron gates, separating the aisles from the altar, by French Huguenot Jean Tijou (both men also worked on Hampton Court Palace).

Walk around the altar, with its massive gilded oak **baldacchino**, a kind of canopy with barley-twist columns, to the **American Memorial Chapel**, commemorating the 28,000 Americans based in Britain who lost their lives during WWII. Note the Roll of Honour book turned daily, the state flags in the stained glass and American flora and fauna in the carved wood panelling.

In the south quire aisle, Bill Viola's new and very poignant **video installation** *Martyrs (Earth, Air, Fire, Water)* depicts four figures being overwhelmed by natural forces. A bit further on is an **effigy of John Donne** (1573–1631), metaphysical poet and one-time dean of Old St Paul's that survived the Great Fire.

☑ Don't Miss

Climbing the dome, witnessing the quire ceiling mosaics and visiting the tombs of Admiral Nelson and the Duke of Wellington.

PETER ADAMS/GETTY IMAGES ©

Crypt

On the eastern side of both the north and south transepts are stairs leading down to the crypt and the **OBE Chapel**, where services are held for members of the Order of the British Empire. The crypt has memorials to around 300 of the great and the good, including Florence Nightingale, TE Lawrence (of Arabia) and Winston Churchill, while both the Duke of Wellington and Admiral Nelson are actually buried

Take a Break

The **Crypt Café** (Map p250; Crypt, St Paul's Cathedral, EC4; dishes £5.65-8.25; 9am-5pm Mon-Sat, 10am-4pm Sun; St Paul's) is open for light meals from 9am.

Located here in some form or another since the 13th century, 'London's Larder' has enjoyed an astonishing renaissance in the past 15 years.

The market specialises in high-end fresh products, so you'll find the usual assortment of fruit and vegetable stalls, cheesemongers, butchers, fishmongers, bakeries and delis, as well as gourmet stalls selling spices, nuts, preserves and condiments. Prices tend to be high, but many traders offer free samples, a great perk for visitors and locals alike.

Food window-shopping (and sampling) over, you'll be able to grab lunch from one of the myriad takeaway stalls – anything from sizzling gourmet sausages, chorizo sandwiches, falafel wraps and raclette portions (cheese melted over cured meats and potatoes). There also seems to be an unreasonable number of cake stalls – walking out without a treat will be a challenge! Many of the lunch stalls cluster in Green Market (the area closest to Southwark Cathedral). If you'd rather eat indoors, there are some fantastic cafes and restaurants, too.

The market simply heaves on Saturdays, so get here early for the best pickings or enjoy the craze at lunch time; if you'd like some elbow space to enjoy your takeaway, head to Southwark Cathedral gardens or walk five minutes in either direction along the Thames for river views.

Note that although the full market runs from Wednesday to Saturday, some traders and takeaway stalls do open Mondays and Tuesdays.

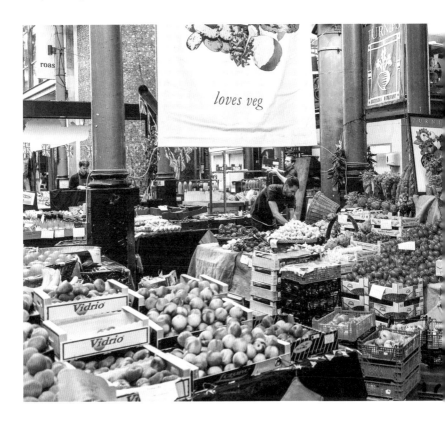

What's Nearby?

Southwark Cathedral

Church

(Map p250; 020-7367 6700; http://cathedral.southwark.anglican.org; Montague Close, SE1; 8am-6pm Mon-Fri, 9am-6pm Sat & Sun; London Bridge) The earliest-surviving parts of this relatively small cathedral are the retrochoir at the eastern end, which contains four chapels and was part of the 13th-century Priory of St Mary Overie, some ancient arcading by the southwest door and an arch that dates to the original Norman church. But most of the cathedral is Victorian. Inside are monuments galore, including a **Shakespeare memorial**. Catch evensong at 5.30pm ... days and Fridays, 4pm o... 3pm on Sundays.

☑ Don't Miss

Grazing on the free samples or eating takeaway in the Southwark Cathedral gardens.

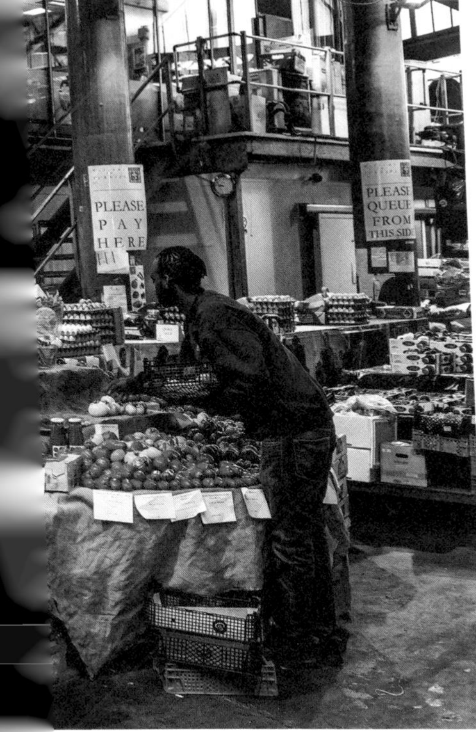

RICHARD I'ANSON/GETTY IMAGES ©

Shard

Notabl...

(Map p250; www.theviewfromtheshard...; London Bridge St, SE1; adult/child £29.95/...; 10am-10pm; London Bridge) Puncturing the skies above London, the dramatic splinter-like form of the Shard has rapidly become an icon of London. The viewing platforms on floors 68, 69 and 72 are open to the public and the views are, as you'd expect from a 244m vantage point, sweeping, but they come at a hefty price – book online at least a day in advance to save £5.

To take in the view for less, visit one of the building's restaurants or bars; you'll pay less than half the viewing-platform ticket price for breakfast or a cocktail at Oblix (p179), where the views are still spectacular.

HMS Belfast

Historic Ship

(Map p250; www.iwm.org.uk/visits/hms-belfast; Queen's Walk, SE1; adult/child £14.50/7.25; 10am-6pm Mar-Oct, to 5pm Nov-Feb; London Bridge) HMS *Belfast* is a magnet for naval-gazing kids of all ages. This large, light cruiser – launched in 1938 – served in WWII, helping to sink the German battleship *Scharnhorst*, shelling the Normandy coast on D-Day, and later participated in the Korean War. Her 6in guns could bombard a target 14 land miles distant. Displays offer a great insight into what life on board was like, in peace times and during military engagements.

There are excellent audioguides (included in your admission fee) featuring anecdotes from former crew members.

✕ Take a Break

Arabica Bar & Kitchen (p144) serves up contemporary Middle Eastern fare.

Shakespeare's Globe

On the South Bank, Shakespeare's Globe attempts to re-create an Elizabethan open-air theatre experience; the resulting venue is a triumph of authenticity, right down to the nail-less construction and English oak beams.

Great For...

☑ Don't Miss

The chance to see actor's treading the boards, either open-air in the Globe or undercover in the Playhouse.

The Globe

Unlike other venues for Shakespearean plays, the new Globe was designed to resemble the original as closely as possible, painstakingly constructed with 600 oak pegs (not a nail or a screw in the house), specially fired Tudor bricks, and thatching reeds from Norfolk that pigeons supposedly don't like. Even the plaster contains goat hair, lime and sand, as it did in Shakespeare's time. It even means having the arena open to the fickle London skies and roar of passing aircraft, leaving the 700 'groundlings' to stand in London's notorious downpours.

Despite the worldwide popularity of Shakespeare over the centuries, the Globe was almost a distant memory when American actor (and, later, film director) Sam Wanamaker came searching for it in 1949.

Exterior of the theatre

Need to Know

Map p250; www.shakespearesglobe.com; 21 New Globe Walk, SE1; adult/child £13.50/8; 9am-5.30pm; Blackfriars, Southwark or London Bridge

Take a Break

Nearby Borough Market (p88) is an embarrassment of riches when it comes to food.

★ Top Tip

The best way to enjoy the Globe is to come and watch a play!

Undeterred by the fact that the theatre's foundations had vanished beneath a row of heritage-listed Georgian houses, Wanamaker set up the Globe Playhouse Trust in 1970 and began fundraising for a memorial theatre. Work started only 200m from the original Globe site in 1987, but Wanamaker died four years before it opened in 1997.

Sam Wanamaker Playhouse

The Globe also opened the Sam Wanamaker Playhouse in 2014, an indoor Jacobean theatre. Shakespeare wrote for both outdoor and indoor theatre, and the playhouse had always been part of the Globe's ambitions.

Tours

Visits include tours of the Globe (which depart half-hourly, generally in the morning so as not to clash with performances) and sometimes the Playhouse, as well as access to the exhibition space beneath the theatre, which has fascinating exhibits about Shakespeare and theatre in the 17th century (including costumes and props), and fun live talks and demonstrations. Or you can of course take in a play (p195).

What's Nearby?

Rose Theatre Theatre

(Map p250; 020-7261 9565; www.rosetheatre.org.uk; 56 Park St, SE1; 10am-5pm Sat; London Bridge) FREE The Rose, for which Christopher Marlowe and Ben Jonson wrote their greatest plays and in which Shakespeare learned his craft, is unique: its original 16th-century foundations were discovered in 1989 beneath an office building and given a protective concrete cover. Administered by the nearby Globe Theatre, the Rose is open to the public only when matinées are being performed at the Globe and can only be visited as part of a group.

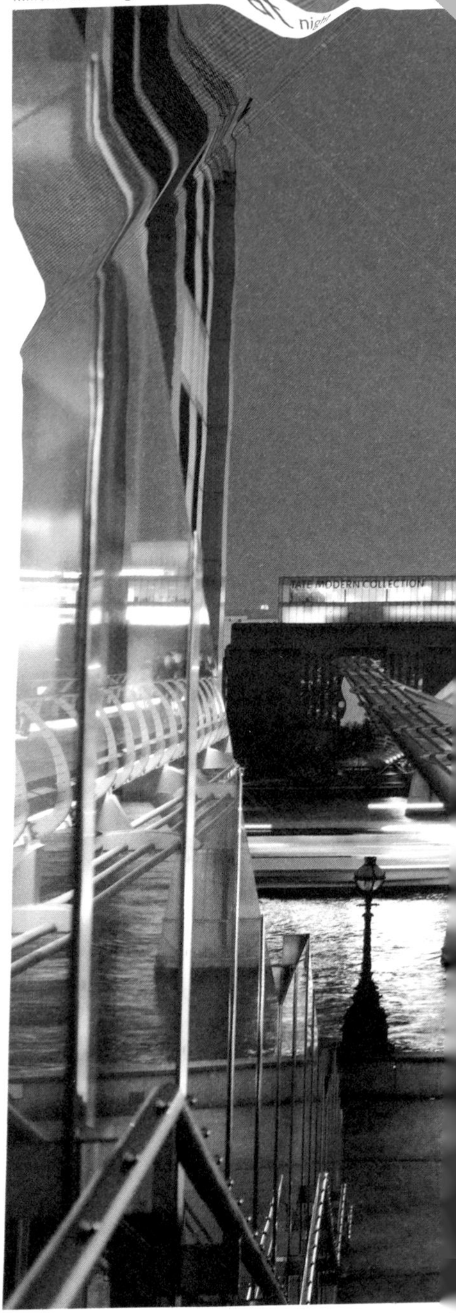

Tate Modern

London's world-class modern and contemporary art museum remains a firm favourite with visitors as much for its superb Pritzker Prize–winning conversion of the former Bankside Power Station as for its contents. This phenomenally successful gallery combines stupendous architecture and a seminal collection of 20th-century modern art. A huge extension opened in summer 2016, dramatically increasing its display space.

Great For...

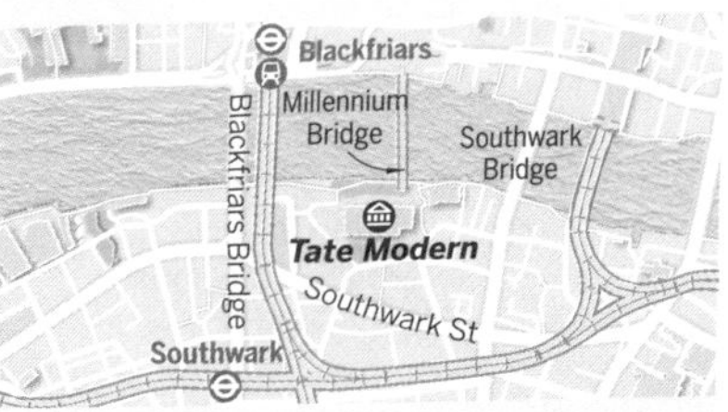

Need to Know

Map p250; www.tate.org.uk; Queen's Walk, SE1; 10am-6pm Sun-Thu, to 10pm Fri & Sat; ; Blackfriars, Southwark or London Bridge; FREE

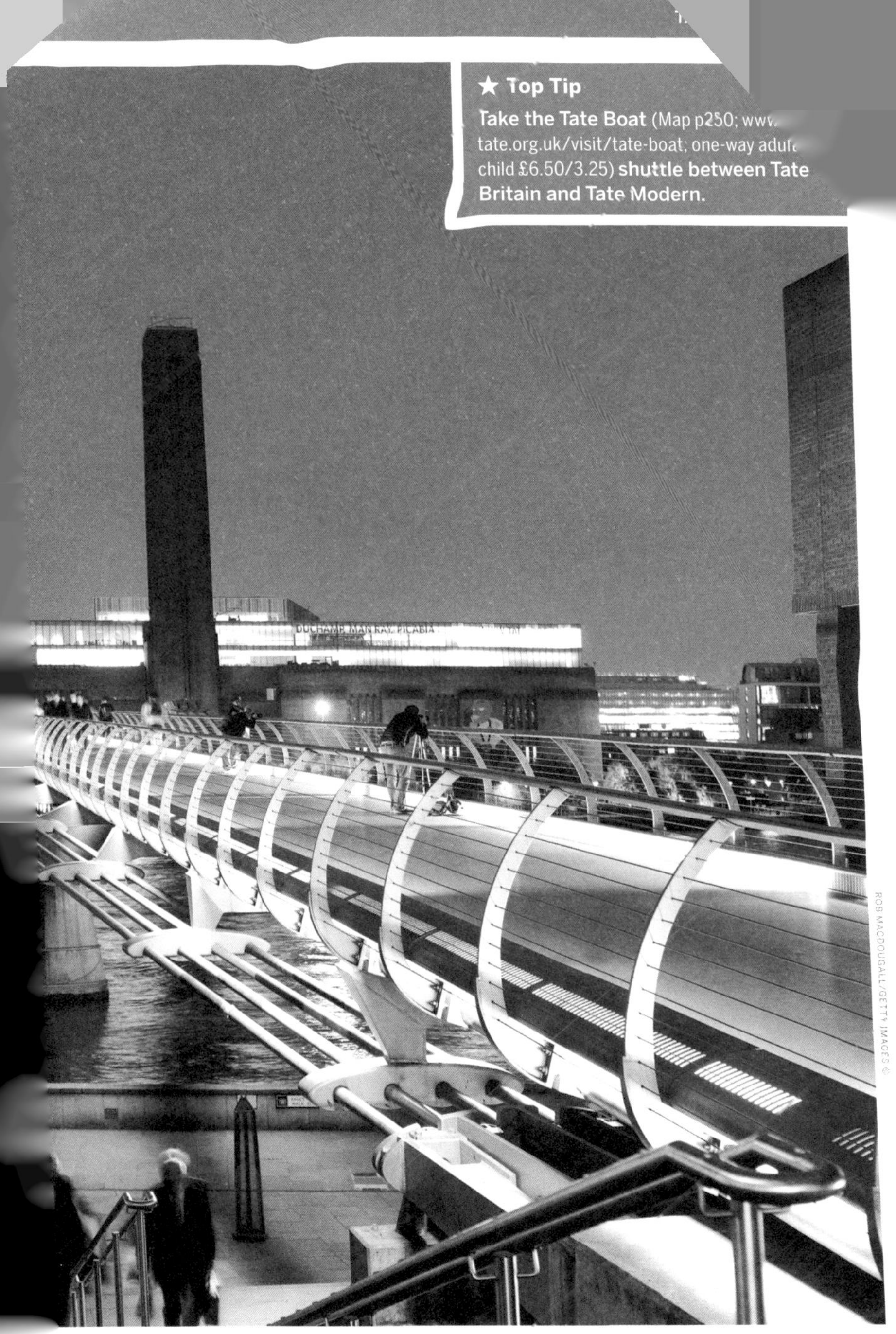

★ Top Tip

Take the Tate Boat (Map p250; www.tate.org.uk/visit/tate-boat; one-way adult/child £6.50/3.25) **shuttle between Tate Britain and Tate Modern.**

ROB MACDOUGALL/GETTY IMAGES ©

...ation

...n-long Tate Modern is an imposing ... ne conversion of the empty Bank- ... Power Station – all 4.2 million bricks of ... – into an art gallery was a masterstroke of design. The 'Tate Modern effect' is clearly as much about the building and its location (cue the ever-popular balconies on level 3 with magnificent views of St Paul) as about the mostly 20th-century art inside. The new Tate Modern Project extension is similarly constructed of brick, but artistically devised as a lattice through which interior lights will be visible at eventide.

Turbine Hall

The first thing to greet you as you pour down the ramp off Holland St (the main entrance) is the astounding 3300-sq-metre Turbine Hall (enter from the river entrance and you'll end up on the more muted level 2). Originally housing the power station's humongous electricity generators, this vast space has become the commanding venue for large-scale installation art and temporary exhibitions. Some art critics swipe at its populism, particularly the 'participatory art' (Carsten Höller's funfair-like slides *Test Site*; Doris Salcedo's enormous *Shibboleth* fissure in the floor; and Robert Morris' climbable geometric sculpture), but others insist this makes art more accessible. Originally visitors were invited to trample over Ai Weiwei's thoughtful and compelling *Sunflower Seeds* – a huge carpet of hand-painted ceramic seeds – until it was discovered people were making off with them in their shoes and turn-ups (to later

Exterior of the Tate Modern

appear on eBay), and the dust emitted by the 'seeds' was diagnosed a health risk.

Permanent Collection

Tate Modern's permanent collection is arranged by both theme and chronology on levels 2, 3 and 4 of the main building and in the extension. More than 60,000 works are on constant rotation, which can be frustrating if you'd like to see one particular piece, but is thrilling for repeat visitors. Helpfully, you can check the excellent website to see whether a specific work is on display – and where.

☑ Don't Miss

Turbine Hall, Special Exhibitions and views of St Paul's Cathedral from level 3 balconies

JULIAN LOVE/GETTY IMAGES ©

The curators have at their disposal paintings by Georges Braque, Henri Matisse, Piet Mondrian, Andy Warhol, Mark Rothko and Jackson Pollock, as well as pieces by Joseph Beuys, Damien Hirst, Rebecca Horn, Claes Oldenburg and Auguste Rodin.

Special Exhibitions

Special exhibitions have included retrospectives on Henri Matisse, Edward Hopper, Frida Kahlo, Roy Lichtenstein, August Strindberg, Nazism and 'Degenerate' Art, and Joan Miró.

Tours

Audioguides (in five languages) are available for £4; they contain explanations of about 50 artworks across the galleries and offer suggested tours for adults or children. Free guided highlights tours depart at 11am, noon, 2pm and 3pm daily.

What's Nearby?

Golden Hinde Historic Ship

(Map p250; ☎020-7403 0123; www.goldenhinde.com; St Mary Overie Dock, Cathedral St, SE1; self-guided tours adult/child £6/4.50, events adult/child £7/5; ⏰10am-5.30pm; 👪; ⊖London Bridge) Stepping aboard this replica of Sir Francis Drake's famous Tudor ship will inspire genuine admiration for the admiral and his rather short (average height: 1.6m) crew, which counted between 40 and 60. It was in a tiny five-deck galleon just like this that Drake and his crew circumnavigated the globe from 1577 to 1580. Visitors can explore the ship by themselves or join a guided tour led by a costumed actor – children love these.

✕ Take a Break

Enjoy a taste of Eastern Europe at the exquisite Baltic (p143).

Walking Tour: East End Eras

This route offers an insight into the old and new of East London. Wander through and soak up the unique character of its neighbourhoods.

Start: ⊖Bethnal Green
Distance: 3.6 miles
Duration: 2½ hours

2 On beautifully preserved **Cyprus St** you'll get a taste of what Victorian Bethnal Green would have looked like.

1 The **Old Ford Rd** area was bombed during WWII, and tower blocks were subsequently erected on the bomb sites.

3 Just over Regent's Canal lies **Victoria Park** (www.towerhamlets.gov.uk/victoriapark; Grove Rd, E3; 7am-dusk; ⊖Hackney Wick). Take the left path along the lake to the **Dogs of Alcibiades** howling on plinths.

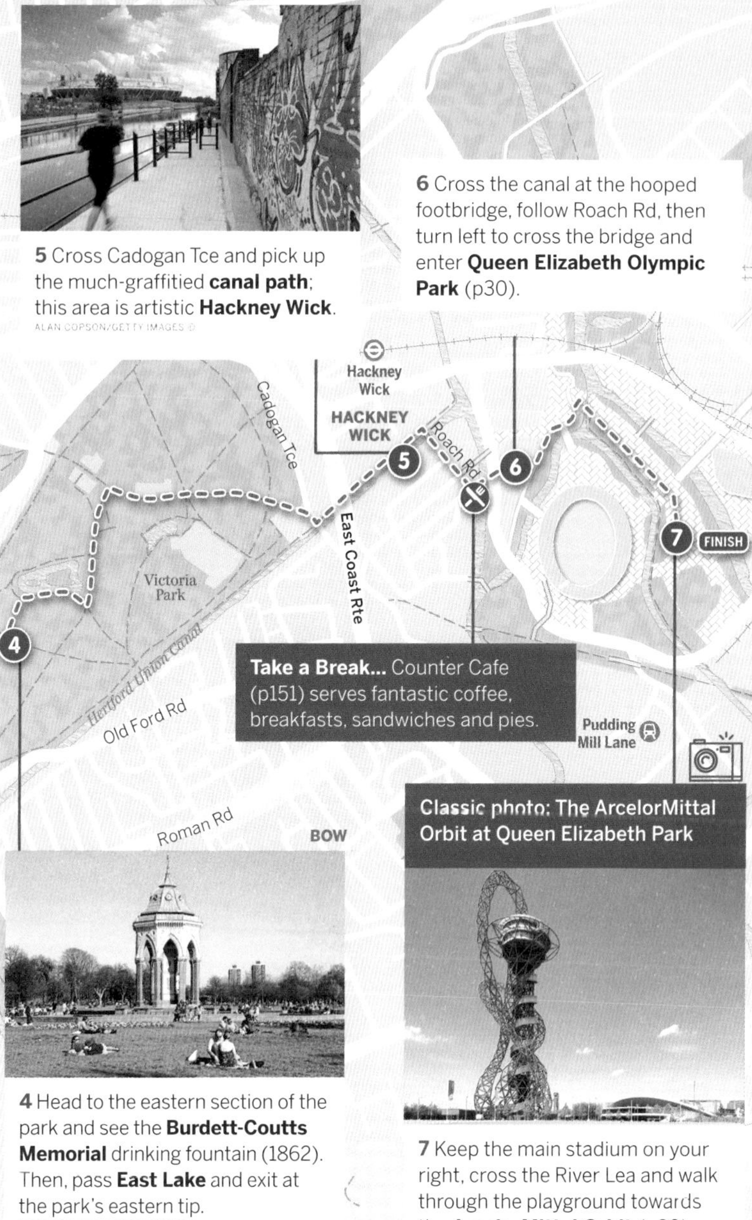

5 Cross Cadogan Tce and pick up the much-graffitied **canal path**; this area is artistic **Hackney Wick**.

ALAN COPSON/GETTY IMAGES ©

6 Cross the canal at the hooped footbridge, follow Roach Rd, then turn left to cross the bridge and enter **Queen Elizabeth Olympic Park** (p30).

Take a Break... Counter Cafe (p151) serves fantastic coffee, breakfasts, sandwiches and pies.

Classic photo: The ArcelorMittal Orbit at Queen Elizabeth Park

4 Head to the eastern section of the park and see the **Burdett-Coutts Memorial** drinking fountain (1862). Then, pass **East Lake** and exit at the park's eastern tip.

PAT TUSON/ALAMY STOCK PHOTO ©

7 Keep the main stadium on your right, cross the River Lea and walk through the playground towards the **ArcelorMittal Orbit** (p30).

RON ELLIS/SHUTTERSTOCK ©

The South Bank and Tower Bridge

The South Bank

Ever since the London Eye came up in 2000, the South Bank has become a magnet for visitors and the area is always a buzz of activity. A roll-call of riverside sights stretches along the Thames, commencing with the London Eye, running past the cultural enclave of the Southbank Centre and onto the Tate Modern, the Millennium Bridge and Shakespeare's Globe.

Great For...

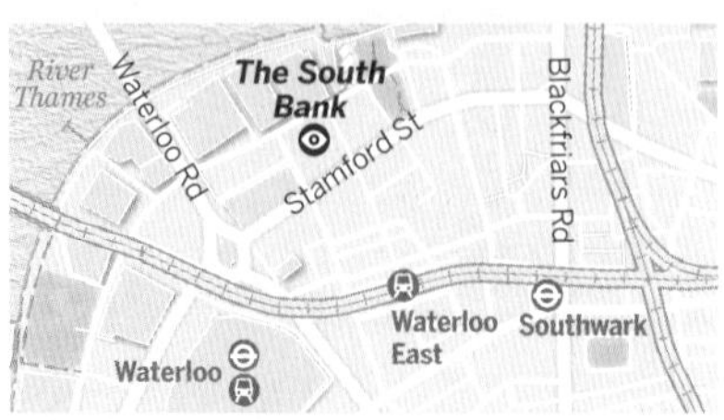

Need to Know

Waterloo or Southwark

★ **Top Tip**

Book online for the London Eye and London Dungeon to skip queues.

JOAS SOUZA PHOTOGRAPHER JOASPH/GETTY IMAGES ©

The South Bank has a great vibe. As well as top attractions, there is plenty to take in whilst enjoying a stroll: views of the north bank of London (including great views of the Houses of Parliament and Big Ben), street artists, office workers on their lunchtime run, and boats toing and froing along the Thames. Two to three days for the South Bank is optimum but if you're in a rush, one day may do for a (frazzling) whistle-stop look at the main sights.

There are also tremendous shops at the National Theatre (p194) and the Southbank Centre.

London Eye

Standing 135m high in a fairly flat city, the **London Eye** (Map p250; 0871 781 3000; www.londoneye.com; adult/child £21.50/15.50; 10am-8pm; Waterloo) affords views 25 miles in every direction, weather permitting. Interactive tablets provide great information (in six languages) about landmarks as they come up in the skyline. Each rotation takes a gracefully slow 30 minutes. At peak times (July, August and school holidays) it may seem like you'll spend more time in the queue than in the capsule however. Save time and money by buying tickets online.

Southbank Centre

The flagship venue of the **Southbank Centre** (Map p250; 020-7960 4200; www.southbankcentre.co.uk; Belvedere Rd, SE1; ; Waterloo), Europe's largest centre for performing and visual arts, is the **Royal Festival Hall** (Map p250; £6-60;). Its gently curved facade of glass and Portland stone is more humane than its 1970s brutalist

View of the city from the London Eye

neighbours. It is one of London's leading music venues and the epicentre of life on this part of the South Bank, hosting cafes, restaurants, shops and bars.

Just north, the austere **Queen Elizabeth Hall** is a brutalist icon, the second-largest concert venue in the centre (closed until late 2017). Underneath its elevated floor is a graffiti-decorated skateboarders' hang-out.

London Dungeon

Older kids tend to love the **London Dungeon** (Map p250; www.thedungeons.com/london; County Hall, Westminster Bridge Rd, SE1; adult/child £25.95/20.95; 10am-5pm, to 6pm Sat & Sun; Waterloo or Westminster), as the terrifying queues during school holidays and weekends testify. It's all spooky music, ghostly boat rides, macabre hangman's drop-rides, fake blood and actors dressed up as torturers and gory criminals (including Jack the Ripper and Sweeney Todd). Beware the interactive bits.

☑ Don't Miss

The astounding views from the London Eye.

PAWEL LIBERA/GETTY IMAGES ©

What's Nearby?

Roupell Street — Street

(Map p250; Roupell St, SE1; Waterloo)
Waterloo station isn't exactly scenic, but wander around the back steets of this transport hub and you'll find some amazing architecture. Roupell St is an astonishingly pretty row of workers' cottages, all dark bricks and coloured doors, dating back to the 1820s. The street is so uniform it looks like a film set.

The same architecture extends to Theed and Whittlesey Sts (which run parallel to Roupell St to the north). The terraced houses were developed for artisan workers by John Palmer Roupell, a gold refiner, between the 1820s and the 1840s. They have survived WWII damage and the many developments of the area intact.

Imperial War Museum — Museum

(www.iwm.org.uk; Lambeth Rd, SE1; 10am-6pm; Lambeth North) FREE Fronted by a pair of intimidating 15-inch naval guns, this riveting museum is housed in what was the Bethlehem Royal Hospital, also known as Bedlam. Although the museum's focus is on military action involving British or Commonwealth troops largely during the 20th century, it rolls out the carpet to war in the wider sense. The highlight of the collection is the state-of-the-art **First World War Galleries**, opened in 2014 to mark the centenary of the war's outbreak.

The museum is a short tube or bus ride from the South Bank and well worth the effort for anyone interested in WWI or WWII.

Take a Break

For tip-top coffee in a bohemian setting, head to Scootercaffe (p142).

JON ARNOLD/GETTY IMAGES ©

Hyde Park

London's largest royal park spreads itself over 142 hectares of neat gardens, wild grasses and glorious trees. As well as being a fantastic green space in the middle of London, it is home to a handful of fascinating sights.

Great For...

☑ **Don't Miss**

The opulence of Apsley House, the Albert Memorial and Kensington Palace.

Henry VIII expropriated Hyde Park from the church in 1536, after which it emerged as a hunting ground for kings and aristocrats; later it became a popular venue for duels, executions and horse racing. It was the first royal park to open to the public in the early 17th century, the famous venue of the Great Exhibition in 1851, and during WWII it became a vast potato bed. These days, as well as being an exquisite park, it is an occasional concert and music-festival venue.

Speakers' Corner

Frequented by Karl Marx, Vladimir Lenin, George Orwell and William Morris, **Speakers' Corner** (Map p249; Park Lane; ⊖Marble Arch), in the northeastern corner of Hyde Park, is traditionally the spot for oratorical acrobatics and soapbox ranting.

It's the only place in Britain where demonstrators can assemble without police

Albert Memorial, Kensington Gardens

ELAN FLEISHER/GETTY IMAGES ©

permission, a concession granted in 1872 after serious riots 17 years before when 150,000 people gathered to demonstrate against the Sunday Trading Bill before Parliament, only to be unexpectedly ambushed by police concealed within Marble Arch.

The Serpentine

Hyde Park is separated from Kensington Gardens by the L-shaped **Serpentine** (Map p249; Knightsbridge or South Kensington), a small lake. It hosted the triathlon swimming during the 2012 Olympics.

The Serpentine Galleries

Straddling the Serpentine lake, the **Serpentine Galleries** (Map p249; www.serpentinegalleries.org; Kensington Gardens, W2; 10am-6pm Tue-Sun; Lancaster Gate or Knightsbridge) FREE may look like quaint historical buildings, but they are one of London's most important contemporary-art galleries. Damien Hirst, Andreas Gursky, Louise Bourgeois, Gabriel Orozco, Tomoko Takahashi and Jeff Koons have all exhibited here.

The original exhibition space is the 1930s former tea pavillion located in Kensington Gardens. In 2013, the gallery opened the **Serpentine Sackler Gallery** (Map p249; www.serpentinegalleries.org; West Carriage Drive, W2; 10am-6pm Tue-Sun; Lancaster Gate) FREE within the Magazine, a former gunpowder depot, across the Serpentine Bridge in Hyde Park. Built in 1805, it has been augmented with a daring, undulating extension designed by Pritzker Prize–winning architect Zaha Hadid.

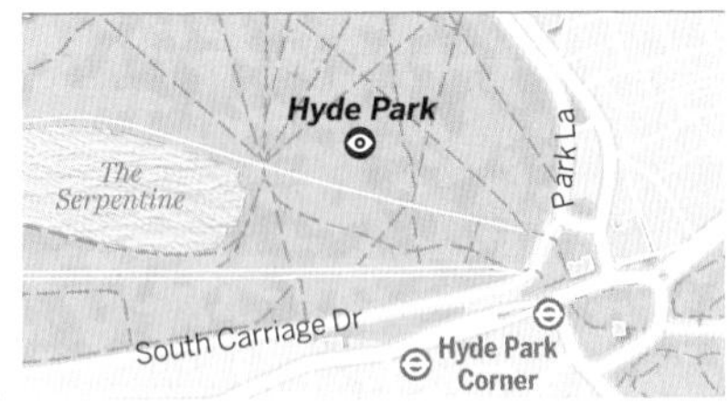

Need to Know

Map p249; www.royalparks.org.uk/parks/hyde-park; 5am-midnight; Marble Arch, Hyde Park Corner or Queensway

Take a Break

Stop off at the **Orangery** (Map p249; 020-3166 6113; www.orangerykensingtonpalace.co.uk; mains £12.50-16, afternoon tea £26; 10am-6pm;), in the grounds of Kensington Palace, for afternoon tea or a pastry.

★ Top Tip

Being so central, Hyde Park is an ideal picnic stop between sights.

Diana, Princess of Wales Memorial Fountain

This **memorial fountain** (Map p249; Knightsbridge) is dedicated to the late Princess of Wales. Envisaged by the designer Kathryn Gustafson as a 'moat without a

castle' and draped 'like a necklace' around the southwestern edge of Hyde Park near the Serpentine Bridge, the circular double stream is composed of 545 pieces of Cornish granite, its waters drawn from a chalk aquifer more than 100m below ground. Unusually, visitors are actively encouraged to splash about, to the delight of children.

A **solar shuttle** (Map p249; ☎020-7262 1330; www.solarshuttle.co.uk; adult/child £5/3) ferries passengers from the Serpentine Boathouse to the fountain at weekends from March to September (every day from mid-July to late August).

Gun Salutes

Royal Gun Salutes are fired in Hyde Park on 10 June for the Duke of Edinburgh's birthday and on 14 November for the Prince of Wales' birthday. The salutes are fired at midday and include 41 rounds (21 is standard, but being a royal park, Hyde Park gets a bonus 20 rounds).

What's Nearby?

Kensington Palace Palace

(Map p249; www.hrp.org.uk/kensingtonpalace; Kensington Gardens, W8; adult/child £17.50/free; 10am-6pm Mar-Oct, to 5pm Nov-Feb; ⊖High St Kensington) Built in 1605, the palace became the favourite royal residence under William and Mary of Orange in 1689, and remained so until George III became king and relocated to Buckingham Palace. Today, it is still a royal residence, with the likes of the Duke and Duchess of Cambridge (Prince William and his wife Catherine) and Prince Harry living there. A large part of the palace is open to the public, however, including the King's and Queen's State Apartments.

Kensington Gardens

The **King's State Apartments** are the most lavish, starting with the **Grand Staircase**, a dizzying feast of trompe l'œil. The beautiful **Cupola Room**, once the venue of choice for music and dance, is arranged with gilded statues and a gorgeous painted ceiling. The **Drawing Room** is beyond, where the king and courtiers would entertain themselves with cards.

Kensington Gardens Park

(Map p249; www.royalparks.org.uk/parks/kensington-gardens; 6am-dusk; Queensway or Lancaster Gate) Immediately west of Hyde Park and across the Serpentine lake, these picturesque 275-acre gardens are technically part of Kensington Palace. The park is a gorgeous collection of manicured lawns, tree-shaded avenues and basins. The largest is the **Round Pond**, close to the palace. Also worth a look are the lovely fountains in the **Italian Gardens** (Map p249), believed to be a gift from Prince Albert to Queen Victoria.

☑ Don't Miss

The 'Summer Pavilion' (June to October); an architect who has never built in the UK is annually commissioned to build a pavilion for the Serpentine Galleries.

EURASIA PRESS/GETTY IMAGES ©

Apsley House Historic Building

(Map p249; www.english-heritage.org.uk/visit/places/apsley-house/; 149 Piccadilly, Hyde Park Corner, W1; adult/child £8.30/5, with Wellington Arch £10/6; 11am-5pm Wed-Sun Apr-Oct, 10am-4pm Sat & Sun Nov-Mar; Hyde Park Corner) This stunning house, containing exhibits about the Duke of Wellington, victor of Waterloo against Napoleon Bonaparte, was once the first building to appear when entering London from the west and was therefore known as 'No 1 London'. Wellington memorabilia, including the duke's death mask, fills the basement **gallery**, while there's an astonishing collection of china and silver, and paintings by Velasquez, Rubens, Van Dyck, Brueghel, Murillo and Goya on the 1st-floor Waterloo Gallery.

Albert Memorial Monument

(Map p249; Kensington Gardens; tours adult/concession £8/7; tours 2pm & 3pm 1st Sun of month Mar-Dec; Knightsbridge or Gloucester Rd) This splendid Victorian confection on the southern edge of Kensington Gardens is as ostentatious as the subject. Queen Victoria's German husband Albert (1819–61) was purportedly humble. Albert explicitly insisted he did not want a monument; ignoring the good prince's wishes, the Lord Mayor instructed George Gilbert Scott to build the 53m-high, gaudy Gothic memorial in 1872.

Take a Break

If you're after somewhere more colourful (and some shade), head to the **Rose Garden** (Map p249; Hyde Park; Hyde Park Corner or Knightsbridge), a beautifully landscaped garden with flowers year-round.

Victoria & Albert Museum

The Museum of Manufactures, as the V&A was known when it opened in 1852, was part of Prince Albert's legacy to the nation in the aftermath of the successful Great Exhibition of 1851. Its aims were the 'improvement of public taste in design' and 'applications of fine art to objects of utility'. It's done a fine job so far.

Great For...

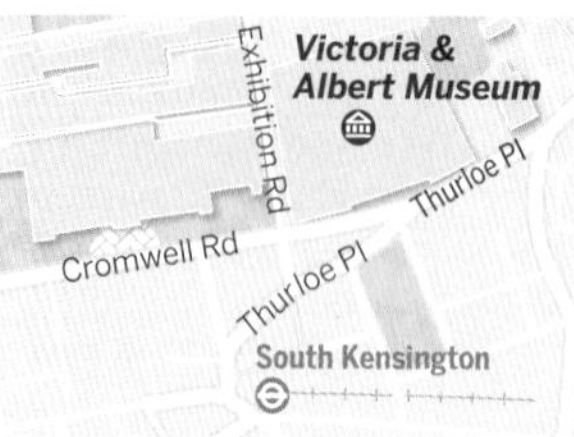

Need to Know

Map p249; www.vam.ac.uk; Cromwell Rd, SW7; 10am-5.45pm Sat-Thu, to 10pm Fri; South Kensington; FREE

★ Top Tip

The V&A's temporary exhibitions are reliably fantastic, so factor some time to check them out.

Collection

Through 146 galleries, the museum houses the world's greatest collection of decorative arts, from ancient Chinese ceramics to modernist architectural drawings, Korean bronze and Japanese swords, cartoons by Raphael, gowns from the Elizabethan era, ancient jewellery, a Sony Walkman – and much, much more.

Tours

Several free one-hour guided tours leave the main reception area every day. Times are prominently displayed; alternatively, check the website for details.

Entrance

Entering under the stunning blue-and-yellow blown-glass **chandelier** by Dale Chihuly, you can grab a museum map (£1 donation requested) at the information desk. (If the 'Grand Entrance' on Cromwell Rd is too busy, there's another around the corner on Exhibition Rd, or you can enter from the tunnel in the basement, if arriving by tube.)

Level One

The street level is mostly devoted to art and design from India, China, Japan, Korea and Southeast Asia, as well as European art. One of the museum's highlights is the **Cast Courts** in rooms 46a and 46b, containing staggering plaster casts collected in the Victorian era, such as Michelangelo's *David,* acquired in 1858.

The **T.T. Tsui Gallery** (rooms 44 and 47e) displays lovely pieces, including a beautifully lithe wooden statue of Guanyin seated in *lalitasana* pose from AD 1200; also check out a leaf from the 'Twenty views of the Yuanmingyuan Summer Palace' (1781–86), revealing the Haiyantang and the 12 animal heads of the fountain (now ruins) in Beijing. Within the subdued lighting of the **Japan Gallery** (room 45) stands a fearsome suit of armour in the Domaru style. More than 400 objects are within the **Islamic Middle East Gallery** (room 42), including ceramics, textiles, carpets, glass and woodwork from the 8th century up to the years before WWI. The exhibition's highlight is the gorgeous mid-16th-century **Ardabil Carpet**.

For fresh air, the landscaped **John Madejski Garden** is a lovely shaded inner courtyard. Cross it to reach the original **Refreshment Rooms** (Morris, Gamble and Poynter Rooms), dating from the 1860s and redesigned by McInnes Usher McKnight Architects (MUMA), who also renovated the **Medieval and Renaissance galleries** (1350–1600) to the right of the Grand Entrance.

☑ Don't Miss

Chinese ceramics, Japanese swords, Elizabethan gowns, and ancient jewellery.

Levels Two & Four

The **British Galleries**, featuring every aspect of British design from 1500 to 1900, are divided between levels 2 (1500–1760) and 4 (1760–1900). Level 4 also boasts the **Architecture Gallery** (rooms 127 to 128a), which vividly describes architectural styles via models and videos, and the spectacular brightly illuminated **Contemporary Glass Gallery** (room 129).

Level Three

The **Jewellery Gallery** (rooms 91 to 93) is outstanding; the mezzanine level – accessed via the glass-and-perspex spiral staircase – glitters with jewel-encrusted swords, watches and gold boxes. The **Photographs Gallery** (room 100) is one of the nation's best, with access to over 500,000 images collected since the mid-19th century. **Design Since 1946** (room 76) celebrates design classics, from a 1985 Sony credit-card radio to a 1992 Nike 'Air Max' shoe, Peter Ghyczy's Garden Egg Chair from 1968 and the now-ubiquitous selfie stick.

Level Six

Among the pieces in the **Ceramics Gallery** (rooms 136 to 146) – the world's largest – are standout items from the Middle East and Asia. The **Dr Susan Weber Gallery** (rooms 133 to 135) celebrates furniture design over the past six centuries.

Take a Break

The **V&A Café** (mains £6.95-11.50; 10am-5.15pm Sat-Thu, to 9.30pm Fri;), in the magnificent Refreshment Rooms, dates from the 1860s.

Natural History Museum

This colossal building is infused with the irrepressible Victorian spirit of collecting, cataloguing and interpreting the natural world. The museum building is as much a reason to visit as the world-famous collection within. Seasonal events and excellent temporary exhibitions complete the package, making this one of the very best museums in London, especially for families.

Great For...

☑ Don't Miss

Fascinating displays about Planet Earth, outstanding Darwin Centre and architecture straight from a Gothic fairy tale.

Hintze Hall

This grand central hall resembles a cathedral nave – quite fitting for a time when the natural sciences were challenging the biblical tenets of Christian orthodoxy. Naturalist and first superintendent of the museum Richard Owen celebrated the building as a 'cathedral to nature'.

From summer 2017, the hall will be dominated by the skeleton of a blue whale, displayed in a diving position for dramatic effect. It replaces the diplodocus skeleton cast that has been the hall's main resident since the 1960s.

Blue Zone

Undoubtedly the museum's star attraction, the **Dinosaurs Gallery** takes you on an impressive overhead walkway, past a dromaeosaurus (a small and agile meat eater)

The museum's architectural detail

ILEANA_BT/SHUTTERSTOCK ©/GETTY IMAGES ©

before reaching a roaring animatronic T-Rex and then winding its way through skeletons, fossils, casts and fascinating displays about how dinosaurs lived and died.

Another highlight of this zone is the **Mammals & Blue Whale Gallery**, with its life-size blue whale model and extensive displays on cetaceans.

Green Zone

While children love the Blue Zone, adults may prefer the Green Zone, especially the **Treasures in Cadogan Gallery**, on the first floor, which houses the museum's most prized possessions, each with a unique history. Exhibits include a chunk of moon rock, an Emperor penguin egg collected by Captain Scott's expedition and a first edition of Charles Darwin's *On the Origin of Species*.

Need to Know

Map p249; www.nhm.ac.uk; Cromwell Rd, SW7; 10am-5.50pm; South Kensington; FREE

Take a Break

The **Queen's Arms** (Map p249; www.thequeensarmskensington.co.uk; 30 Queen's Gate Mews, SW7; noon-11pm), just around the corner from the Royal Albert Hall, beckons with a cosy interior and a right royal selection of ales and ciders on tap.

★ Top Tip

Families can borrow an 'explorer backpack' or buy a themed discover trail (£1).

Equally rare and exceptional are the gems and rocks held in the **Vault**, including a Martian meteorite and the largest emerald ever found.

Take a moment to marvel at the trunk section of a 1300-year-old **giant sequoia tree** on the second floor: its size is mind-boggling.

Back on the ground floor, the **Creepy Crawlies Gallery** is fantastic, delving into every aspect of insect life and whether they are our friends or foe (both!).

Red Zone

This zone explores the ever-changing nature of our planet and the forces shaping it. The **earthquake simulator** (in the **Volcanoes & Earthquakes Gallery**), which re-creates the 1995 Kobe earthquake in a grocery store (of which you can see footage) is a favourite, as is the **From the**

Beginning Gallery, which retraces Earth's history.

In **Earth's Treasury**, you can find out more about our planet's mineral riches and how they are being used in our everyday lives, from jewellery to construction and electronics.

Access to most of the galleries in the Red Zone is via **Earth Hall** and a very tall escalator that disappears into a large Earth metal sculpture. The most intact **stegosaurus fossil skeleton** ever found is displayed at the base.

Orange Zone

The **Darwin Centre** is the beating heart of the museum: this is where the museum's millions of specimens are kept and where its scientists work. The top two floors of the amazing '**cocoon**' building are dedicated to explaining the kind of research the museum does (and how) – windows allow you to see the researchers at work.

If you'd like to find out more, pop into the **Attenborough studio** (named after famous naturalist and broadcaster David Attenborough) for one of the daily talks with the museum's scientists. The studio also shows films throughout the day.

Exhibitions

The museum hosts regular exhibitions (admission fees apply), some of them on a recurrent basis. **Wildlife Photographer of the Year** (adult/child £12.60/6.30; ⌚Nov-Aug), with its show-stopping images, recently celebrated its 50th year, and **Sensational Butterflies**, a tunnel tent on the East Lawn that swarms with what must originally have been called 'flutter-bys', has become a firm

Earth Hall, Red Zone

summer favourite. In winter, the same lawn turns into a very popular **ice-skating rink**.

What's Nearby?

Science Museum — Museum

(Map p249; www.sciencemuseum.org.uk; Exhibition Rd, SW7; 10am-6pm; South Kensington) FREE With seven floors of interactive and educational exhibits, this scientifically spellbinding museum will mesmerise adults and children alike, covering everything from early technology to space travel. A perennial favourite is **Exploring Space**, a gallery featuring genuine rockets and satellites and a full size replica of 'Eagle', the lander that took Neil Armstrong and Buzz Aldrin to the Moon in 1969. The **Making the Modern World Gallery** next door is a visual feast of locomotives, planes, cars and other revolutionary inventions.

The fantastic **Information Age Gallery** on level 2 showcases how information and communication technologies – from the telegraph to smartphones – have transformed our lives since the 19th century. Standout displays include wireless messages sent by a sinking *Titanic*, the first BBC radio broadcast and a Soviet BESM 1965 supercomputer.

The 3rd-floor **Flight Gallery** (free tours 1pm most days) is a favourite place for children, with its gliders, hot-air balloons and aircraft, including the *Gipsy Moth*, which Amy Johnson flew to Australia in 1930. This floor also features a **Red Arrows 3D flight simulation theatre** (adult/child £6/5) and **Fly 360 degree flight simulator capsules** (£12 per capsule). On the same floor is a new Interactive gallery, formerly the home of Launchpad, which is packed with state-of-the-art interactive exhibits.

If you've kids under the age of five, pop down to the basement and the **Garden**, where there's a fun-filled play zone, including a water-play area, besieged by tots in orange waterproof smocks.

☑ Don't Miss

From Halloween to January, a section by the East Lawn of the museum is transformed into a glittering and highly popular ice rink.

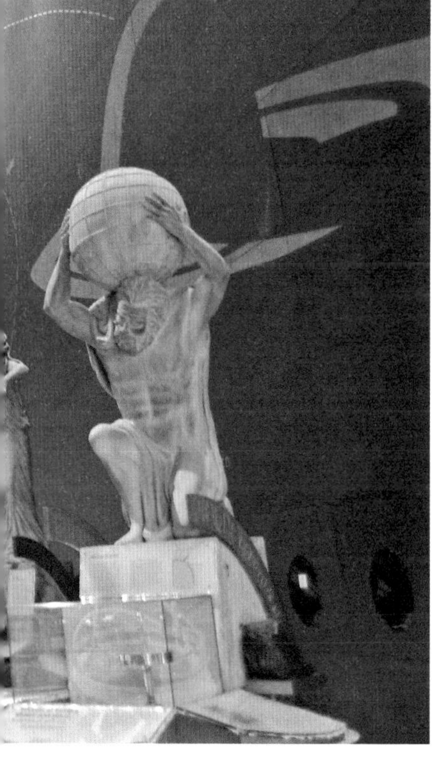

BABAK TAFRESHI/GETTY IMAGES ©

Take a Break

A slice of English countryside, the beautiful **Wildlife Garden** next to the West Lawn encompasses a range of British lowland habitats, including a meadow with farm gates and a bee tree where a colony of honey bees fills the air.

Royal Observatory from Greenwich Park

IR STONE/SHUTTERSTOCK ©

Royal Observatory & Greenwich Park

The Royal Observatory is where the study of the sea, the stars and time converge. The prime meridian charts its line through the grounds of the observatory, chosen quite arbitrarily in 1884, dividing the globe into the eastern and western hemispheres.

Great For...

☑ Don't Miss

Straddling hemispheres and time zones as you stand on either side of the actual meridian line in the Meridian Courtyard.

Royal Observatory

Unlike most other attractions in Greenwich, the Royal Observatory contains free-access areas (Weller Astronomy Galleries, Great Equatorial Telescope) and ones you pay for (Meridian Line, Flamsteed House).

Flamsteed House & Meridian Courtyard

Charles II ordered construction of the Christopher Wren–designed Flamsteed House, the original observatory building, on the foundations of Greenwich Castle in 1675 after closing the observatory at the Tower of London. Today it contains the magnificent **Octagon Room** and the rather simple apartment where the Astronomer Royal, John Flamsteed, and his family lived. Here you'll also find the brilliant new **Time Galleries**, explaining how the longitude

Time Ball

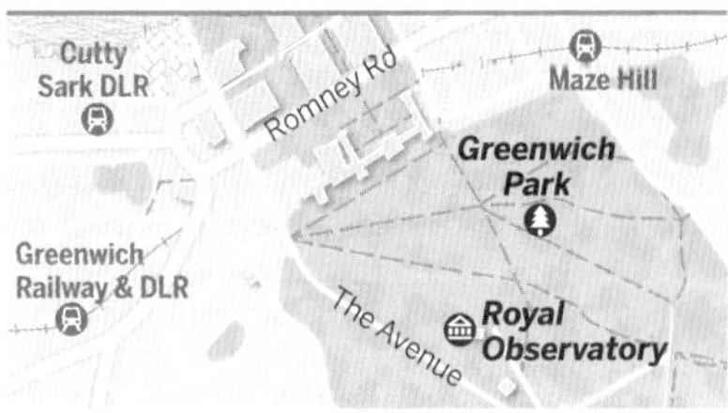

Need to Know

www.rmg.co.uk; Greenwich Park, Blackheath Ave, SE10; adult/child £9.50/5, with Cutty Sark £16.80/7.70; 10am-5pm Oct-Jun, to 6pm Jul-Sep; DLR Cutty Sark or DLR Greenwich, Greenwich)

Take a Break

Enjoy locally brewed beer and lovely food at the **Old Brewery** (020-3327 1280; www.oldbrewerygreenwich.com).

★ Top Tip

Get here before 1pm on any day of the week to see the red time ball at the top of the Royal Observatory drop.

problem – how to accurately determine a ship's east-west location – was solved through astronomical means and the invention of the marine chronometer.

In the Meridian Courtyard, where the globe is decisively sliced into east and west, visitors can delightfully straddle both hemispheres, with one foot on either side of the meridian line. Every day the red **Time Ball** at the top of the Royal Observatory drops at 1pm, as it has done ever since 1833.

Astronomy Centre & Planetarium

The southern half of the observatory contains the highly informative (and free) **Weller Astronomy Galleries**, where you can touch the oldest object you will ever encounter: part of the Gibeon meteorite, a mere 4.5 billion years old. Other engaging exhibits include an orrery (a mechanical model of the solar system, minus the as-yet-discovered Uranus and Neptune) from 1780, astronomical documentaries, a first edition of Newton's *Principia Mathematica* and the opportunity to view the Milky Way in multiple wavelengths. To take stargazing further, pick up a Skyhawk telescope from the shop.

The state-of-the-art **Peter Harrison Planetarium** (020-8312 6608; www.rmg.co.uk/whats-on/planetarium-shows; adult/child £7.50/5.50; Greenwich, DLR Cutty Sark) – London's only planetarium – can cast entire heavens onto the inside of its roof. It runs at least five informative shows a day.

Greenwich Park

The **park** (www.royalparks.org.uk; King George St, SE10; 6am-6pm winter, to 8pm spring & autumn, to 9pm summer; Greenwich or Maze Hill, DLR Cutty Sark) is one of London's loveliest expanses of green, with a rose garden, picturesque walks, Anglo-Saxon tumuli and

astonishing views from the crown of the hill near the Royal Observatory towards Canary Wharf, the financial district across the Thames. Greenwich Park hosted the 2012 Olympic Games equestrian events.

Covering 74 hectares, this is the oldest enclosed royal park and is partly the work of André Le Nôtre, the landscape architect who designed the palace gardens of Versailles. The view of central London from the statue of General James Wolfe, celebrated for his victory over the French at the Battle of Quebec in Canada in 1759, is one of the best in the city.

Ranger's House (Werhner Collection)

This elegant Georgian **villa** (EH; 020-8294 2548; www.english-heritage.org.uk; Greenwich Park, Chesterfield Walk, SE10; adult/child £7.20/4.30; guided tours only at 11am & 2pm Sun-Wed late Mar-Sep; Greenwich, DLR Cutty Sark), built in 1723, once housed the park's ranger and now contains a collection of 700 works of fine and applied art (medieval and Renaissance paintings, porcelain, silverware, tapestries) amassed by Julius Wernher (1850–1912), a German-born railway engineer's son who struck it rich in the diamond fields of South Africa in the 19th century. The Spanish Renaissance jewellery collection is the best in Europe, and the rose garden fronting the house makes a visit in June even more special.

What's Nearby?

Old Royal Naval College Historic Building

(www.ornc.org; 2 Cutty Sark Gardens, SE10; grounds 8am-6pm; DLR Cutty Sark) FREE

Painted Hall, Old Royal Naval College

Designed by Christopher Wren, the Old Royal Naval College is a magnificent example of monumental classical architecture. Parts are now used by the University of Greenwich and Trinity College of Music, but you can still visit the **chapel** and the extraordinary **Painted Hall**, which took artist Sir James Thornhill 19 years to complete. Hour-long, yeomen-led tours (£6) of the complex leave at noon daily, taking in areas not otherwise open to the public.

The complex was built on the site of the 15th-century Palace of Placentia, the birthplace of Henry VIII and Elizabeth I. This Tudor connection, along with Greenwich's industrial and maritime history, is explored in the **Discover Greenwich** (www.ornc.org; Pepys Building, King William Walk, SE10; 10am-5pm) FREE centre. The tourist office is based here, along with a cafe/restaurant and microbrewery.

JOAS SOUZA PHOTOGRAPHER - JOASPH/GETTY IMAGES ©

Cutty Sark Museum

(020-8312 6608; www.rmg.co.uk/cuttysark; King William Walk, SE10; adult/child £12.15/6.30, with Royal Observatory £16.80/7.70; 10am-5pm; DLR Cutty Sark) This Greenwich landmark, the last of the great clipper ships to sail between China and England in the 19th century, is now fully operational after six years and £25 million of extensive renovations largely precipitated by a disastrous fire in 2007. The exhibition in the ship's hold tells her story as a tea clipper at the end of the 19th century.

Launched in 1869 in Scotland, she made eight voyages to China in the 1870s, sailing out with a mixed cargo and coming back with a bounty of tea. As you make your way up, there are films, interactive maps and plenty of illustrations and props to get an idea of what life on board was like.

National Maritime Museum Museum

(www.rmg.co.uk/national-maritime-museum; Romney Rd, SE10; 10am-5pm; DLR Cutty Sark) FREE Narrating the long and eventful history of seafaring Britain, the museum's exhibits are arranged thematically and highlights include *Miss Britain III* (the first boat to top 100mph on open water) from 1933, the 19m-long golden state barge built in 1732 for Frederick, Prince of Wales, the huge ship's propeller and the colourful figureheads installed on the ground floor. Families will love these, as well as the ship simulator and the children's gallery on the 2nd floor.

Adults are likely to prefer the fantastic (and slightly more serene) galleries such as **Voyagers: Britons and the Sea** on the ground floor, or the award-winning **Nelson, Navy, Nation 1688–1815**, which focuses on the history of the Royal Navy during the conflict-ridden 17th century. It provides an excellent look at the legendary national hero; the coat in which Nelson was fatally wounded during the Battle of Trafalgar takes pride of place.

Take a Break

The **Astronomy Cafe**, next to the Planetarium, serves light meals.

A guide dressed as a Tudor in front of the palace

Day Trip: Hampton Court Palace

London's most spectacular Tudor palace, this 16th-century icon concocts an imposing sense of history, from the huge kitchens and grand living quarters to the spectacular gardens, complete with a 300-year-old maze. Tag along with a themed tour led by a costumed historian or grab one of the audio tours to delve into Hampton Court and its residents' tumultuous history.

Great For...

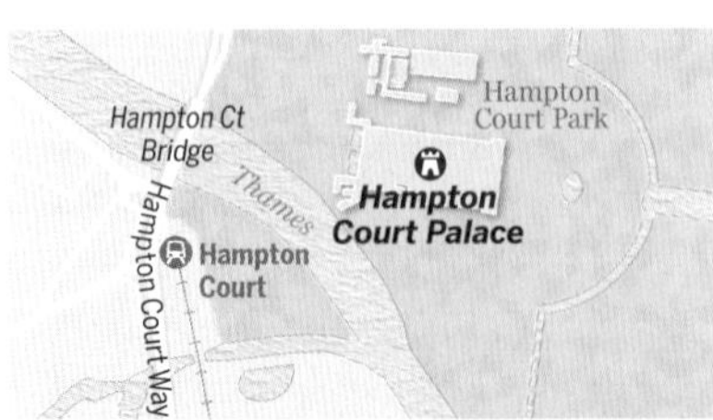

Need to Know

www.hrp.org.uk/HamptonCourtPalace; adult/child/family £17.50/8.75/43.80; 10am-6pm Apr-Oct, to 4.30pm Nov-Mar; Hampton Court Palace, Hampton Court

★ Top Tip

Ask one of the red-tunic-garbed warders for anecdotes and information.

TONY C FRENCH/GETTY IMAGES ©

Hampton Court Palace was built by Cardinal Thomas Wolsey in 1515, but was coaxed from him by Henry VIII just before Wolsey (as chancellor) fell from favour. It was already one of the most sophisticated palaces in Europe when, in the 17th century, Sir Christopher Wren was commissioned to build an extension. The result is a beautiful blend of Tudor and 'restrained baroque' architecture.

Entering the Palace

Passing through the magnificent main gate, you arrive first in the **Base Court** and beyond that the **Clock Court**, named after its 16th-century astronomical clock. The panelled rooms and arched doorways in the **Young Henry VIII's Story** upstairs from Base Court provide a rewarding introduction: note the Tudor graffiti on the fireplace. Off Base Court to the right as you enter, and acquired by Charles I in 1629, Andrea Magenta's nine-painting series *The Triumphs of Caesar* portray Julius Caesar returning to Rome in a triumphant procession.

Henry VIII's Apartments

The stairs inside Anne Boleyn's Gateway lead up to Henry VIII's Apartments, including the stunning **Great Hall**. The **Horn Room**, hung with impressive antlers, leads to the **Great Watching Chamber**, where guards controlled access to the king. Henry VIII's dazzling gemstone-encrusted **crown** has been re-created – the original was melted down by Oliver Cromwell – and sits in the **Royal Pew** (10am-4pm Mon-Sat, 12.30-1.30pm Sun), which overlooks the beautiful **Chapel Royal** (still a place of worship after 450 years).

Hampton Court Palace and gardens

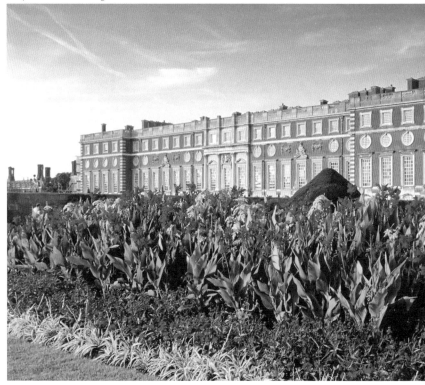

Tudor Kitchens & Great Wine Cellar

Also dating from Henry's day are the delightful Tudor kitchens, once used to rustle up meals for a royal household of some 1200 people. Don't miss the Great Wine Cellar, which handled the 300 barrels each of ale and wine consumed here annually in the mid-16th century.

Cumberland Art Gallery

The restored and recently opened Cumberland Suite off Clock Court is the venue for a staggering collection of artworks from the Royal Collection, including Rembrandt's *Self-portrait in a Flat Cap* (1642) and Sir Anthony van Dyck's *Charles I on Horseback* (c 1635–6).

PAWEL LIBERA/GETTY IMAGES ©

William III's & Mary II's Apartments

A tour of William III's Apartments, completed by Wren in 1702, takes you up the grand **King's Staircase**. Highlights include the **King's Presence Chamber**, dominated by a throne backed with scarlet hangings. During a devastating fire in 1986 that gutted an entire wing of the palace, staff were ready to cut the huge portrait of William III from its frame with knives, if necessary. The sumptuous **King's Great Bedchamber**, with a bed topped with ostrich plumes, and the **King's Closet** (where His Majesty's toilet has a velvet seat) should not be missed. Restored and reopened in 2014, the unique **Chocolate Kitchens** were built for William and Mary in around 1689.

William's wife Mary II had her own apartments, accessible via the fabulous **Queen's Staircase** (decorated by William Kent).

Georgian Private Apartments

The Georgian Rooms were used by George II and Queen Caroline on the court's last visit to the palace in 1737. Do not miss the fabulous Tudor **Wolsey Closet** with its early 16th-century ceiling and painted panels, commissioned by Henry VIII.

Garden & Maze

Beyond the palace are the stunning gardens; keep an eye out for the **Real Tennis Court**, dating from the 1620s. Originally created for William and Mary, the **Kitchen Garden** is a magnificent, recently opened re-creation.

No one should leave Hampton Court without losing themselves in the 800m-long **maze** (adult/child/family £4/2.50/12; 10am-5.15pm Apr-Oct, to 3.45pm Nov-Mar, also accessible to those not entering the palace.

Take a Break

Hampton Court Palace presses up against 445-hectare **Bushy Park** (www.royalparks.gov.uk), a semiwild expanse with herds of red and fallow deer.

Columbia Road Flower Market

ELENA DIJOUR/SHUTTERSTOCK ©

A Sunday in the East End

The East End has a colourful and multicultural history. Waves of migrants (French Protestants, Jewish, Bangladeshi) have left their mark on the area, which, added to the Cockney heritage and the 21st-century hipster phenomenon, has created an incredibly vibrant neighbourhood.

Great For...

☑ Don't Miss

The area's food offerings are as diverse as its population, from curry houses to modern British cuisine.

On Sundays, this whole area feels like one giant, sprawling market. It is brilliant fun, but pretty exhausting, so pace yourself – there are plenty of cafes and restaurants to sit down, relax and take in the atmosphere.

Columbia Road Flower Market

A wonderful explosion of colour and life, this weekly **market** (Map p255; www.columbiaroad.info; Columbia Rd, E2; 8am-3pm Sun; Hoxton) sells a beautiful array of flowers, pot plants, bulbs, seeds and everything you might need for the garden. It's a lot of fun and the best place to hear proper Cockney barrow-boy banter ('We got flowers cheap enough for ya muvver-in-law's grave' etc). It gets really packed, so go as early as you can, or later on, when the vendors sell off the cut flowers cheaply.

Fresh vegetables for sale at Brick Lane Market

ELENA DIJOUR/SHUTTERSTOCK ©

Brick Lane Market

Head south towards **Brick Lane Market** (Map p255; www.visitbricklane.org; Brick Lane, E1; 9am-5pm Sun; Shoreditch High St), which spills out into the surrounding streets with everything from household goods and bric-a-brac to secondhand clothes, cheap fashion and ethnic food. The best range and quality of products are to be found in the beautiful Old Truman Brewery's markets: **Sunday UpMarket** (Map p255; www.sundayupmarket.co.uk; Old Truman Brewery, 91 Brick Lane, E1; 10am-5pm Sun; Shoreditch High St) and **Backyard Market** (Map p255; www.backyardmarket.co.uk; 146 Brick Lane, E1; 11am-5pm Sat & Sun; Shoreditch High St), where young designers sell their creations, along with arts and crafts and cracking food stalls.

Need to Know

The area is as its best on Sundays, when the area's markets are in full swing.

Take a Break

If you've worked up an appetite, Tayyabs (p149) does stupendous Pakistani food.

★ Top Tip

To avoid market overdose on a Sunday, choose between Brick Lane or Old Spitalfields Market.

Brick Lane's Famous Bagel

This relic (p149) of the Jewish East End still makes a brisk trade serving dirt-cheap homemade bagels (filled with salmon, cream cheese and/or salt beef), and the best time to have one is after a night on the tiles and a morning traipsing through the market throngs.

Old Spitalfields Market

Traders have been hawking their wares here since 1638 and it's still one of London's best markets. Today's covered **market** (Map p255; www.oldspitalfieldsmarket.com; Commercial St, E1; 10am-5pm; Shoreditch High St) was built in the late 19th century, with the more modern development added in 2006. Sundays are the biggest and best days, but Thursdays are good for antiques and Fridays for independent fashion. There are plenty of food stalls, too.

Brick Lane Great Mosque

After lunch, walk over to this fascinating **mosque** (Brick Lane Jamme Masjid; Map p255; www.bricklanejammemasjid.co.uk; 59 Brick Lane,

E1; ⊖Shoreditch High St or Liverpool St). No building symbolises the different waves of immigration to Spitalfields quite as well as this one. Built in 1743 as the New French Church for the Huguenots, it was a Methodist chapel from 1819 until it was transformed into the Great Synagogue for Jewish refugees from Russia and Central Europe in 1898. In 1976, it changed faiths yet again, becoming the Great Mosque. Look for the sundial, high up on the Fournier St frontage.

Whitechapel Gallery

From Brick Lane Mosque, continue on to **Whitechapel Gallery** (020-7522 7888; www.whitechapelgallery.org; 77-82 Whitechapel High St, E1; 11am-6pm Tue, Wed & Fri-Sun, to 9pm Thu; ⊖Aldgate East) FREE. A firm favourite of art students and the avant-garde cognoscenti, this ground-breaking gallery doesn't have a permanent collection, but is devoted to hosting edgy exhibitions of contemporary art. It made its name by staging exhibitions by both established and emerging artists, including the first UK shows by Pablo Picasso, Jackson Pollock, Mark Rothko and Frida Khalo. The gallery's ambitiously themed shows change every couple of months (check online) and there's often also live music, talks and films on Thursday evenings.

What's Nearby?

Geffrye Museum Museum

(Map p255; www.geffrye-museum.org.uk; 136 Kingsland Rd, E2; 10am-5pm Tue-Sun; ⊖Hoxton) FREE If you like nosing around other people's homes, you'll love this museum, entirely devoted to middle-class

Brick Lane and the Old Truman Brewery

domestic interiors. Built in 1714 as a home for poor pensioners, these beautiful ivy-clad almshouses have been converted into a series of living rooms, dating from 1630 to the present day. The rear garden is also organised by era, mirroring the museum's exploration of domesticity through the centuries. There's also a very impressive walled herb garden, featuring 170 different plants.

Dennis Severs' House Museum

(Map p255; ☎020-7247 4013; www.dennissevershouse.co.uk; 18 Folgate St, E1; day/night £10/15; ⊙noon-4pm Sun, noon-2pm & 5-9pm Mon, 5-9pm Wed; ⊖Shoreditch High St) This extraordinary Georgian House is set up as if its occupants had just walked out the door. There are half-drunk cups of tea, lit candles and, in a perhaps unnecessary attention to detail, a full chamber pot by the bed. More than a museum, it's an opportunity to meditate on the minutiae of everyday Georgian life through silent exploration.

Did You Know?

Because of its immigrant communities, the East End is a diverse area to eat, drink and explore.

BY ARCAID/UIG/GETTY IMAGES ©

Old Truman Brewery Historic Building

(Map p255; www.trumanbrewery.com; 91 Brick Lane, E1; ⊖Shoreditch High St) Founded here in the 17th century, Truman's Black Eagle Brewery was, by the 1850s, the largest brewery in the world. Spread over a series of brick buildings and yards straddling both sides of Brick Lane, the complex is now completely given over to edgy markets, pop-up fashion stores, vintage-clothes shops, indie record hunters, cafes, bars and live-music venues. Beer may not be brewed here any more, but it certainly is consumed.

After decades of decline, Truman's Brewery finally shut up shop in 1989 – temporarily as it turned out, with the brand subsequently resurrected in 2010 in new premises in Hackney Wick. In the 1990s, the abandoned brewery premises found new purpose as a deadly cool hub for boozy Brit-poppers, and while it may not have quite the same caché today, it's still plenty popular.

Several of the buildings are heritage listed, including the Director's House at 91 Brick Lane (built in the 1740s); the old Vat House directly opposite, with its hexagonal bell tower (c 1800); and the Engineer's House right next to it (at 150 Brick Lane), dating from the 1830s.

Take a Break

In the evening, check out **93 Feet East** (www.93feeteast.co.uk; 150 Brick Lane, E1) on Brick Lane for DJs and cocktails.

St Pancras Station

King's Cross & Euston

Formerly a dilapidated red-light district, King's Cross used to be a place better avoided. Fast-forward a couple of decades, though, and the area has metamorphosed, now boasting cool hang-outs and luxury hotels.

Great For...

☑ **Don't Miss**

The intriguing manuscripts in the Sir John Ritblatt Gallery at the British Library.

Along with some excellent sights, the area has become a great place to hang out. Particularly popular are the plaza at the front of King's Cross station; **Granary Square** (Map p256; www.kingscross.co.uk; Stable St, N1; ⊖King's Cross St Pancras), at the back of King's Cross station; and the AstroTurf-covered steps by Regent's Canal near Granary Sq.

British Library Library

(Map p256; www.bl.uk; 96 Euston Rd, NW1; galleries 9.30am-6pm Mon, Fri & Sat, to 8pm Tue-Thu, 11am-5pm Sun; ⊖King's Cross St Pancras) FREE Consisting of low-slung red-brick terraces and fronted by a large plaza featuring an oversized statue of Sir Isaac Newton, Colin St John Wilson's British Library building is a love-it-or-hate-it affair (Prince Charles once famously likened it to a secret-police academy). Completed in 1998, it's home to

An entrance to the British Library

CHRISDORNEY/SHUTTERSTOCK ©

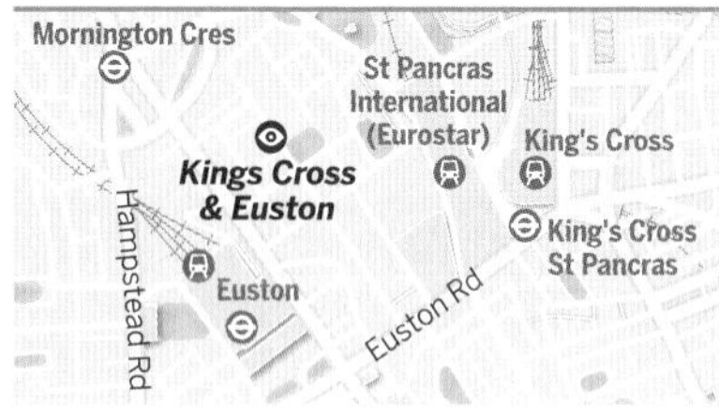

Need to Know

Map p256; King's Cross St Pancras or Euston

Take a Break

Grain Store (p152), with its creative European cuisine, is a good example of King's Cross regeneration.

★ Top Tip

Harry Potter fans will want to seek out the Platform 9¾ sign at King's Cross station.

some of the greatest treasures of the written word, including the Codex Sinaiticus (the first complete text of the New Testament), Leonardo da Vinci's notebooks and a copy of the Magna Carta (1215).

The most precious manuscripts are held in the **Sir John Ritblat Gallery**, including the stunningly illustrated Jain sacred texts, explorer Captain Scott's final diary and Shakespeare's First Folio (1623). Music fans will love the Beatles' handwritten lyrics, and original scores by Bach, Handel, Mozart and Beethoven.

Wellcome Collection Museum

(Map p256; www.wellcomecollection.org; 183 Euston Rd, NW1; 10am-6pm Tue, Wed & Fri-Sun, to 10pm Thu; Euston Sq) FREE Focusing on the interface of art, science and medicine, this clever museum is surprisingly fascinating. There are interactive displays where you can scan your face and watch it stretched into the statistical average, wacky modern sculptures inspired by various medical conditions, and downright creepy things, such as an actual cross section of a body and enlargements of parasites (fleas, body lice, scabies) at terrifying proportions.

St Pancras Station & Hotel Historic Building

(Map p256; 020-8241 6921; Euston Rd, NW1; tour per person £20; tours 10.30am, noon, 2pm & 3.30pm Sat & Sun; King's Cross St Pancras) Looking at the jaw-dropping Gothic splendour of St Pancras, it's hard to believe that the 1873 Midland Grand Hotel languished empty for years and even faced demolition in the 1960s. Now home to a five-star hotel, 67 luxury apartments and the Eurostar terminal, the entire complex has been returned to its former glory. Tours take you on a fascinating journey through the building's history, from its inception as the southern terminus for the Midlands Railway line.

Walking Tour: A Northern Point of View

This walk takes in North London's most interesting locales, including celebrity-infested Primrose Hill and chaotic Camden Town, home to loud guitar bands and the last of London's cartoon punks.

Start: ⊖Chalk Farm
Distance: 4km
Duration: 2 hours

Classic photo: London's skyline from atop Primrose Hill

2 In **Primrose Hill**, walk to the top of the park where you'll find a classic view of central London's skyline.

VISITBRITAIN/PAWEL LIBERA/GETTY IMAGES ©

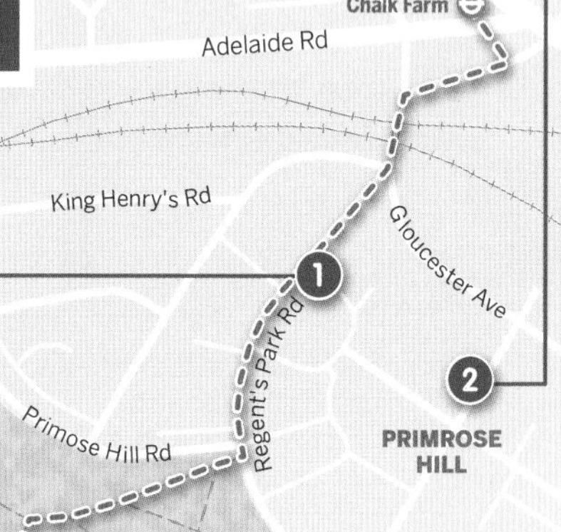

1 Affluent **Regent's Park Rd** is home to many darlings of the women's mags, so keep your eyes open for famous faces.

BASIC ELEMENTS PHOTOGRAPHY/GETTY IMAGES ©

3 Walk downhill towards the London Zoo (p32), past the zoo's large aviary, quaint boats, superb mansions and converted industrial buildings.

RICHARD NEWSTEAD/GETTY IMAGES ©

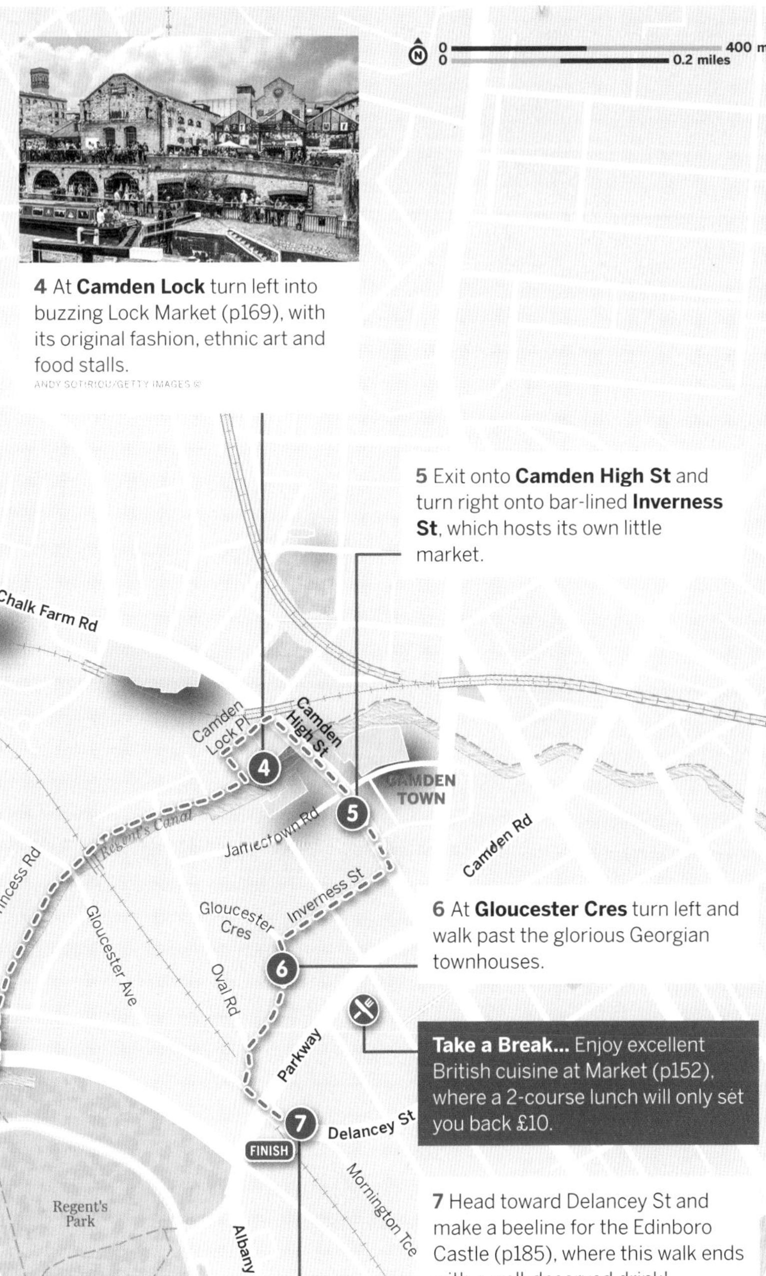

4 At **Camden Lock** turn left into buzzing Lock Market (p169), with its original fashion, ethnic art and food stalls.

ANDY SOTIRIOU/GETTY IMAGES ©

5 Exit onto **Camden High St** and turn right onto bar-lined **Inverness St**, which hosts its own little market.

6 At **Gloucester Cres** turn left and walk past the glorious Georgian townhouses.

Take a Break... Enjoy excellent British cuisine at Market (p152), where a 2-course lunch will only set you back £10.

7 Head toward Delancey St and make a beeline for the Edinboro Castle (p185), where this walk ends with a well-deserved drink!

LEADENHALL
LEADENHALL MARKET

DINING OUT

Top-notch restaurants, gastropubs, afternoon tea and more

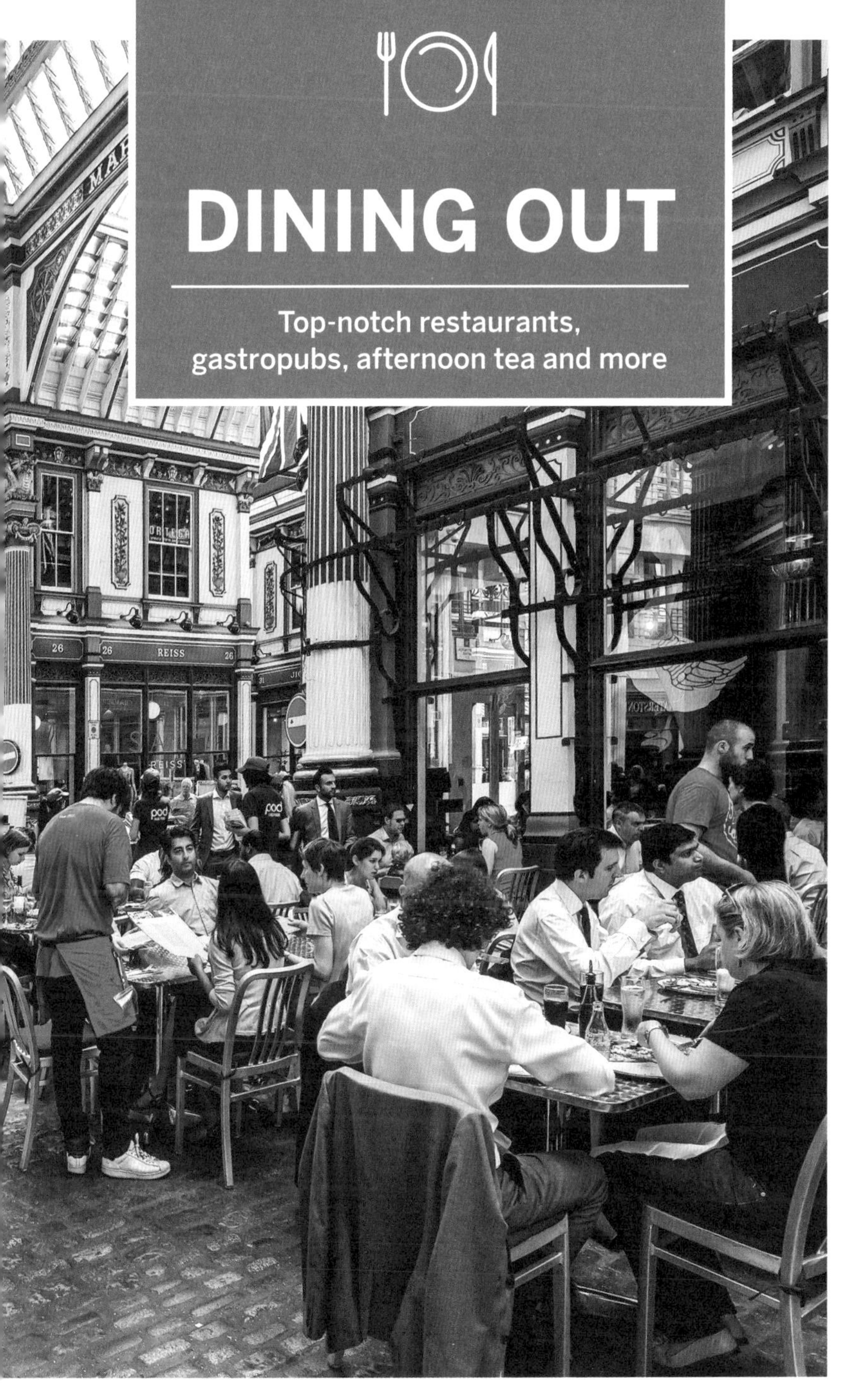

Dining Out

Once the laughing stock of the cooking world, London has got its culinary act together in the last 20 years and is today an undisputed dining destination. There are plenty of top-notch, Michelin-starred restaurants, but it is the sheer diversity on offer that is head-spinning: from Afghan to Zambian, London is a virtual A to Z of world cuisine.

You'll find that there are restaurants to suit every budget – and every occasion. Dinner in a fabulous restaurant is part and parcel of a great trip to London, but make sure you also sample the cheap and cheerful fare on offer in market stalls, and sit down in one of the capital's tip-top cafes.

In This Section

Price Ranges

These symbols indicate the average cost of a main course at a restaurant:

£ less than £10
££ £10–20
£££ more than £20

Tipping

Most restaurants add a 'discretionary' service charge (usually 12.5%) onto the bill; if it isn't and you would like to tip, 10% is about right.

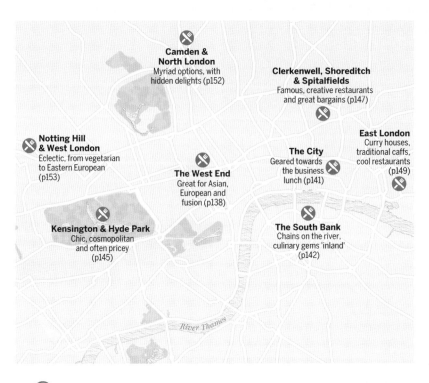

Camden & North London
Myriad options, with hidden delights (p152)

Clerkenwell, Shoreditch & Spitalfields
Famous, creative restaurants and great bargains (p147)

Notting Hill & West London
Eclectic, from vegetarian to Eastern European (p153)

The West End
Great for Asian, European and fusion (p138)

The City
Geared towards the business lunch (p141)

East London
Curry houses, traditional caffs, cool restaurants (p149)

Kensington & Hyde Park
Chic, cosmopolitan and often pricey (p145)

The South Bank
Chains on the river, culinary gems 'inland' (p142)

River Thames

Best Blogs & Websites

Open Table (www.opentable.com) One of the main restaurant booking websites in London.

Time Out (www.timeout.com/london) Restaurant listings and reviews.

London Eater (www.londoneater.com) London food blog with lush pics.

Classic Dishes

Pie & Mash A pie, usually beef, served with mashed potato and jellied eel (we dare you!). Typical East London fare.

Sunday Roast Roast meat (beef, chicken, lamb) with a smorgasbord of vegetables and sauces; best enjoyed in a gastropub on a Sunday.

The Best...

Experience London's top restaurants and cafes

By Budget

£

Shoryu (p140) Perfectly executed bowls of *tonkotsu ramen*.

Café Below (p142) One of London's most atmospheric locations with excellent value to boot.

Pimlico Fresh (p147) Perky cafe with an accent on good-value fine food.

Polpo (p147) Addictive selection of Italian tapas.

Watch House (p144) Ace sandwiches, fine coffee and a lovely setting.

££

Tom's Kitchen (p145) Relaxing ambience warm staff, excellent food: you can't go wrong.

Palomar (p140) Excellent Jerusalem food for sharing with a foodie friend.

Baltic (p143) Fabulous taste of Eastern Europe in a gorgeous, minimalist setting.

Empress (p151) If ever there was a gastropub to try, this is it.

£££

Dinner by Heston Blumenthal (p145) A supreme fusion of perfect British food, eye-catching design and celeb stature.

Arabica Bar & Kitchen (p144) A modern, and utterly divine, take on Middle Eastern cuisine.

Clove Club (p148) A modern British cuisine tour de force.

Ledbury (p153) A long-standing modern British restaurant, with two Michelin stars to prove it.

For Views

Duck & Waffle (p142) Hearty British dishes from the top of Heron Tower, round the clock.

Portrait (p150) Classic views to Nelson's Column and beyond, down Whitehall to Big Ben.

Skylon (p143) Majestic riverside views from the South Bank with a side of Modern European fare.

For British

St John (p148) The restaurant that inspired the revival of British cuisine.

Market (p152) Smart, seasonal and delightfully understated modern British fare.

Rabbit (p147) Make it to King's Rd for some of the best British food in London.

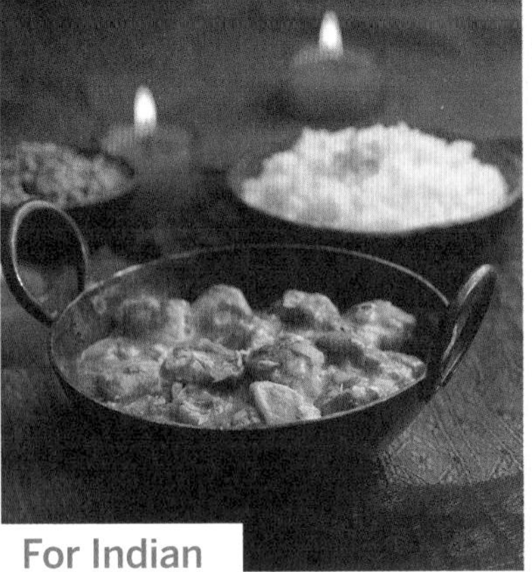

For Indian

Tayyabs (p149) Long-standing Punjabi favourite in the East End.

Dishoom (p141) Bombay caff food as it really is served and eaten.

Gymkhana (p141) Splendid club-style Raj environment, top cuisine.

For European

Dabbous (p138) A modern take on European cuisine, in an even more modern setting.

Morito (p147) Splendid Spanish-style tapas.

Ottolenghi (p153) King of Mediterranean flavours (and fantastic desserts, too).

Cafes

Scootercaffe (p142) An Aladdin's cave of fairy lights and thrift-shop furniture with a great vibe.

Tomtom Coffee House (p147) No one takes their coffee more seriously than these guys.

Prufrock Coffee (p147) The coffee here is so good they've opened a barista school.

Towpath (p150) Canal-side alfresco lattes: welcome to London.

Gastropubs

Anchor & Hope (p143) Flying the gastropub flag on the South Bank for the best part of a decade.

Perkin Reveller (p142) Fantastically named Thames-side top spot with classic British menu.

Empress (p151) Choice East End spot with an excellent modern British menu.

The West End

Westminster & St James's

Vincent Rooms Modern European £
(020-7802 8391; www.centrallondonvenues.co.uk; Westminster Kingsway College, Vincent Sq, SW1; mains £8-12; noon-2pm Mon-Fri, 6.30-9pm Wed & Thu; Victoria) Care to be a guinea pig for student chefs at Westminster Kingsway College, where celebrity chefs Jamie Oliver and Ainsley Harriott were trained? Service is eager to please, the atmosphere in both the Brasserie and the Escoffier Room smarter than expected, and the food (including veggie options) ranges from wonderful to exquisite – at prices that put other culinary stars to shame.

Cafe Murano Italian ££
(Map p252; 020-3371 5559; www.cafemurano.co.uk; 33 St James's St, SW1; mains £9-40, 2/3-course set meal £18/22; noon-3pm & 5.30-11pm Mon-Sat; Green Park) The setting may be somewhat demure (but busy) at this superb restaurant, but with such a sublime North Italian menu on offer, it sees no need to make nods to being flash and of-the-moment. You get what you come for, and the beef carpaccio, crab linguine and lamb ragu are as close to culinary perfection as you can get. Reserve.

Inn the Park British ££
(Map p252; 020-7451 9999; www.innthepark.com; St James's Park, SW1; mains £14-29; 8am-9pm; ; Charing Cross or St James's Park) This stunning wooden cafe and restaurant in St James's Park is run by Irish wonderchef Oliver Peyton and offers cakes and tea as well as excellent British food, with the menu changing monthly. The terrace, which overlooks one of the park's fountains and views of Whitehall's grand buildings, is wonderful in warm weather.

Bloomsbury

Lady Ottoline Gastropub ££
(Map p256; 020-7831 0008; www.theladyottoline.com; 11a Northington St, WC1; mains £11-18; noon-11pm Mon-Sat, to 5pm Sun; Chancery Lane) Bloomsbury can sometimes seem a culinary wasteland, but this buzzy gastropub (named after a patron of the Bloomsbury Set) is a pleasant exception. You can eat in the noisy pub downstairs, but the cosy dining room above is more tempting. Favourites like beer-battered fish and chips and pork and cider pie are excellent.

Fitzrovia

Busaba Eathai Thai £
(Map p256; 020-7299 7900; www.busaba.com; 22 Store St, WC1; mains £8-15; noon-11pm Mon-Thu, to 11.30pm Fri & Sat, to 10pm Sun; ; Goodge St) The Store St branch of this hugely popular minichain is slightly less hectic than some of the other West End outlets, but it retains all the features that have made the chain a roaring success. Think sleek Asian interior, large communal wooden tables, and heavenly cheap and tasty Thai dishes, like *pad thai* noodles, green and red curries, and fragrant noodle soups.

Franco Manca Pizza £
(Map p256; www.francomanca.co.uk; 98 Tottenham Court Rd, W1; mains £4-7; 11.30am-11pm Mon-Thu, 11.30am-11.30pm Fri & Sat, noon-10pm Sun; Goodge St) It's first come, first served at Franco Manca, which has come a long way since first feeding Brixton on slow-rising sourdough pizzas several years back. The six-pizza choice menu may seem lightweight, but you really don't need to look any further, it's the real deal.

Dabbous Modern European ££
(Map p256; 020-7323 1544; www.dabbous.co.uk; 39 Whitfield St, W1; set lunch/dinner £35/56; noon-3pm & 5.30-11.30pm Tue-Sat; ; Goodge St) This award-winning eatery is the creation of Ollie Dabbous, everyone's favourite new chef, so book ahead for dinner or come for lunch (four courses £28). The combination of flavours is inspired – squid with buckwheat, pork with mango, rhubarb with lavender – and at first seems at odds with the industrial, hard-edged decor. But it all works exceedingly well. Reservations essential.

Fino — Spanish ££

(Map p256; ☎020-7813 8010; www.finorestaurant.com; 33 Charlotte St, enter from Rathbone St, W1; tapas £3-13; ⏰noon-2.30pm Mon-Fri, 6-10.30pm Mon-Sat; ⊖Goodge St) Set in a glamorous basement with a fabulous bar, Fino is a tapas restaurant with a difference. The menu changes daily, but expect to find *morcilla* (blood sausage), *presa iberica* (tender Iberian pork), *prawn and piquillo pepper tortilla* and other delightful and innovative Spanish dishes. For groups, consider the whole slow roast suckling pig (but give 48 hours notice).

Soho & Chinatown

Koya — Noodles £

(Map p252; www.koya.co.uk; 49 Frith St, W1; mains £7-15; ⏰noon-3pm & 5.30-10.30pm; ⊖Tottenham Court Rd, Leicester Sq) Arrive early or late if you don't want to queue at this excellent Japanese eatery. Londoners come for their fill of authentic udon noodles (served hot or cold, in soup or with a cold sauce), the efficient service and very reasonable prices. The *saba* udon noodles with generous chunks of smoked mackerel and topped with watercress is a gorgeous dish.

Nordic Bakery — Scandinavian £

(Map p252; www.nordicbakery.com; 14a Golden Sq, W1; snacks £4-5; ⏰7.30am-8pm Mon-Fri, 8.30am-8pm Sat, 9am-7pm Sun; ⊖Piccadilly Circus) This is the perfect place to escape the chaos that is Soho and relax in the dark-wood-panelled space on the south side of a delightful 'secret' square. Lunch on Scandinavian smoked-fish sandwiches or goat's cheese and beetroot salad, or have an afternoon break with tea or coffee and rustic oatmeal cookies.

Brasserie Zédel — French ££

(Map p252; ☎020-7734 4888; www.brasseriezedel.com; 20 Sherwood St, W1; mains £8-30; ⏰11.30am-midnight Mon-Sat, to 11pm Sun; 📶; ⊖Piccadilly Circus) This brasserie in the renovated art deco ballroom of a former Piccadilly hotel is the French-est eatery west of Calais. Choose from among the usual favourites, including *choucroute alsacienne* (sauerkraut

British Cuisine in a Nutshell

England might have given the world baked beans on toast, mushy peas and chip butties (hot chips or fries between two slices of buttered white bread), but that's hardly the whole story.

Modern British food has become a cuisine in its own right, by championing traditional (and sometimes underrated) ingredients such as root vegetables, smoked fish, shellfish, game, sausages and black pudding (a kind of sausage stuffed with oatmeal, spices and blood). Dishes can be anything from game served with a traditional vegetable such as Jerusalem artichoke, to seared scallops with orange-scented black pudding, or roast pork with chorizo on rosemary mash.

England does a mean dessert, and establishments serving British cuisine revel in these indulgent treats. Favourites include bread-and-butter pudding, sticky toffee pudding (a steamed pudding that contains dates and is topped with a divine caramel sauce), the alarmingly named spotted dick (a steamed suet pudding with currants and raisins), Eton mess (meringue, cream and strawberries mixed into a gooey, heavenly mess), and seasonal musts such as Christmas pudding (a steamed pudding with candied fruit and brandy) and fruity crumbles (rhubarb, apple etc).

Sticky toffee pudding

Chefs at work, Palomar

with sausages and charcuterie, £14) and duck leg confit with Puy lentils. The set menus (£8.95/11.75 for two/three courses) and *plats du jour* (dish of the day; £12.95) offer excellent value, in a terrific setting.

Palomar Jewish ££

(Map p252; 020-7439 8777; 34 Rupert St, W1; mains £6-19; noon-2.30pm Mon-Sat & noon-3.30pm Sun, 5.30-11pm Mon-Wed, 5.30-11.30pm Thu-Sat; ; Piccadilly Circus) The buzzing vibe at this good-looking celebration of modern-day Jerusalem cuisine (in all its inflections) is infectious, but we could enjoy the dishes cooked up here in a deserted warehouse and still come back for more. The polenta Jerusalem style and aubergine and feta *bourekas* (flaky pastry parcels) were fantastic, but portions are smallish, so sharing is the way to go. Reservations essential.

Bocca di Lupo Italian ££

(Map p252; 020-7734 2223; www.boccadilupo.com; 12 Archer St, W1; mains £8-28; 12.30-3pm & 5.30-11pm Mon-Sat, 12.15-3.15pm & 5.15-9.30pm Sun; Piccadilly Circus) Hidden in a dark Soho backstreet, Bocca radiates elegant sophistication. The menu has dishes from across Italy (and informs you which region they're from), and every main course can be ordered as a large or small portion. There's a good choice of Italian wines and fantastic desserts. It's often full, so make sure to book.

Covent Garden & Leicester Square

Shoryu Noodles £

(Map p252; www.shoryuramen.com; 9 Regent St, SW1; mains £9-15; 11.15am-midnight Mon-Sat, to 10.30pm Sun; Piccadilly Circus) Compact, well-mannered noodle parlour Shoryu draws in reams of noodle diners to feast at its wooden counters and small tables. It's busy, friendly and efficient, with informative staff. Fantastic *tonkotsu* ramen is the name of the game here, sprinkled with *nori* (dried, pressed seaweed), spring onion, *nitamago* (soft-boiled eggs) and sesame seeds. No bookings.

Dishoom Indian £

(Map p252; ☎020-7420 9320; www.dishoom.com; 12 Upper St Martin's Lane, WC2; mains £5-17; ⏰8am-11pm Mon-Thu, 8am-midnight Fri, 9am-midnight Sat, 9am-11pm Sun; 📶; ⊖Covent Garden) This laid-back eatery takes the fast-disappearing old-style 'Bombay cafe' and gives it the kiss of life. Distressed with a modern twist (all ceiling fans and Bollywood photos), you'll find yummy favourites like *sheekh kabab* and *haleem* (slow-cooked lamb, cracked wheat, barley and lentils), okra fries and snack foods like *bhel* (Bombay mix and puffed rice with pomegranate and lime).

Delaunay Brasserie ££

(Map p250; ☎020-7499 8558; www.thedelaunay.com; 55 Aldwych, WC2; mains £6-28; ⏰7am-midnight Mon-Fri, 8am-midnight Sat, 9am-11pm Sun; ⊖Temple or Covent Garden) This smart brasserie across from Bush House is a kind of Franco-German hybrid, where schnitzels and wieners sit happily beside croque-monsieurs and *choucroute alsacienne* (Alsace sauerkraut). Even more relaxed is the adjacent **Counter** (Map p250; ⏰7am-8pm Mon-Wed, 7am-10.30pm Thu & Fri, 10.30am-10.30pm Sat, 11am-5.30pm Sun), where you can drop in for chicken noodle soup and a New York–style hot dog.

Brunch is from 11am to 5pm at the weekend and afternoon tea (£23.75, or £33.50 with Champagne) is daily from 3pm.

Mayfair

Gymkhana Indian ££

(Map p252; ☎020-3011 5900; www.gymkhanalondon.com; 42 Albemarle St, W1; mains £8-28, 2/3-course lunch £25/30; ⏰noon-2.30pm & 5.30-10.30pm Mon-Sat; 📶; ⊖Green Park) The rather sombre setting is all British Raj: ceiling fans, oak ceiling, period cricket photos and hunting trophies, but the menu is lively, bright and inspiring. Game gets its very own menu, but for lovers of variety, the seven-course tasting menu (£65) is the way to go. The bar is open to 1am.

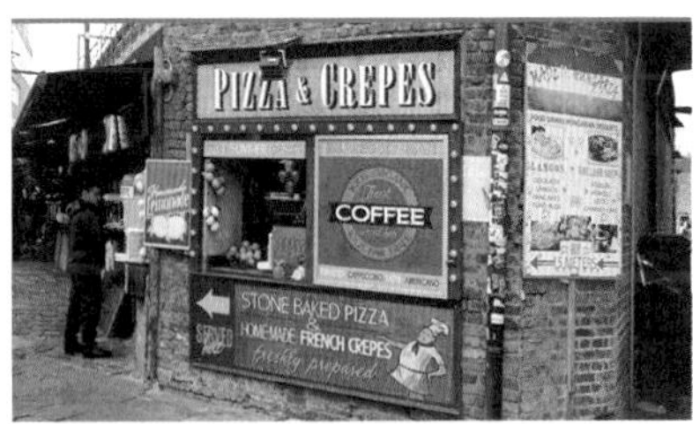

Food Markets

The boom in London's eating scene has extended to its markets, which come in three broad categories: food stalls that are part of a broader market and appeal to visitors keen to soak up the atmosphere – Spitalfields (p125), Borough (p88) or Camden (p169), for example; farmers markets, which sell pricey local and/or organic products (check out www.lfm.org.uk for a selection of the best); and the many colourful food markets, where the oranges and lemons come from who knows where and the barrow boys and girls speak with perfect Cockney accents (such as Berwick St in Soho).

Food stall near Camden Lock Market

The City

Bea's of Bloomsbury Cafe £

(Map p250; ☎020-7242 8330; www.beasofbloomsbury.com; 83 Watling St, EC4; afternoon teas £9-24; ⏰7.30am-7pm Mon-Fri, from 10.30am Sat & Sun; ⊖St Paul's) Bea's made its name with its signature cupcakes, so it was only natural for it to offer a full afternoon tea, too. This branch of the Bloomsbury institution is tiny but original, with great cake displays and boutique decor. It's at One New Change and is an excellent place to refuel after visiting St Paul's.

Café Below Cafe £

(Map p250; ☎020-7329 0789; www.cafebelow.co.uk; St Mary-le-Bow, Cheapside, EC2; mains £8-12, 3-course set dinner £20; ⏰7.30am-2.30pm Mon & Tue, to 9.15pm Wed-Fri; ; ⊖Mansion House, St Paul's) This atmospheric cafe-restaurant, in the crypt of one of London's most famous churches, offers excellent value and such tasty dishes as pan-fried sea bream with chermoula (spicy North African sauce) and aubergine Parmigiana. There are as many vegetarian choices as meat ones. Summer sees tables outside in the shady courtyard.

Perkin Reveller Brasserie ££

(☎020-3166 6949; www.perkinreveller.co.uk; The Wharf, Tower of London, EC3; mains £15-26; ⏰10am-9pm Mon-Sat, to 5pm Sun; ⊖Tower Hill) The location of this minimalist building on the Thames, southeast of the Tower of London and at the foot of Tower Bridge, is hard to beat – indeed, the restaurant's bar actually spreads into an arch under Tower Bridge. The food – mostly classic British (Morecambe Bay potted shrimp, fish and chips, high-end pies) – matches the A-list spot.

Duck & Waffle Brasserie ££

(Map p250; ☎020-3640 7310; www.duckandwaffle.com; 40th fl, Heron Tower, 110 Bishopsgate, EC2; mains £10-19; ⏰24hr; ⊖Liverpool St) If you like your views with sustenance round the clock, this is the place for you. Perched atop Heron Tower, just down from Liverpool St Station, it serves European and British dishes (shellfish, roast chicken, some unusual seafood concoctions such as pollack meatballs) in small and large sizes by day, waffles by night, and round-the-clocktails.

The South Bank

Waterloo

Scootercaffe Cafe £

(132 Lower Marsh, SE1; ⏰8.30am-11pm Mon-Fri, 10am-midnight Sat, 10am-11pm Sun; ; ⊖Waterloo) A well-established fixture on the up-and-coming Lower Marsh road, this funky cafe-bar and former scooter repair shop with a Piatti scooter in the window serves killer hot chocolates, coffee and decadent cocktails. Unusually, you're allowed to bring

Street food in Camden Town

MARCO PRATI/SHUTTERSTOCK ©

take-away food. The tiny patio at the back is perfect to soak up the sun.

Skylon Modern European ££

(Map p250; 020-7654 7800; www.skylon-restaurant.co.uk; 3rd fl, Royal Festival Hall, Southbank Centre, Belvedere Rd, SE1; 2-/3-course menu grill £18/21, restaurant £42/48; grill noon-11pm Mon-Sat & noon-10.30pm Sun, restaurant noon-2.30pm & 5.30-10.30pm Mon-Sat & noon-4pm Sun; ; Waterloo) This excellent restaurant inside the Royal Festival Hall is divided into grill and fine-dining sections by a large bar (p179). The decor is cutting-edge 1950s: muted colours and period chairs (trendy then, trendier now) while floor-to-ceiling windows bathe you in magnificent views of the Thames and the City. Booking is advised.

Bankside & Southwark

Baltic Eastern European ££

(Map p250; 020-7928 1111; www.balticrestaurant.co.uk; 74 Blackfriars Rd, SE1; mains £10-19; noon-3pm & 5.30-11.15pm Tue-Sun, 5.30-11.15pm Mon; Southwark) In a bright and airy, high-ceilinged dining room with glass roof and wooden beams, Baltic is travel on a plate: dill and beetroot, dumplings and blini, pickle and smoke, rich stews and braised meat. From Poland to Georgia, the flavours are authentic and the dishes beautifully presented. The wine and vodka lists are equally diverse.

Anchor & Hope Gastropub ££

(Map p250; www.anchorandhopepub.co.uk; 36 The Cut, SE1; mains £12-20; noon-2.30pm Tue-Sat, 6-10.30pm Mon-Sat, 12.30-3pm Sun; Southwark) A stalwart of the South Bank food scene, the Anchor & Hope is a quintessential gastropub: elegant but not formal, and utterly delicious (European fare with a British twist). Think salt marsh lamb shoulder cooked for seven hours, wild rabbit with anchovies, almonds and rocket, and panna cotta with rhubarb compote.

Union Street Cafe Italian £££

(Map p250; 020-7592 7977; www.gordonramsay.com/union-street-cafe; 47-51 Great Suffolk St, SE1; mains £11-25, 1-/2-course lunch menu £12/19; 12-3pm & 6-11pm Mon-Fri, 12-4pm & 6-10.30pm Sat, 12-5pm Sun; ; Southwark) There's not a scrap of snootiness about this canteen-style Gordon Ramsay bistro. The dining room works the industrial chic look and staff are positively lovely.

★ Top Food Markets

Borough Market (p88)
Portobello Road Market (p168)
Maltby Street Market (p184)
Broadway Market (p168)
Old Spitalfields Market (p125)

Left and below: Borough Market

On the plate, it's a yummy mix of classic antipasti, pasta, meats and more unusual Italian dishes. Sunday brunch deserves a special mention: kids go free and for £12, it's free-flowing prosecco. Hurrah!

London Bridge

Arabica Bar & Kitchen — Middle Eastern £££

(Map p250; ☎020-3011 5151; www.arabicabarandkitchen.com; 3 Rochester Walk, Borough Market, SE1; dishes £4-14; ⏰11am-11pm Mon-Wed, 8.30am-11pm Thu-Sat; 📶; ⊖London Bridge) Pan Middle-Eastern cuisine is a well-rehearsed classic these days, but Arabica Bar & Kitchen has managed to bring something fresh to its table: the decor is contemporary and bright, the food delicate and light, with an emphasis on sharing (two to three small dishes per person). The downside of this tapas approach is that the bill adds up quickly.

Bermondsey

Watch House — Cafe £

(www.watchhousecoffee.com; 193 Bermondsey St, SE1; mains from £5; ⏰7am-6pm Mon-Fri, 8am-6pm Sat, 9am-5pm Sun; 📶; ⊖Borough) Saying that the Watch House nails the sandwich wouldn't really do justice to this tip-top cafe: the sandwiches really are delicious (with artisan breads from a local baker). But there is also great coffee, treats for the sweet-toothed, and the small but lovely setting: a renovated 19th-century watch house where guards looked out for grave robbers in the next-door cemetery.

M Manze — British £

(www.manze.co.uk; 87 Tower Bridge Rd, SE1; mains £3-7; ⏰11am-2pm Mon-Thu, 10am-2.30pm Fri & Sat; ⊖Borough) Dating to 1902, M Manze started off as an ice-cream seller before moving on to selling its legendary staples: pies (minced beef). It's a classic operation, from the ageing tile work to the traditional working-man's menu: pie and mash (£3.70), pie and liquor (£2.95) and you can take your eels jellied or stewed (£4.65).

Sumptuously presented Dinner is a gastronomic tour de force

Dinner by Heston Blumenthal

Kensington & Hyde Park

Knightsbridge & South Kensington

Tom's Kitchen Modern European ££
(020-7349 0202; www.tomskitchen.co.uk; 27 Cale St, SW3; mains £10-28, 2-/3-course lunch menu £16.50/19.50; 8am-2.30pm & 6-10.30pm Mon-Fri, 10am-3.30pm & 6-10.30pm Sat & Sun; ; South Kensington) Recipe for success: mix one part relaxed and smiling staff, one part light and airy decor to two parts divine food and voilà, you have Tom's Kitchen. Classics such as grilled steaks, burgers, slow-cooked lamb and chicken schnitzel are cooked to perfection, while seasonal fares such as the homemade ricotta or baked scallops with sea herbs are sublime.

Ognisko Polish ££
(Map p249; 020-7589 0101; www.ognisko restaurant.co.uk; 55 Prince's Gate, Exhibition Rd, SW7; mains £11-17; 12.30-3pm & 5.30-11.15pm; South Kensington) Ognisko has been a stalwart of the Polish community in London since 1940 (it's part of the Polish Hearth Club). The grand dining room is stunning, bathed in light from tall windows and adorned with modern art and chandeliers, and the food couldn't be more authentic: try the delicious *pierogi* (dumplings stuffed with cheese and potatoes) or the blinis.

Dinner by Heston Blumenthal Modern British £££
(Map p249; 020-7201 3833; www.dinnerby heston.com; Mandarin Oriental Hyde Park, 66 Knightsbridge, SW1; 3-course set lunch £38, mains £28-42; noon-2.30pm & 6.30-10.30pm; ; Knightsbridge) Sumptuously presented Dinner is a gastronomic tour de force, taking diners on a journey through British culinary history (with inventive modern inflections). Dishes carry historical dates to convey context, while the restaurant interior is a design triumph, from the glass-walled kitchen and its overhead clock mechanism to the large windows looking onto the park. Book ahead.

Breakfast

The Brits were always big on breakfast – they even invented one, the full English breakfast. It's something of a protein overload, but there's nothing quite like it to mop up the excesses of a night on the tiles. A typical plate will include bacon, sausages, baked beans in tomato sauce, eggs (fried or scrambled), mushrooms, tomatoes and toast (maybe with Marmite). You'll find countless brightly lit, grotty cafes – nicknamed 'greasy spoons' – serving these monster plates. They're also a must in gastropubs.

Making a comeback on the breakfast table is porridge (boiled oats in water or milk, served hot), sweet or savoury. Top-end restaurants serving breakfast have played a big part in glamming up what was essentially poor folk's food. It's great with banana and honey, fruit compote or even plain with some chocolate powder.

Hyde Park & Kensington Gardens

Magazine International ££
(Map p249; 020-72987552; www.magazine-restaurant.co.uk; Serpentine Sackler Gallery, West Carriage Dr, W2; mains £13-24, 2-/3-course lunch menu £17.50/21.50; 8am-6pm Tue-Sat, from 9am Sun; Lancaster Gate or Knightsbridge) Located in the ethereally beautiful extension of the **Serpentine Sackler Gallery** (p105), Magazine is no ordinary museum cafe. The food is as contemporary and elegant as the building, and artworks from current

London on a Plate

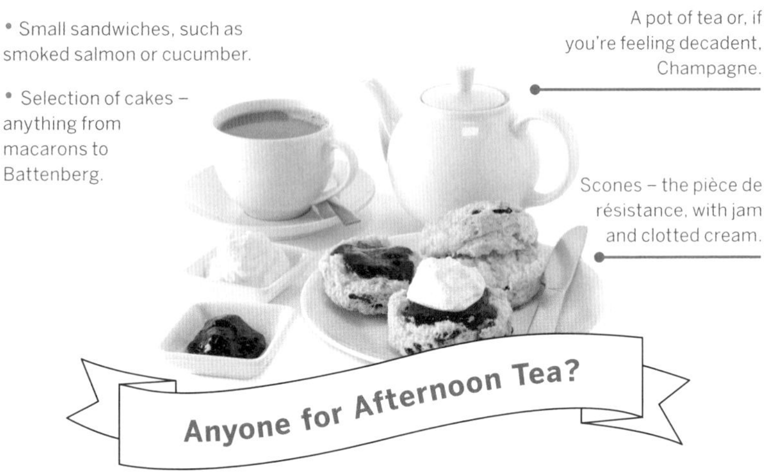

• Small sandwiches, such as smoked salmon or cucumber.
• Selection of cakes – anything from macarons to Battenberg.
A pot of tea or, if you're feeling decadent, Champagne.
Scones – the pièce de résistance, with jam and clotted cream.
Anyone for Afternoon Tea?

TRAVELLINGLIGHT/GETTY IMAGES ©

Afternoon Tea in London

Afternoon tea has become all the rage in the last few years, and you can see why: it's convivial, fun and ever-so-slightly naughty (all those sweets in one sitting!), if slightly overpriced (£20 to £30 per person). It is usually served in top-end restaurants and hotels at weekends, between 3pm and 6pm. It's best to skip lunch (and you probably won't need much dinner either). Bookings are essential pretty much everywhere, especially in winter.

VISITBRITAIN/ANDREW PICKETT/GETTY IMAGES ©

★ Top Three Afternoon Tea Destinations

Portrait (Map p252; ☎020-7312 2490; www.npg.org.uk/visit/shop-eat-drink.php; 3rd fl, National Portrait Gallery, St Martin's Pl, WC2; afternoon tea £28-40; ⏰10-11am, 11.45am-2.45pm & 3.30-4.45pm daily, 5.30-8.15pm Thu, Fri & Sat; ⊖Charing Cross) **Lovely afternoon tea with great views of the city.**

Bea's of Bloomsbury (Map p250; ☎020-7242 8330; www.beasofbloomsbury.com; 83 Watling St, EC4; afternoon tea £25-35; ⏰7.30am-7pm Mon-Fri, from 10.30am Sat & Sun; ⊖St Paul's) **One of the original and best; cakes are its forte.**

Delaunay (Map p250; ☎020-7499 8558; www.thedelaunay.com; 55 Aldwych, WC2; afternoon tea £10-30; ⏰7am-midnight Mon-Fri, 8am-midnight Sat, 9am-11pm Sun; ⊖Temple, Covent Garden) **Wonderful old-style brasserie serving daily afternoon tea.**

exhibitions add yet another dimension. The afternoon tea (£17.50) is particularly original: out with cucumber sandwiches, in with beef tartare and goat's curd.

Min Jiang Chinese £££
(Map p249; 020-7361 1988; www.minjiang.co.uk; Royal Garden Hotel, 10th fl, 2-24 Kensington High St, W8; mains £12-68; noon-3pm & 6-10.30pm; ; High St Kensington) Min Jiang serves up seafood, excellent wood-fired Peking duck (half/whole £32/58) and sumptuously regal views over Kensington Palace and Gardens. The menu is diverse, with a sporadic accent on spice (the Min Jiang is a river in Sichuan).

Chelsea & Belgravia

Rabbit Modern British ££
(www.rabbit-restaurant.com; 172 King's Rd, SW3; mains £6-24; noon-midnight Tue-Sat, noon-4pm Sun, 6-11pm Mon; ; Sloane Sq) Three brothers grew up on a farm. One became a farmer, another a butcher, while the third worked in hospitality. Noticing how complementary their trades were, they teamed up and founded Rabbit. Genius! Rabbit is a breath of fresh air in upmarket Chelsea: the restaurant rocks the agri-chic (yes) look and the creative, seasonal modern British cuisine is fabulous.

Victoria & Pimlico

Tomtom Coffee House Cafe £
(Map p249; www.tomtom.co.uk; 114 Ebury St, SW1; 8am-6pm Sun-Tue, to 9pm Wed-Sat, shorter hours in winter; Victoria) Tomtom has built its reputation on its amazing coffee: not only are the drinks fabulously presented (forget ferns and hearts in your latte, here it's peacocks fanning their tails), the selection is dizzying, from the usual espresso-based suspects to filter, and a full choice of beans. You can even spice things up with a bonus tot of cognac or scotch (£3).

Pimlico Fresh Cafe £
(86 Wilton Rd, SW1; mains from £4.50; 7.30am-7.30pm Mon-Fri, 9am-6pm Sat & Sun; Victoria) This friendly two-room cafe will see you right whether you need breakfast (French toast, bowls of porridge laced with honey or maple syrup), lunch (homemade quiches and soups, 'things' on toast) or just a good old latte and cake.

Clerkenwell, Shoreditch & Spitalfields

Clerkenwell

Polpo Italian £
(Map p255; 020-7250 0034; www.polpo.co.uk; 3 Cowcross St, EC1M; dishes £6-10; noon-11pm Mon-Sat, to 4pm Sun; Farringdon) Occupying a sunny spot on semi-pedestrianised Cowcross St, this sweet little place serves rustic Venetian-style meatballs, *pizzette*, grilled meat and fish dishes. Portions are larger than your average tapas but a tad smaller than a regular main – perfect for a light meal for one, or as part of a feast split between friends.

Prufrock Coffee Cafe £
(Map p255; www.prufrockcoffee.com; 23-25 Leather Lane, EC1N; mains £4-7; 8am-6pm Mon-Fri, 10am-5pm Sat & Sun; ; Farringdon) Not content with being one of the kings of London's coffee-bean scene (it offers barista training and workshops in 'latte art'), Prufrock also dishes up delicious breakfasts, lunches and cuppa-friendly pastries and snacks. Judging by the number of laptops, plenty of customers treat it as their office.

Morito Tapas ££
(Map p255; 020-7278 7007; www.morito.co.uk; 32 Exmouth Market, EC1R; tapas £4.50-9.50; noon-11pm Mon-Sat, to 4pm Sun; ; Farringdon) This diminutive eatery is a wonderfully authentic take on a Spanish tapas bar. Seats are at the bar, along the window, or on one of the small tables inside or out. It's relaxed, convivial and often completely crammed. The food is excellent.

Gastropubs

While not so long ago the pub was where you went for a drink, with maybe a packet of potato crisps to soak up the alcohol, the birth of the gastropub in the 1990s means that today just about every establishment serves full meals. But the quality varies widely, from defrosted-on-the-premises to Michelin-star worthy.

Pork pie with relish
DIANA MILLER/GETTY IMAGES ©

St John British ££

(Map p255; 020-7251 0848; www.stjohnrestaurant.com; 26 St John St, EC1M; mains £17-20; noon-3pm & 6-11pm Mon-Fri, 6-11pm Sat, 1-3pm Sun; Farringdon) Whitewashed brick walls, high ceilings and simple wooden furniture keep diners free to concentrate on St John's famous nose-to-tail dishes. Serves are big, hearty and a celebration of England's culinary past. Don't miss the signature roast bone marrow and parsley salad.

Medcalf British ££

(Map p255; 020-7833 3533; www.medcalfbar.co.uk; 40 Exmouth Market, EC1R; mains £13-18; noon-3pm & 5.30pm-midnight Mon-Sat, to 5pm Sun; Farringdon) Housed in a beautifully converted butcher shop dating back to 1912, Medcalf serves up tasty and well-realised British fare, such as hand-picked Dorset crab and Welsh rarebit. In summer, tables spill out onto the pavement.

Finsbury & St Luke's

Look Mum No Hands! Cafe £

(Map p255; 020-7253 1025; www.lookmumnohands.com; 49 Old St, EC1V; dishes £4-9; 7.30am-10pm Mon-Fri, 9am-10pm Sat & Sun; ; Barbican) Cyclists and noncyclists alike adore this cafe-workshop set in a light-filled space looking out onto Old St. Excellent homemade pies and wholesome salads are accompanied by daily specials, baguettes, cakes, pastries and good coffee. There are also a few outdoor tables and it'll loan you a lock if you need to park your wheels.

Hoxton & Shoreditch

Sông Quê Vietnamese £

(Map p255; www.songque.co.uk; 134 Kingsland Rd, E2; mains £7-10; noon-3pm & 5.30-11pm Mon-Fri, noon-11pm Sat & Sun; Hoxton) With the kind of demand for seats that most London restaurants can only dream of, this no-frills, hospital-green Vietnamese joint often has a line of people waiting. Service is abrupt, but the food is great, with two dozen types of *pho* (noodle soup) to choose from.

Allpress Espresso Cafe £

(Map p255; www.allpressespresso.com; 58 Redchurch St, E2; dishes £4-6; 8am-5pm; Shoreditch High St) Part of the great Antipodean takeover of London cafes, this distant outpost of a New Zealand brand serves perfectly crafted coffee from its neat-as-a-pin roastery. Also on the menu are pastries, cakes, sandwiches and a particularly good breakfast platter.

Clove Club Modern British £££

(Map p255; 020-7729 6496; www.thecloveclub.com; 380 Old St, EC1V; 3-course lunch £35, 5-course dinner £65; noon-2pm Tue-Sat, 6-9.30pm Mon-Sat; ; Old St) From humble origins as a supper club in a Dalston flat, the Clove Club has transformed into this incredibly impressive Michelin-starred restaurant in Shoreditch Town Hall. Hold onto your hats as you're taken on a culinary canter through multiple courses of intricately arranged, well-thought-out, flavoursome food – including numerous unbidden amuse-bouches and palate cleansers. Sensational

Spitalfields

Nude Espresso Cafe £

(Map p255; www.nudeespresso.com; 26 Hanbury St, E1; dishes £4-12; 7am-6pm Mon-Fri, 9.30am-5pm Sat & Sun; Shoreditch High St) A simply styled, cosy cafe serving top-notch coffee along with cooked breakfasts, light lunches and sweet treats. If it's just coffee you're after, head to its giant-sized roastery directly across the road.

Brick Lane Beigel Bake Bakery £

(Map p255; 159 Brick Lane, E2; bagels £1-4; 24hr; Shoreditch High St) This relic of the Jewish East End still makes a brisk trade serving dirt-cheap homemade bagels (filled with salmon, cream cheese and/or salt beef) to hungry shoppers and late-night boozers.

this relic still makes a brisk trade serving dirt-cheap homemade bagels

Hawksmoor Steak £££

(Map p255; 020-7426 4850; www.thehawksmoor.com; 157 Commercial St, E1; mains £13-30, noon-2.30pm & 5-10.30pm Mon-Sat, noon-4.30pm Sun; ; Shoreditch High St) You could easily miss discreetly signed Hawksmoor, but confirmed carnivores will find it worth seeking out. The dark wood, bare bricks and velvet curtains make for a handsome setting in which to gorge yourself on the best of British meat. The Sunday roasts (£20) are legendary.

East London

Whitechapel

Tayyabs Pakistani ££

(020-7247 9543; www.tayyabs.co.uk; 83-89 Fieldgate St, E1; mains £5-16; noon-11.30pm; ; Whitechapel) This buzzing (OK, crowded) Punjabi restaurant is in another league to its Brick Lane equivalents. *Seekh* kebabs, masala fish and other starters served on sizzling hot plates are delicious, as are accompaniments such as dhal, naan

View into London's famous bagel joint, Brick Lane Beigel Bake

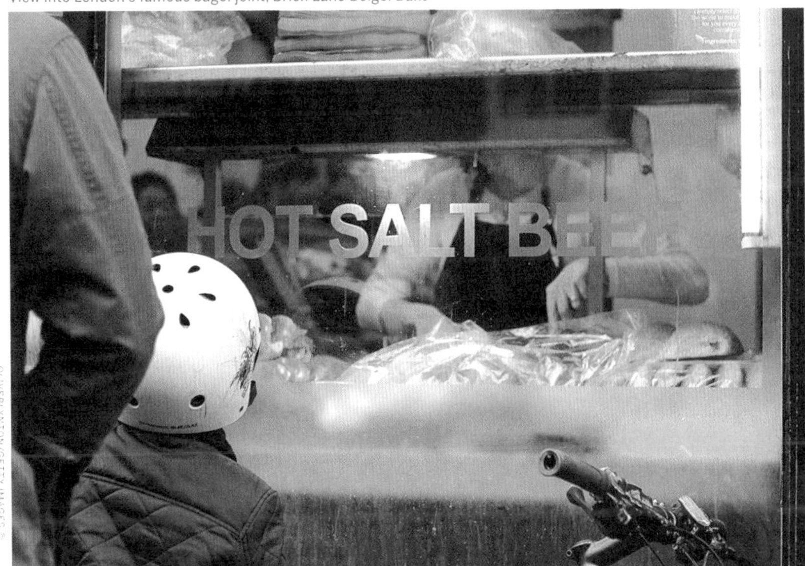

Museum Restaurants

National Dining Rooms (Map p252; 020-7747 2525; www.peytonandbyrne.co.uk; 1st fl, Sainsbury Wing, National Gallery, Trafalgar Sq, WC2; mains £12.50-17.50; 10am-5.30pm Sat-Thu, to 8.30pm Fri; Charing Cross) Chef Oliver Peyton's restaurant at the National Gallery styles itself as 'proudly and resolutely British', and what a great idea. The menu features an extensive and wonderful selection of British cheeses for a light lunch. For something more filling, go for the monthly changing County Menu, honouring regional specialities from across the British Isles. Set lunch is £19.50/23.50 for two/three courses.

Portrait (Map p252; 020-7312 2490; www.npg.org.uk/visit/shop-eat-drink.php; 3rd fl, National Portrait Gallery, St Martin's Pl, WC2; mains £17.50-26, 2/3-course menu £26.50/31.50; 10-11am, 11.45am-2.45pm & 3.30-4.45pm daily, 5.30-8.15pm Thu, Fri & Sat; Charing Cross) This stunningly located restaurant above the excellent National Portrait Gallery – with views over Trafalgar Sq and Westminster – is a great place to relax after a morning or afternoon at the gallery. The brunch (10am to 11.30am) and afternoon tea (3.30pm to 4.45pm) come highly recommended.

Wallace (020-7563 9505; www.peytonandbyrne.co.uk/the-wallace-restaurant/index.html; Hertford House, Manchester Sq, W1; mains £14-26; 10am-4.30pm Mon-Sun, 6-9.30pm Fri-Sat) There are few more idyllically placed restaurants than this brasserie in the enclosed courtyard of the Wallace Collection. The emphasis is on seasonal French-inspired dishes, with the daily menu offering two- or three-course meals for £22/26. Afternoon tea is £17.

and raita. On the downside, it can be noisy, service can be haphazard and queues often snake out the door.

Bethnal Green

Corner Room Modern British **££**
(020-7871 0460; www.townhallhotel.com; Patriot Sq, E2; mains £10-15, 2/3-course lunch £19/23; 7.30-10am, noon-3pm & 6-10pm; Bethnal Green) Someone put this baby in the corner, but we're certainly not complaining. Tucked away on the 1st floor of the Town Hall Hotel, this relaxed restaurant serves expertly crafted dishes with complex yet delicate flavours, highlighting the best of British seasonal produce.

Brawn British, French **££**
(Map p255; 020-7729 5692; www.brawn.co; 49 Columbia Rd, E2; mains £14-18; noon-3pm Tue-Sun, 6-10.30pm Mon-Sat; Hoxton) There's a Parisian bistro feel to this relaxed corner restaurant, yet the menu walks a fine line between British and French traditions. Hence oxtail and veal kidney pie sits alongside plaice Grenobloise, and souffles are filled with Westcombe cheddar. Try its legendary spicy Scotch egg starter – a Brit classic delivered with French finesse.

De Beauvoir Town

Towpath Cafe **£**
(Map p255; rear 42-44 De Beauvoir Cres, N1; mains £6-9; 9am-5.30pm Tue-Sun; Haggerston) Occupying four small units on the Regent's Canal towpath, this simple cafe is a super place to sip a cuppa and watch the ducks and narrowboats glide by. The food's excellent too, with delicious frittatas and brownies on the counter and cooked dishes chalked up on the blackboard daily.

Duke's Brew & Que American **££**
(020-3006 0795; www.dukesbrewandque.com; 33 Downham Rd, N1; mains £12-27; 6-10pm Mon-Fri, 11am-3pm & 5-9.30pm Sat & Sun; Haggerston) The house speciality at this attractive 18th-century pub is ribs – pork or beef – smoked over hickory and lovingly barbecued until the meat falls off the bone. Washed down with a beer from the nearby

Beavertown Brewery, it is lip-smackin' food par excellence. The weekend brunch is similarly delicious with pancakes and whopper omelettes filled with BBQ cuts.

Dalston

Rotorino — Italian ££

(020-7249 9081; www.rotorino.com; 434 Kingsland Rd, E8; mains £9-17; 6-11pm Mon-Fri, noon-3pm & 6-11pm Sat, noon-9pm Sun; Dalston Junction) Decked out with blue tiles, 1950s lino and exposed brick, Rotorino's chic interior comes as a welcome surprise, especially after stepping off such a shabby section of Kingsland Rd. The menu is full of delicious, robust Italian dishes, divided into antipasto-style 'starters', 'pasta', 'wood grill' and 'stove'.

Mangal Ocakbasi — Turkish ££

(www.mangal1.com; 10 Arcola St, E8; mains £8-15; noon-midnight; Dalston Kingsland) Mangal is the quintessential Turkish *ocakbasi* (open-hooded charcoal grill, the mother of all BBQs): cramped, smoky and serving superb mezze, grilled lamb chops, quail and a lip-smacking assortment of kebabs.

Hackney & Hackney Wick

Counter Cafe — Cafe £

(www.counterproductive.co.uk; 7 Roach Rd, E3; dishes £4-8; 8am-5pm; ; Hackney Wick) Housed within the Stour Space gallery and directly overlooking the Olympic stadium, this friendly canal-side cafe serves fantastic coffee, breakfasts, sandwiches and pies. The mismatched, thrift-store furniture, art-clad walls and relaxed atmosphere make it a favourite with the local artistic community.

Empress — Modern British ££

(020-8533 5123; www.empresse9.co.uk; 130 Lauriston Rd, E9; mains £15-16; 10am-9.30pm Sun, 6-10.15pm Mon, noon-3.30pm & 6-10.15pm Tue-Fri, 10am-3.30pm & 6-10.15pm Sat; 277) This upmarket pub conversion belts out excellent modern British cuisine under the watchful eye of chef Elliott Lidstone. On Mondays there's a £10 main-plus-drink deal and on weekends it serves an excellent brunch.

Celebrity Chefs

London's food renaissance was partly led by a group of telegenic chefs who built food empires around their names and their TV programs. Gordon Ramsay is the most (in)famous of the lot, but his London venues are still standard-bearers for top-quality cuisine. Other big names include campaigning star Jamie Oliver; Tom Aitken (p145), who champions British products; and Heston Blumenthal (p145), whose mad-professor-like experiments with food (molecular gastronomy, as he describes it) have earned him rave reviews.

Chef Jamie Oliver
MARK CUTHBERT/UK PRESS/GETTY IMAGES ©

Formans — Modern British ££

(020-8525 2365; www.formans.co.uk; Stour Rd, E3; mains £15-20, brunch £6-10; 7-11pm Thu & Fri, 10am-2pm & 7-11pm Sat, noon-5pm Sun; ; Hackney Wick) Curing fish since 1905, riverside Formans boasts prime views over the Olympic stadium and has a gallery overlooking its smokery. The menu includes a delectable choice of smoked salmon (including its signature 'London cure'), plenty of other seafood and a few nonfishy things. There's a great selection of British wines and spirits, too.

Camden & North London

King's Cross & Euston

Grain Store International ££

(Map p256; 020-7324 4466; www.grainstore.com; 1-3 Stable St, N1C; weekend brunch £6-17, lunch £11-17, dinner £15-17; noon-2.30pm & 6-10.30pm Mon-Sat, 11am-3.45pm Sun; ; King's Cross St Pancras) Fresh seasonal vegetables take top billing at Bruno Loubet's bright and breezy Granary Sq restaurant. Meat does appear but it lurks coyly beneath leaves, or adds crunch to mashes. The creative menu gainfully plunders from numerous cuisines to produce dishes that are simultaneously healthy and delicious.

Caravan International ££

(Map p256; 020-7101 7661; www.caravankingscross.co.uk; 1 Granary Sq, N1C; mains £10-17; 8am-10.30pm Mon-Fri, 10am-11.30pm Sat, 10am-4pm Sun; ; King's Cross St Pancras) Housed in the lofty Granary Building, Caravan is a vast, industrial-chic destination for tasty bites from around the world. You can opt for several small plates to share meze/tapas style, or stick to main-sized plates.

Camden Town

Chin Chin Labs Ice Cream £

(Map p256; www.chinchinlabs.com; 49-50 Camden Lock Pl, NW1; ice cream £4-5; noon-7pm Tue-Sun; Camden Town) This is food chemistry at its absolute best. Chefs prepare the ice-cream mixture and freeze it on the spot by adding liquid nitrogen. Flavours change regularly and match the seasons (spiced hot cross bun, passionfruit and coconut etc). Sauces and toppings are equally creative. It's directly opposite the giant Gilgamesh statue inside Camden Lock Market.

Market Modern British ££

(Map p256; 020-7267 9700; www.marketrestaurant.co.uk; 43 Parkway, NW1; 2-course lunch £10, mains £15-19; noon-2.30pm & 6-10.30pm Mon-Sat, 11am-3pm Sun; Camden Town) This fabulous restaurant is an ode to great, simple British food, with a measure of French sophistication thrown in. The light and airy space (bare brick walls, steel

Caravan

Vegetarians & Vegans

London has been one of the best places for vegetarians to dine out since the 1970s, initially due mostly to its many Indian restaurants, which, for religious reasons, always cater for people who don't eat meat. A number of dedicated vegetarian restaurants have since cropped up, offering imaginative, filling and truly delicious meals. Most nonvegetarian places generally offer a couple of dishes for those who don't eat meat; vegans, however, will find it harder outside Indian or dedicated establishments.

tables and basic wooden chairs) reflects this stripped-back approach.

Islington

Ottolenghi Bakery, Mediterranean ££
(020-7288 1454; www.ottolenghi.co.uk; 287 Upper St, N1; breakfast £6-10, lunch £12-17, dinner £9-13; 8am-10.30pm Mon-Sat, 9am-7pm Sun; ; Highbury & Islington) Mountains of meringues tempt you through the door, where a sumptuous array of baked goods and fresh salads greets you. Meals are as light and bright as the brilliantly white interior design, with a strong influence from the eastern Mediterranean.

Trullo Italian ££
(020-7226 2733; www.trullorestaurant.com; 300-302 St Paul's Rd, N1; mains £16-22; 12.30-3pm daily, 6-10.30pm Mon-Sat; Highbury & Islington) Trullo's homemade pasta is delicious, but the main attraction here is the charcoal grill, which churns out the likes of succulent Italian-style pork chops, steaks and fish. The service is excellent, too.

Notting Hill & West London

Geales Seafood ££
(020-7727 7528; www.geales.com; 2 Farmer St, W8; 2-/3-course express lunch £9.95/12.95, mains £8.50-23; noon-3pm Tue-Fri, 6-10.30pm Mon-Fri, noon-10.30pm Sat, noon-9.30pm Sun; Notting Hill Gate) Frying since 1939, Geales enjoys a quiet location, tucked away on the corner of Hillgate Village. The succulent fish in crispy batter is a fine catch from a menu which also runs to other British faves such as pork belly with apple sauce and crackling, and beef and bacon pie. Look out for the good-value express lunch.

Mazi Greek ££
(020-7229 3794; www.mazi.co.uk; 12-14 Hillgate St, W8; mains £10-26; noon-3pm Wed-Sun, 6.30-10.30pm Mon & Tue, 6.30-11pm Wed-Sun; Notting Hill Gate) Mazi has shaken up the Greek tradition along pretty Hillgate St, concocting a lively menu of modern and innovative (many of sharing size) platters in a bright and neat setting, with a small back garden (for summer months) and an all-Greek wine list. It's both small and popular, so reservations are important.

Ledbury French £££
(020-7792 9090; www.theledbury.com; 127 Ledbury Rd, W11; 4-course set lunch £50, 4-course dinner £95; noon-2pm Wed-Sun & 6.30-9.45pm daily; ; Westbourne Park, Notting Hill Gate) Two Michelin stars and swooningly elegant, Brett Graham's artful French restaurant attracts well-heeled diners in jeans with designer jackets. Dishes – such as Herdwick lamb with salt baked turnips, ewe's milk and garlic shoots, or flame grilled mackerel with pickled cucumber, celtic mustard and shiso – are triumphant. London gastronomes have the Ledbury on speed-dial, so reservations are crucial.

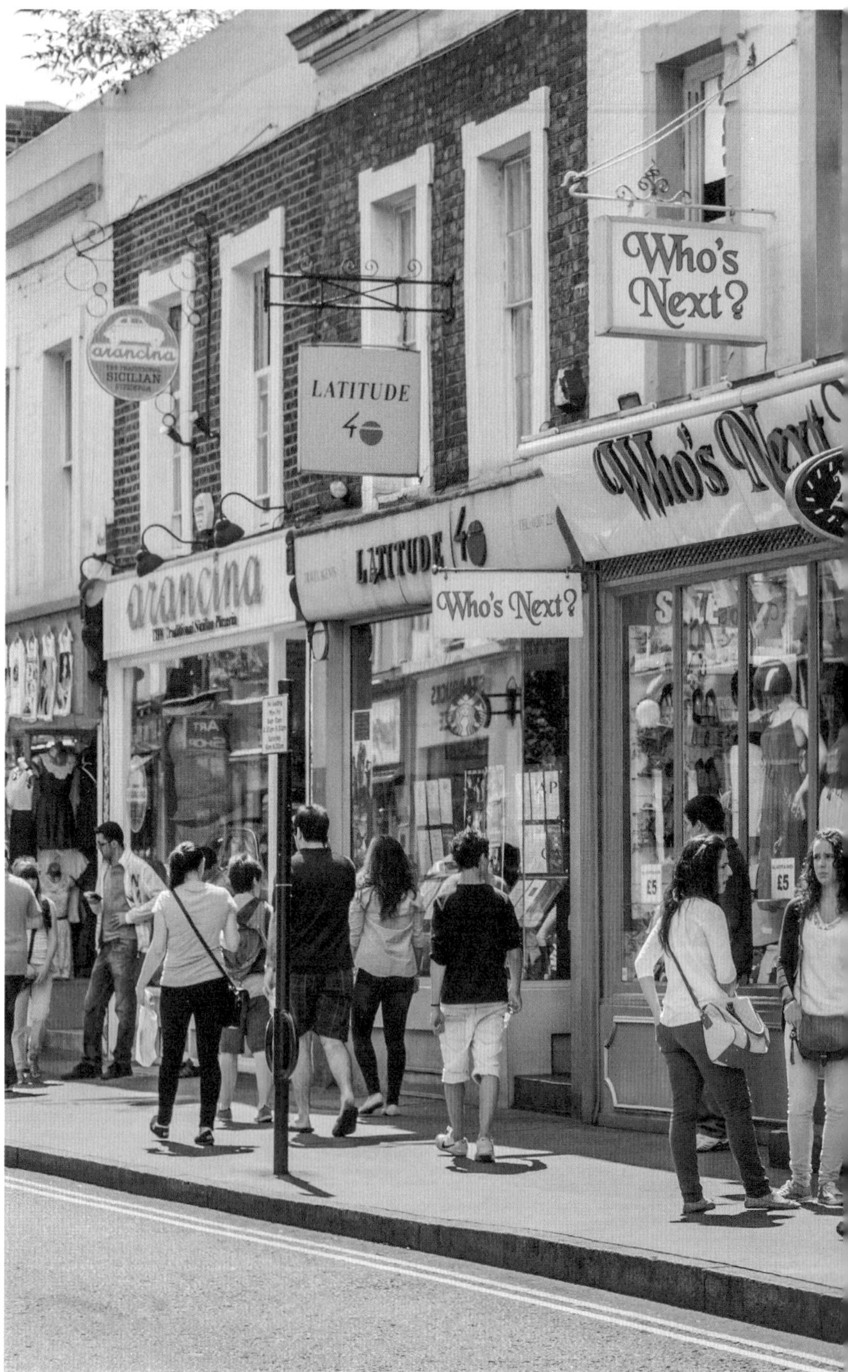

MAREMAGNUM/GETTY IMAGES ©

TREASURE HUNT

Begin your shopping adventure

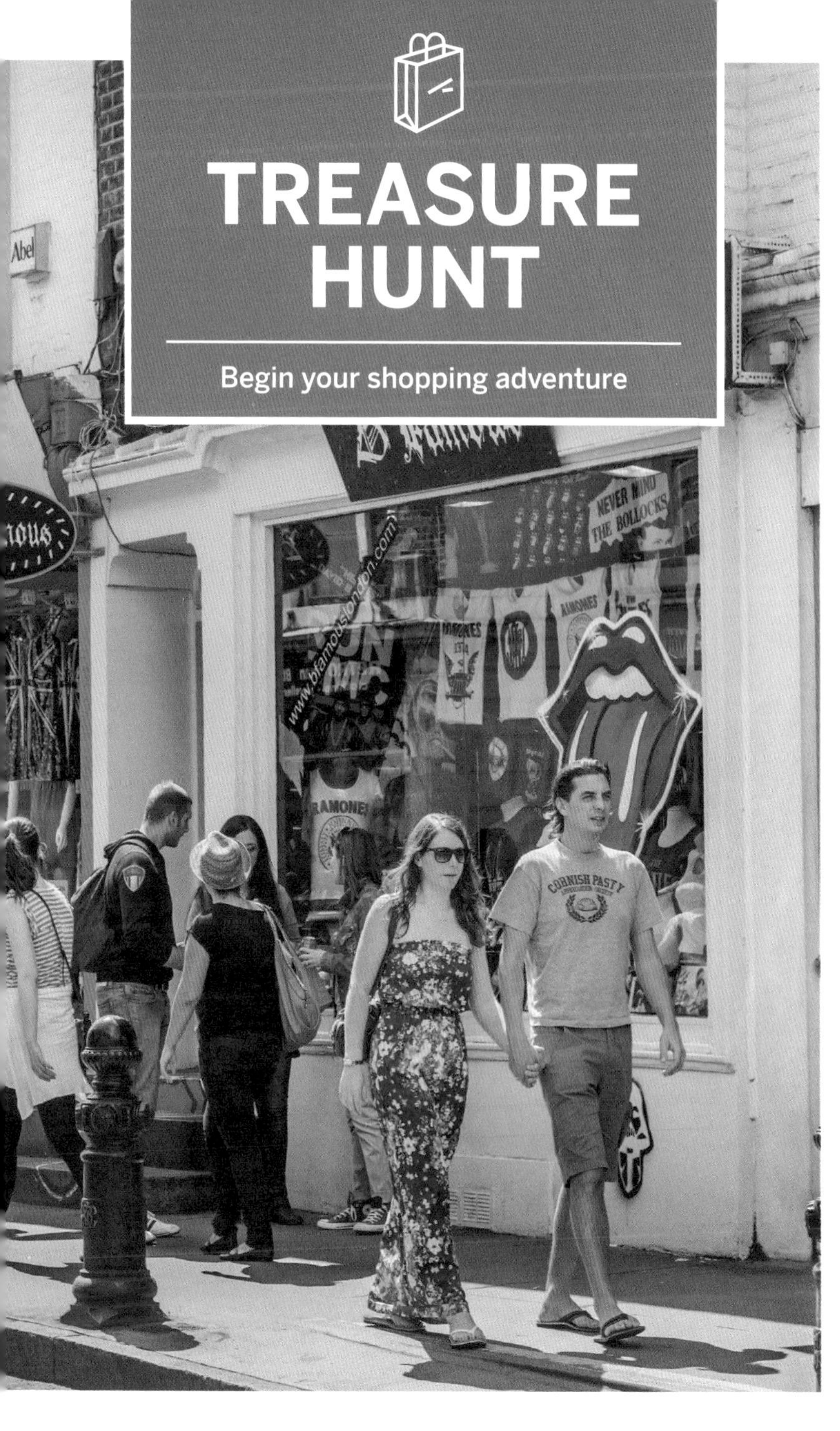

Treasure Hunt

From charity-shop finds to designer bags, there are thousands of ways to spend your hard-earned cash in London. Many of the big-name shopping attractions, such as Harrods and Hamleys, and famous designers, such as Stella McCartney and Paul Smith, have become must-sees in their own right. Chances are that with so many temptations, you'll give your wallet a full workout.

One of the biggest draws for visitors are the capital's famed markets. A treasure trove of small designers, unique jewellery pieces, original framed photographs and posters, colourful vintage pieces and bric-a-brac, they are the antidote to impersonal, carbon-copy shopping centres.

In This Section

Taxes & Refunds

In certain circumstances visitors from non-EU countries are entitled to claim back the 20% value-added tax (VAT) they have paid on purchased goods. The rebate applies only to items purchased in stores displaying a 'tax free' sign.

For information on how to apply, see www.gov.uk/tax-on-shopping/taxfree-shopping.

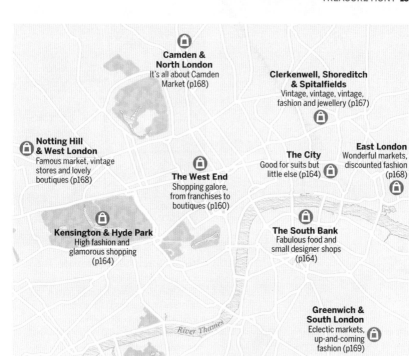

Camden & North London
It's all about Camden Market (p168)

Clerkenwell, Shoreditch & Spitalfields
Vintage, vintage, vintage, fashion and jewellery (p167)

Notting Hill & West London
Famous market, vintage stores and lovely boutiques (p168)

The West End
Shopping galore, from franchises to boutiques (p160)

The City
Good for suits but little else (p164)

East London
Wonderful markets, discounted fashion (p168)

Kensington & Hyde Park
High fashion and glamorous shopping (p164)

The South Bank
Fabulous food and small designer shops (p164)

River Thames

Greenwich & South London
Eclectic markets, up-and-coming fashion (p169)

Opening Hours

Shops generally open from 9am or 10am to 6pm or 7pm Monday to Saturday.

The majority of stores in the most popular shopping strips also open on Sunday, typically from noon to 6pm (sometimes 10am to 4pm).

Shops in the West End open till 9pm on Thursday.

Sales

With the growing popularity of online shopping, sales now often start earlier and last longer, but there are two main sales seasons in the UK (which both last about a month):

Winter sales Start on Boxing Day (26 December)

Summer sales July

The Best...

Experience London's best shopping

Vintage

Beyond Retro (p168) London vintage empire with a rock and roll heart.

Bang Bang Clothing Exchange (p160) On-trend vintage designer pieces.

British Red Cross (p166) Kensington cast-offs of exceptional quality.

Retrobates Vintage (p169) Duds for a dinner at Downton.

Bookshops

Foyles (p161) A brilliant selection covering most bases.

Daunt Books (p163) Guides, maps and tales from every corner of the world.

Hatchards (p160) The oldest, and still one of the best, bookshops in London.

Gosh! (p161) Comic fans have found their match.

Fashion Shops

Selfridges (p160) Everything from streetwear to high fashion under one roof.

Burberry Outlet Store (p168) A slightly cheaper take on the classic Brit brand.

Topshop (p160) Setting trends like no one else on the High Street.

Department Stores

Selfridges (p160) Over 100 years of retail innovation.

Liberty (p161) Fabric, fashion and much, much more.

Harrods (p164) Enormous, overwhelming and indulgent, with a world-famous food hall.

Fortnum & Mason (p160) A world of food in luxuriously historic surroundings.

Cosmetics

Penhaligon's (p160) Classic British perfumer, with highly personalised service.

Jo Loves (p166) The latest venture of famed scent-maker Jo Malone.

Molton Brown (p161) A reference in soaps, creams, lotions and more.

Markets

Camden Market (p169) Authentic antiques to tourist tat – and everything in between.

Portobello Road Market (p168) Classic Notting Hill sprawl, perfect for vintage everything.

Old Spitalfields Market (p125) One of London's best for young fashion designers.

Sunday UpMarket (p125) Up-and-coming designers, cool tees and terrific food.

Broadway Market (p168) Local market known for its food but with plenty else besides.

Greenwich Market (p169) Food, food, glorious food, with shopping to be had too.

★ Lonely Planet's Top Choices

Silver Vaults (p164) The world's largest collection of silver, from cutlery to jewellery.

Fortnum & Mason (p160) The world's most glamorous grocery store.

Camden Market (p169) Every shade of exotic and alternative: steampunk fashion, navel jewellery, Moroccan lamps.

Harrods (p164) Garish, stylish, kitsch, yet perennially popular department store.

Sister Ray (p163) A top independent music shop, with an ever-changing selection of vinyls and CDs.

The West End

Westminster & St James's

Penhaligon's Accessories

(Map p252; www.penhaligons.com; 16-17 Burlington Arcade, W1; 10am-6pm Mon-Fri, to 6.30pm Sat, 11am-5pm Sun; Piccadilly Circus or Green Park) Ensconced within stunningly historic Burlington Arcade, Penhaligon's is a classic British perfumery. Attendants enquire about your favourite smells, take you on an exploratory tour of the shop's signature range and help you discover new scents in their traditional perfumes, home fragrances and bath and body products. Everything is made in Cornwall.

Fortnum & Mason Department Store

(Map p252; www.fortnumandmason.com; 181 Piccadilly, W1; 10am-9pm Mon-Sat, noon-6pm Sun; Piccadilly Circus) With its classic eau de nil colour scheme, London's oldest grocery store (into its fourth century) refuses to yield to modern times. Its staff are still clad in old-fashioned tailcoats, its glamorous food hall supplied with hampers, cut marmalade, speciality teas and so forth.

Hatchards Books

(Map p252; 187 Piccadilly, W1; 9.30am-7pm Mon-Sat, noon-6pm Sun; Green Park or Piccadilly Circus) London's oldest bookshop dates to 1797. Holding three royal warrants (hence the portrait of the Queen), it's a stupendous independent bookstore, with a solid supply of signed editions and bursting at its smart seams with very browseable stock. There's a strong selection of first editions on the ground floor as well as regular literary events.

Bloomsbury & Fitzrovia

Bang Bang Clothing Exchange Vintage

(Map p256; www.bangbangclothingexchange.com; 21 Goodge St, W1; 10am-6.30pm Mon-Fri, 11am-6pm Sat; Goodge St) Got some designer or high-street or vintage pieces you're tired of? Bang Bang exchanges, buys and sells. As the exchange says of

British Designers

British designers are well established in the fashion world, with Stella McCartney (p163), Vivienne Westwood, Paul Smith, Burberry, Mulberry and Alexander McQueen (the design house behind Princess Catherine's wedding dress) now household names. For the best selection, head to **Selfridges** (www.selfridges.com; 400 Oxford St, W1; 9.30am-9pm Mon-Sat, 11.30am-6pm Sun); otherwise most designers have their own boutique in London.

CARL DE SOUZA/AFP/GETTY IMAGES ©

itself, 'think of Alexander McQueen cocktail dresses rubbing shoulders with Topshop shoes and 1950s jewellery'. Indeed.

Soho & Chinatown

Topshop Clothing

(Map p252; www.topshop.co.uk; 36-38 Great Castle St, W1; 9am-9pm Mon-Sat, 11.30am-6pm Sun; Oxford Circus) The 'It'-store when it comes to clothes and accessories, venturing boldly into couture in recent years, Topshop encapsulates London's supreme skill at bringing catwalk fashion to the youth market affordably and quickly.

Hamleys Toys

(Map p252; www.hamleys.com; 188-196 Regent St, W1; 10am-9pm Mon-Fri, 9.30am-9pm Sat, noon-6pm Sun; Oxford Circus) Claiming to be the world's oldest (and some say, the largest) toy store, Hamleys moved to its address on Regent St in 1881. From the ground floor – where staff glide UFOs and foam boomerangs through the air with practised nonchalance – to Lego World and a cafe on the 5th floor, it's a layer cake of playthings.

Liberty Department Store

(Map p252; www.liberty.co.uk; Great Marlborough St, W1; 10am-8pm Mon-Sat, noon-6pm Sun; Oxford Circus) An irresistible blend of contemporary styles in an old-fashioned mock-Tudor atmosphere, Liberty has a huge cosmetics department and an accessories floor, along with a breathtaking lingerie section, all at very inflated prices. A classic London souvenir is a Liberty fabric print, especially in the form of a scarf.

Gosh! Books

(Map p252; www.goshlondon.com; 1 Berwick St, W1; 10.30am-7.30pm; Piccadilly Circus) Draw up here for graphic novels, manga, newspaper-strip collections and children's books, such as the Tintin and Asterix series. It's also perfect for finding presents for kids and teenagers.

Covent Garden & Leicester Square

Cambridge Satchel Company Accessories

(Map p252; www.cambridgesatchel.com; 31 James St, WC2; 10am-7pm Mon-Sat, 11am-7pm Sun; Covent Garden) The classic British leather-satchel concept morphed into a trendy and colourful him-or-her array of backpacks, totes, clutches, tiny satchels, work bags, music bags, mini satchels, two-in-one satchels and more.

Foyles Books

(Map p252; www.foyles.co.uk; 107 Charing Cross Rd, WC2; 9.30am-9pm Mon-Sat, 11.30am-6pm Sun; Tottenham Court Rd) This is London's most legendary bookshop, where you can bet on finding even the most obscure of titles. In 2014, the store moved just down the road into the spacious former home of Central St Martins. Thoroughly redesigned, its stunning new home is a joy to explore.

Molton Brown Beauty

(Map p252; www.moltonbrown.co.uk; 18 Russell St, WC2; 10am-7pm Mon-Sat, 11am-6pm Sun;

Grand Entrance to Fortnum & Mason

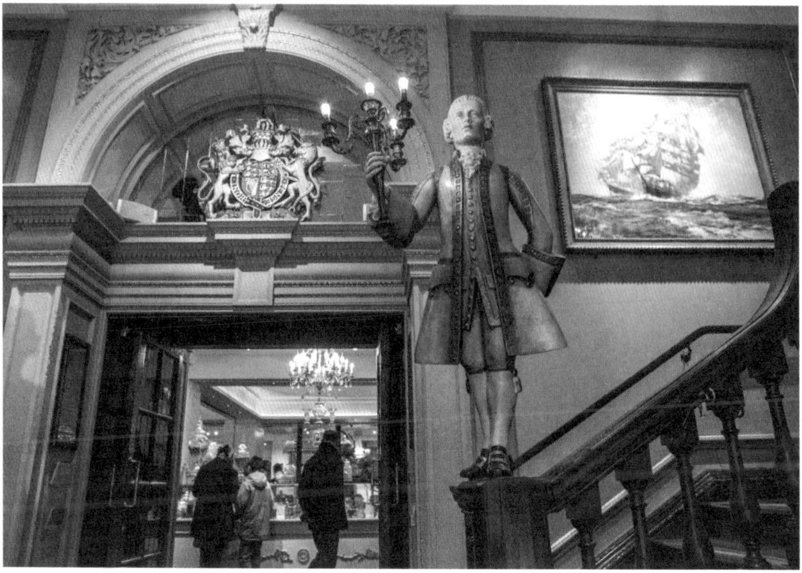

Rough Trade East

this record store is still the best place to come for music of an indie or alternative bent

Covent Garden) A fabulously fragrant British natural beauty range, Molton Brown is *the* choice for boutique hotel, posh restaurant and 1st-class airline bathrooms. Its skin-care products offer plenty of pampering for both men and women. In this store you can also have a facial as well as pick up home accessories.

Ted Baker Fashion

(Map p252; www.tedbaker.com; 9-10 Floral St, WC2; 10.30am-7.30pm Mon-Wed, Fri & Sat, to 8pm Thu, 10am-7pm Sat, noon-6pm Sun; Covent Garden) The one-time Glasgow-based tailor shop has grown into a superb brand of clothing, with elegant menswear and womenswear. Ted's forte is its formal wear, with beautiful dresses for women (lots of daring prints and exquisite material) and sharp tailoring for men. The casual collections (denim, beachwear etc) are excellent, too.

Paul Smith Fashion

(Map p252; www.paulsmith.co.uk; 40-44 Floral St, WC2; 10.30am-6.30pm Mon-Wed, to 7pm Thu & Fri, 10am-7pm Sat, 12.30-5.30pm Sun; Covent Garden) Paul Smith represents the best of British classics with innovative twists. Superstylish menswear, suits and tailored shirts are all laid out on open shelves in this walk-in closet of a shop. Smith also does womenswear, with sharp tailoring for an androgynous, almost masculine, look.

Marylebone

Cath Kidston Homewares, Clothing

(Map p256; www.cathkidston.com; 51 Marylebone High St, W1; 10am-7pm Mon-Sat, 11am-5pm Sun; Baker St) If you favour the preppy look, you'll love Cath Kidston with her signature floral prints and 1950s fashion (dresses above the knee and cinched at the waist, cardigans, shawls and old-fashioned pyjamas). There is also a range of homewares.

Cadenhead's Whisky & Tasting Shop — Drink

(www.whiskytastingroom.com; 26 Chiltern St, W1; Baker St) Scotland's oldest independent bottler of pure, nonblended whisky from local distilleries, this excellent shop is a joy for anyone with a passion for *uisge* (the Gaelic word for 'water'). All bottled whiskies derive from individually selected casks, without any filtrations, additions or colouring, guaranteeing purity. Regular whisky tastings are held downstairs (maximum 12 people).

Daunt Books — Books

(Map p256; www.dauntbooks.co.uk; 83 Marylebone High St, W1; 9am-7.30pm Mon-Sat, 11am-6pm Sun; Baker St) An original Edwardian bookshop, with oak panels and gorgeous skylights, Daunt is one of London's loveliest travel bookshops. It has two floors and stocks general fiction and nonfiction titles as well.

Monocle Shop — Accessories

(020-7486 8770; www.monocle.com; 2a George St, W1; 11am-7pm Mon-Sat, noon-5pm Sun; Bond St) Run by the people behind the design and International current affairs magazine *Monocle*, this shop is pure understated heaven. Costly stuff but if you're a fan of minimalist quality design (clothes, bags, umbrellas and so on), you'll want to stop by. Beautifully bound 1st editions too.

Mayfair

Sting — Fashion

(Map p252; www.thesting.nl; 55 Regent St, W1; 10am-10pm Mon-Sat, noon-6pm Sun; Piccadilly Circus) This Dutch chain is a 'network of brands': most of the clothes it stocks are European labels that are little known in the UK. Spread over three floors are anything from casual sweatpants and fluoro T-shirts to elegant dresses, frilly tops and handsome shirts.

Stella McCartney — Fashion

(Map p252; www.stellamccartney.co.uk; 30 Bruton St, W1; 10am-7pm Mon-Sat; Bond St) Stella McCartney's sharp tailoring, floaty

Independent Music Stores

Britons buy more music per head than any other nation. Independent music stores find it difficult to keep going, especially in central London, but they still exist. Here are some of London's best:

Rough Trade East (Map p255; www.roughtrade.com; Old Truman Brewery, 91 Brick Lane, E1; 8am-9pm Mon-Fri, 11am-7pm Sat & Sun; Shoreditch High St) Although it's no longer directly associated with the legendary record label (home to The Smiths and The Libertines, among many others), this large record store is still the best place to come for music of an indie or alternative bent. Apart from the impressive selection of CDs and vinyl, it also dispenses coffee and stages promotional gigs.

Sister Ray (Map p252; www.sisterray.co.uk; 75 Berwick St, W1; 10am-8pm Mon-Sat, noon-6pm Sun; Oxford Circus or Tottenham Court Rd) If you were a fan of the late, great John Peel on the BBC/BBC World Service, this specialist in innovative, experimental and indie music is just right for you.

Ray's Jazz (Map p252; www.foyles.co.uk; 2nd fl, 107 Charing Cross Rd, WC2; 9.30am-9pm Mon-Sat, 11.30am-6pm Sun; Tottenham Court Rd) Quiet and serene with friendly and helpful staff, this shop on the 2nd floor of Foyles bookshop has one of the best jazz selections in London.

Reckless Records (Map p252; www.reckless.co.uk; 30 Berwick St, W1; 10am-7pm; Oxford Circus or Tottenham Court Rd) Despite its numerous name changes, this outfit hasn't really changed in spirit. It still stocks new and secondhand records and CDs, from punk, soul, dance and independent to mainstream.

Vintage Fashion

The realm of vintage apparel has moved from being sought out by those looking for something offbeat and original, to an all-out mainstream shopping habit. Vintage designer garments and odd bits and pieces from the 1920s to the 1980s are all gracing the rails in some surprisingly upmarket boutique vintage shops.

The less self-conscious charity shops – especially those in areas such as Chelsea, Kensington and Islington – are your best bets for real bargains on designer wear (usually, the richer the area, the better the secondhand shops).

LOLOSTOCK/GETTY IMAGES ©

designs, accessible style and 'ethical' approach to fashion (no leather or fur) is very of-the-moment. This three-storey terraced Victorian home is a minimalist showcase for the designer's current collections. Depending on your devotion and wallet, you'll feel at ease or like a trespasser.

The City

Silver Vaults Handicrafts

(Map p250; 020-7242 3844; http://silvervaultslondon.com; 53-63 Chancery Lane, WC2; 9am-5.30pm Mon-Fri, to 1pm Sat; Chancery Lane) The 30-odd shops that work out of these secure subterranean vaults make up the largest collection of silver under one roof in the world. The different businesses tend to specialise in particular types of silverware, from cutlery sets to picture frames and lots of jewellery.

The South Bank

Waterloo

National Theatre Gift Shop Books

(Map p250; 020-7452 3456; www.nationaltheatre.org.uk; South Bank, SE1; 9.30am-10.45pm Mon-Sat, noon-6pm Sun; Waterloo) You'll find an extensive selection of books covering literature, history, art and more, as well as NT merchandise and unusual gifts. Jewellery and children's gifts are lined up next to fold-out craft beer maps and skull-shaped erasers.

Southbank Centre Shop Homewares

(Map p250; www.southbankcentre.co.uk; Festival Tce, SE1; 10am-9pm Mon-Fri, to 8pm Sat, noon-8pm Sun; Waterloo) This is the place to come for quirky London books, '50s-inspired homewares, original prints and creative gifts for children. The shop is rather eclectic but you're sure to find unique gifts or souvenirs to take home.

Bermondsey

Lovely & British Gifts

(020-7378 6570; www.facebook.com/LovelyandBritish; 132a Bermondsey St, SE1; 10am-3pm Mon, 11.30am-6pm Tue, 10am-6pm Wed-Fri, 10am-5.30pm Sat, 11am-4pm Sun; London Bridge) As the name suggests, this gorgeous Bermondsey boutique prides itself on stocking prints, jewellery and home furnishings from British designers. It's an eclectic mix of vintage and new, with very reasonable prices.

Kensington & Hyde Park

Knightsbridge & South Kensington

Harrods Department Store

(Map p249; www.harrods.com; 87-135 Brompton Rd, SW1; 10am-9pm Mon-Sat, 11.30am-6pm Sun; Knightsbridge) Garish and stylish in

5 Must-Buy Mementos

Tea

The British drink par excellence, with plenty of iconic names and a huge variety to choose from. For lovely packaging too, try Fortnum & Mason (p160) or Harrods (p164).

Vintage Clothes & Shoes

Your London vintage fashion finds will forever be associated with your trip to the city. Dalston has great vintage shops, including Beyond Retro (p168).

British Design

With its cool and understated chic, British design has made a name for itself worldwide. Try the Conran Shop (p166) or Monocle Shop (p163).

Music

The city that produced legends from the Rolling Stones to Amy Winehouse is a brilliant place to buy records. Try Rough Trade East (p163) or Sister Ray (p163).

London Toys

Double-decker buses, Paddington bears, guards in bearskin hats – London's icons make for great souvenirs. Hamleys (p160) is the place to go.

equal measures, perennially crowded Harrods is an obligatory stop for visitors, from the cash-strapped to the big, big spenders. The stock is astonishing, as are many of the price tags. High on kitsch, the 'Egyptian Elevator' resembles something out of an Indiana Jones epic, while the memorial fountain to Dodi and Di (lower ground floor) merely adds surrealism.

Conran Shop Design
(Map p249; www.conranshop.co.uk; Michelin House, 81 Fulham Rd, SW3; 10am-6pm Mon, Tue, Fri & Sat, to 7pm Wed & Thu, noon-6pm Sun; South Kensington) The original design store (going strong since 1987), the Conran Shop is a treasure trove of beautiful things, from radios to sunglasses, kitchenware to children's toys and books, bathroom accessories to greeting cards.

Chelsea & Belgravia

British Red Cross Vintage
(69-71 Old Church St, SW3; 10am-6pm Mon-Sat; Sloane Sq) The motto 'One man's rubbish is another man's treasure' couldn't be truer in this part of London, where the 'rubbish' is made up of designer gowns and cashmere jumpers. Obviously the price tags are a little higher than in your run-of-the-mill charity shop (£40 rather than £5 for a jumper or jacket) but it's still a bargain for the quality.

Pickett Gifts
(Map p249; www.pickett.co.uk; cnr Sloane St & Sloane Tce, SW1; 9.30am-6.30pm Mon-Fri, 10am-6pm Sat; Sloane Sq) Walking into Picketts as an adult is a bit like walking into a sweet shop as a child: the exquisite leather goods are all so colourful and beautiful, you don't really know where to start. Choice items include the perfectly finished handbags, the exquisite roll-up backgammon sets and the men's grooming sets. All leather goods are made in Britain.

Jo Loves Beauty
(Map p249; www.joloves.com; 42 Elizabeth St, SW1; 10am-6pm Mon-Sat, noon-5pm Sun; Victoria) The latest venture of famed British scent-maker Jo Malone, Jo Loves features the entrepreneur's signature candles, fragrances and bath products in a range of delicate scents: Arabian amber, white rose and lemon leaves, oud and

French Connection UK

BEN PRUCHNIE/GETTY IMAGES ©

mango. All products come exquisitely wrapped in red boxes with black bows.

Clerkenwell, Shoreditch & Spitalfields

Clerkenwell

Hatton Garden Jewellery

(Map p255; www.hatton-garden.net; EC1N; Farringdon) If you're in the market for classic settings or unmounted stones, stroll along Hatton Garden – it's chock-a-block with gold, diamond and jewellery shops, especially at the southern end.

Shoreditch

Boxpark Shopping Centre

(Map p255; www.boxpark.co.uk; 2-10 Bethnal Green Rd, E1; 11am-7pm; Shoreditch High St) A great place to find both up-and-coming and established brands, Boxpark is a quirky pop-up shopping mall created from shipping containers. Each of the series of tiny shops inhabits its own container, selling a wide variety of things: fashion, design, gifts, art and wine. Head to the upper level for restaurants, bars and a terrace.

Tatty Devine Jewellery

(Map p255; 020-7739 9191; www.tattydevine.com; 236 Brick Lane, E2; 10am-6.30pm Mon-Sat, to 5pm Sun; Shoreditch High St) Harriet Vine and Rosie Wolfenden make hip and witty jewellery that's become the favourite of many young Londoners. Their original designs feature all manner of flora- and fauna-inspired necklaces, as well as creations sporting moustaches, dinosaurs and bunting. Perspex name necklaces (made to order; from £28) are also a treat.

Labour & Wait Homewares

(Map p255; www.labourandwait.co.uk; 85 Redchurch St, E2; 11am-6pm Tue-Sun; Shoreditch High St) Dedicated to simple and functional, yet scrumptiously stylish, traditional British and European homewares, Labour & Wait specialises in items by independent manufacturers who make their products the old-fashioned way. There are shaving soaps, enamel coffee pots, luxurious lambswool blankets, elegant ostrich-feather dusters and even kitchen sinks.

BEN PRUCHNIE/GETTY IMAGES ©

★ Top Five Chain Stores

Ben Sherman (www.bensherman.com)

French Connection UK (www.frenchconnection.com)

Jigsaw (www.jigsaw-online.com)

Marks & Spencer (www.marksandspencer.co.uk)

Reiss (www.reiss.co.uk)

Left: Jigsaw; Below: Marks & Spencer

OLI SCARFF/GETTY IMAGES ©

East London

Dalston

Beyond Retro Vintage
(☎020-7923 2277; www.beyondretro.com; 92-100 Stoke Newington Rd, N16; ⏰10am-7pm Mon-Sat, 11.30am-6pm Sun; ⊖Dalston Kingsland) A riot of colour, furbelow, frill, feathers and flares, this vast store has every imaginable type of vintage clothing for sale, from hats to shoes. When it all gets too overwhelming, retreat to the licensed cafe. There's a smaller but even cheaper outlet branch in **Bethnal Green** (www.beyondretro.com; 110-112 Cheshire St, E2; ⏰10am-7pm Mon-Sat, 11.30am-6pm Sun; ⊖Shoreditch High St).

Traid Clothing
(www.traid.org.uk; 106-108 Kingsland High St, E8; ⏰10am-6pm; ⊖Dalston Kingsland) Banish every preconception you have about charity shops, for Traid is nothing like the ones you've seen before: big and bright, with not a whiff of mothball. The offerings aren't necessarily vintage but rather quality, contemporary secondhand clothes for a fraction of the usual prices. It also sells its own creations made from offcuts.

Burberry Outlet Store Clothing
(www.burberry.com; 29-31 Chatham Pl, E9; ⏰10am-5pm; ⊖Hackney Central) This outlet shop has excess international stock from the reborn-as-trendy Brit brand's current and last-season collections. Prices are around 30% lower than those in the main shopping centres – but still properly pricey.

Hackney

Broadway Market Market
(www.broadwaymarket.co.uk; Broadway Market, E8; ⏰9am-5pm Sat; 🚌394) There's been a market down this pretty street since the late 19th century. The focus these days is artisan food, arty knick-knacks, books, records and vintage clothing.

Pringle of Scotland Outlet Store Clothing
(www.pringlescotland.com; 90 Morning Lane; ⏰10am-6.30pm Mon-Sat, 11am-5pm Sun; ⊖Hackney Central) There are proper bargains to be had at this excellent outlet store that stocks seconds and end-of-line items from the Pringle range. Expect high-quality merino, cashmere and lambswool knitwear for both men and women.

Camden & North London

King's Cross & Euston

Harry Potter Shop at Platform 9¾ Children
(Map p256; www.harrypotterplatform934.com; King's Cross Station, N1; ⏰8am-10pm; ⊖King's Cross St Pancras) Diagon Alley is impossible to find, so if your junior witches and wizards have come to London seeking a wand of their own, apparate the family directly to King's Cross Station instead. This little wood-paneled store also stocks jumpers sporting the colours of Hogwarts' four houses (Gryffindor having pride of place) and assorted merchandise.

Islington

Camden Passage Market Antiques
(Map p255; www.camdenpassageislington.co.uk; Camden Passage, N1; ⏰8am-6pm Wed & Sat, 11am-6pm Sun-Tue, Thu & Fri; ⊖Angel) Not to be confused with Camden Market, Camden Passage is a pretty cobbled lane in Islington lined with antique stores, vintage clothing boutiques and cafes. Scattered along the lane are four separate market areas devoted to antique curios and whatnots. The main market days are Wednesday and Sunday. Stallholders know their stuff, so bargains are rare.

Notting Hill & West London

Portobello Road Market Clothing, Antiques
(www.portobellomarket.org; Portobello Rd, W10; ⏰8am-6.30pm Mon-Wed, Fri & Sat, to 1pm Thu; ⊖Notting Hill Gate or Ladbroke Grove) Portobello Road Market is an iconic London attraction with an eclectic mix of street food, fruit and veg, antiques, curios, collectibles, vibrant fashion and trinkets. Although the

Which Camden Market?

The four distinct areas at **Camden Market** (Map p256; www.camdenmarket.com; Camden High St, NW1; ⏰10am-6pm; ⊖Camden Town) tend to sell similar kinds of things (numerous T-shirts with variations on the 'Keep Calm & Carry On' theme, for instance), although each has its own specialities and quirks.

Stables Market (Map p256; Chalk Farm Rd, NW1; ⏰10am-6pm; ⊖Chalk Farm) Connected to the Lock Market, the Stables is the best part of the Camden Market complex, with antiques, Asian artefacts, rugs, retro furniture and clothing.

Camden Lock Market (Map p256; www.camdenlockmarket.com; 54-56 Camden Lock Pl, NW1; ⏰10am-6pm; ⊖Camden Town) Right next to the canal lock, this is the original Camden Market, with diverse food stalls, ceramics, furniture, oriental rugs, musical instruments and clothes.

Camden Lock Village (Map p256; Chalk Farm Rd, NW1; ⏰10am-6pm; ⊖Camden Town) Stretched along the canal on the opposite side of the road from the Lock Market, this part of Camden Market is lined with stalls selling bric-a-brac. There are controversial plans to turn it into the 'Borough Market of North London' as part of a development involving the building of offices and 170 apartments in a large building backing the site.

Buck Street Market (cnr Buck & Camden High Sts, NW1; ⏰9am-5.30pm; ⊖Camden Town) While it bills itself as 'The Camden Market', this little covered market isn't part of the main complex. Stalls sell mainly T-shirts, jewellery and tourist tat. It's the closest market to the station, but the least interesting.

shops along Portobello Rd open daily and the fruit and veg stalls (from Elgin Cres to Talbot Rd) only close on Sunday, the busiest day by far is Saturday, when antique dealers set up shop (from Chepstow Villas to Elgin Cres).

Saturday is also when the fashion market (beneath Westway, from Portobello Rd to Ladbroke Rd) is in full swing – although you can also browse for fashion on Friday and Sunday.

Greenwich

Greenwich Market Market

(www.greenwichmarketlondon.com; College Approach, SE10; ⏰10am-5.30pm; DLR Cutty Sark) Greenwich may be one of the smallest of London's ubiquitous markets, but it holds its own in quality. On Tuesdays, Wednesdays, Fridays and weekends, stallholders tend to be small, independent artists, offering original prints, wholesome beauty products, funky jewellery and accessories, cool fashion pieces and so on. On Tuesdays, Thursdays and Fridays, there's also vintage, antiques and collectables.

Arty Globe Gifts, Souvenirs

(www.artyglobe.com; 15 Greenwich Market, SE10; ⏰11am-6pm; DLR Cutty Sark) The unique fisheye-view drawings of various areas of London (and other cities, including New York, Paris and Berlin) by architect Hartwig Braun are works of art and appear on the shopping bags, place mats, notebooks, coasters, mugs and jigsaws available in this tiny shop. They make excellent gifts.

Retrobates Vintage Vintage

(330-332 Creek Rd, SE10; ⏰10.30am-6pm Mon-Fri, to 6.30pm Sat & Sun; DLR Cutty Sark) Each piece is individual at this lovely vintage shop, where glass cabinets are crammed with costume jewellery, old perfume bottles and straw hats, while gorgeous jackets and blazers intermingle on the clothes racks. The men's offering is unusually good for a vintage shop.

PIMM'S
Old Rosie
CLOUDY CIDER
Old Rosie
CLOUDY CIDER
WITH ELDERFLOWER
ANGRAM
ANGRAM

BAR OPEN

Afternoon pints, midnight gin and tonics, and beyond

Bar Open

There is little Londoners like to do more than drinking: from Hogarth's 18th-century Gin Lane prints to former Mayor Boris Johnson's decision to ban all alcohol on public transport in 2008, the capital's history has been shot through with the population's desire to imbibe as much alcohol as possible and party into the night.

The metropolis offers a huge variety of venues to wet your whistle in, from neighbourhood pubs to all-night clubs, and everything in between. Note that when it comes to clubbing, a little planning will help you keep costs down and skip queues.

In This Section

Opening Hours

Pubs usually open at 11am or midday and close at 11pm or midnight, with a slightly earlier closing on a Sunday. On Friday and Saturday, some bars and pubs remain open to around 2am or 3am.

Clubs generally open at 10pm and close between 3am and 7am.

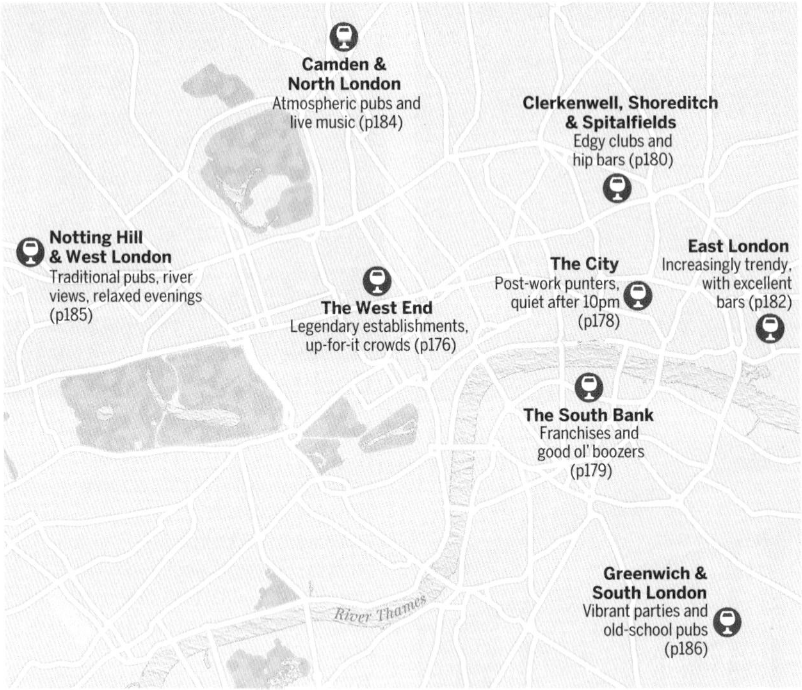

Camden & North London
Atmospheric pubs and live music (p184)

Clerkenwell, Shoreditch & Spitalfields
Edgy clubs and hip bars (p180)

Notting Hill & West London
Traditional pubs, river views, relaxed evenings (p185)

The West End
Legendary establishments, up-for-it crowds (p176)

The City
Post-work punters, quiet after 10pm (p178)

East London
Increasingly trendy, with excellent bars (p182)

The South Bank
Franchises and good ol' boozers (p179)

Greenwich & South London
Vibrant parties and old-school pubs (p186)

River Thames

Costs

Many clubs are free or cheaper midweek. If you want to go to a famous club on a Saturday night, expect to pay around £20. Some places are considerably cheaper if you arrive earlier in the night.

Tipping

Tipping isn't customary.

Blogs/Websites

London on the Inside (www.londontheinside.com)

Skiddle (www.skiddle.com) Comprehensive info on nightclubs, DJs and events.

Time Out (www.timeout.com/london) Has details of bars, pubs and nightlife.

The Best...

Experience London's finest drinking establishments

Cocktail Bars

Dukes Bar (p183) Cocktails, James Bond–style.

LAB (p70) Bespoke cocktails at a long-standing Soho favourite.

Experimental Cocktail Club (p176) Inventive cocktails in a vintage Shanghai-style interior.

Little Bird Gin (p183) Drinks are made with its eponymous gin (a small-batch, citrusy gin distilled in London).

Zetter Townhouse Cocktail Lounge (p180) This eccentric bar serves up unique and unusual tipples.

Pubs

Jerusalem Tavern (p180) Tiny but crammed with antique atmosphere.

Jamaica Wine House (p178) Hidden down a City lane, but well worth seeking out.

Carpenter's Arms (p182) Bags of East End history, great beers and a fab interior.

Dove Freehouse (p184) A huge range of Belgian beers on tap in an Arts and Crafts–style setting.

Cutty Sark Tavern (p186) Beautiful riverside pub with a view of the Thames.

Beer Gardens

Windsor Castle (p186) Come summer, regulars abandon the Windsor's historic interior for the chilled-out garden.

Edinboro Castle (p185) A festive place to stretch out on a summer evening.

For Views

Oblix (p179) It's not even halfway up the Shard, but the views are legendary.

Sky Pod (p178) Sip a cocktail on an open-air terrace, 35 floors above the city.

Kensington Roof Gardens (p185) It may not be a skyscraper, but those gardens...

Clubs

Ministry of Sound (p187) The original super-club is back on top form.

Fabric (p180) A huge venue (literally) for fans of drum and bass, dubstep, house, techno and electronica.

Corsica Studios (p187) A not-for-profit under-ground club that hosts some of London's best Electronic Dance Music (EDM) nights.

XOYO (p180) Excellent and varied gigs, club nights and art events.

Bars

Gordon's Wine Bar (p177) A classic and long-standing London institution in darkened vaults.

Bar Pepito (p185) A delightful, pocket-sized Andalucian bar dedicated to lovers of sherry.

French House (p70) Soho's best boozer, with a steady supply of local eccentrics.

Proud Camden (p185) Occupying a former horse hospital, this bar is one of Camden's best music venues.

★ Lonely Planet's Top Choices

Princess Louise (p177) A stunner of a Victorian pub with snugs and a riot of etched glass.

Worship St Whistling Shop (p180) Fine-dining sophistication in liquid form.

Cat & Mutton (p184) Simultaneously traditional and hip, and always up for a party.

Wine Pantry (p179) Showcasing the best of British wine.

Trafalgar Tavern (p186) Riverside tavern oozing history.

The West End

Bloomsbury

Lamb Pub

(Map p256; www.thelamblondon.com; 94 Lamb's Conduit St, WC1; noon-11pm Mon-Wed, to midnight Thu-Sat, to 10.30pm Sun; Russell Sq) The Lamb's central mahogany bar with beautiful Victorian dividers (also called 'snob screens' as they allowed the well-to-do to drink in private) has been a favourite with locals since 1729. Nearly three centuries later, its popularity hasn't waned, so come early to bag a booth and sample its decent selection of Young's bitters and genial atmosphere.

Queen's Larder Pub

(Map p256; www.queenslarder.co.uk; 1 Queen Sq, WC1; 11.30am-11pm Mon-Sat, noon-10.30pm Sun; Russell Sq) In a lovely square southeast of Russell Sq is this pub, so-called because Queen Charlotte, wife of 'Mad' King George III, rented part of the pub's cellar to store special foods for her husband while he was being treated nearby. It's a tiny but wonderfully cosy pub; there are benches outside for fair-weather fans and a dining room upstairs.

Soho & Chinatown

Experimental Cocktail Club Cocktail Bar

(Map p252; www.experimentalcocktailclub london.com; 13a Gerrard St, W1; 6pm-3am Mon-Sat, to midnight Sun; ; Leicester Sq or Piccadilly Circus) The three-floor Experimental is a sensational cocktail bar in Chinatown with an unmarked, shabby door (it's next to the Four Seasons restaurant). The interior, with its soft lighting, mirrors, bare brick wall and elegant furnishings, matches the sophistication of the cocktails: rare and original spirits, vintage Champagne and homemade fruit syrups. Booking not essential; there's a £5 cover charge after 11pm.

Edge Gay

(Map p252; www.edgesoho.co.uk; 11 Soho Sq, W1; 4pm-1am Mon-Thu, noon-3am Fri & Sat, 4-11.30pm Sun; ; Tottenham Court Rd) Overlooking Soho Sq in all its four-storey glory, the Edge is London's largest gay bar and heaves every night of the week. There

Lamb pub

ROGER HUTCHINGS/ALAMY STOCK PHOTO ©

are dancers, waiters in skimpy outfits, good music and a generally superfriendly vibe. There's a heavy straight presence, as it's so close to Oxford St.

Holborn & the Strand

Princess Louise — Pub

(Map p252; http://princesslouisepub.co.uk; 208 High Holborn, WC1; 11am-11pm Mon-Fri, noon-11pm Sat, noon-6.45pm Sun; Holborn) This late-19th-century Victorian pub is spectacularly decorated with a riot of fine tiles, etched mirrors, plasterwork and a stunning central horseshoe bar. The old Victorian wood partitions give drinkers plenty of nooks and alcoves to hide in. Beers are Sam Smith's only but cost just under £3 a pint, so it's no wonder many elect to spend the whole evening here.

Heaven — Club, Gay

(Map p252; www.heavennightclub-london.com; Villiers St, WC2; 11pm-5am Mon, Thu & Fri, 10pm-5am Sat; Embankment or Charing Cross) This 36-year old, perennially popular gay club under the arches beneath Charing Cross station has always been host to excellent live gigs and club nights. Monday's Popcorn (mixed dance party, all-welcome door policy) has to be one of the best weeknight's clubbing in the capital. The celebrated G-A-Y takes place here on Thursday (G-A-Y Porn Idol), Friday (G-A-Y Camp Attack) and Saturday (plain ol' G-A-Y).

Gordon's Wine Bar — Bar

(Map p252; www.gordonswinebar.com; 47 Villiers St, WC2; 11am-11pm Mon-Sat, noon-10pm Sun; Embankment) Gordon's is a victim of its own success; it is relentlessly busy and unless you arrive before the office crowd does (generally around 6pm), you can forget about getting a table. It's cavernous and dark, and the French and New World wines are heady and reasonably priced. You can nibble on bread, cheese and olives. Outside garden seating in summer.

CATH HARRIES/ALAMY STOCK PHOTO ©

★ Top Five Microbreweries

Meantime (www. meantime.london.com)

Sambrooks (www.sambrooksbrewery.co.uk)

Camden Town Brewery (www.camdentownbrewery.com)

London Fields Brewery (www.londonfieldsbrewery.co.uk)

Beavertown (www.beavertownbrewery.co.uk)

Left: Beers at Meantime; Below: Heaven nightclub

O HALE/REDFERNS/GETTY IMAGES ©

The Pub

The pub (public house) is at the heart of London life and is one of the capital's great social levellers. Virtually every Londoner has a 'local' and looking for your own is a fun part of any visit to the capital.

Pubs in central London are mostly after-work drinking dens, busy from 5pm onwards with the postwork crowd during the week and revellers at weekends. In more residential areas, pubs come into their own at weekends, when long lunches turn into sloshy afternoons and groups of friends settle in for the night. Many also run popular quizzes on week nights. Other pubs entice punters through the doors with live music or comedy. Some have developed such a reputation for the quality of their food that they've been dubbed 'gastropubs'.

You'll be able to order almost anything you like in a pub, from beer to wine, soft drinks, spirits and sometimes hot drinks too. Some specialise in craft beer, offering drinks from local microbreweries, including real ale, fruit beers, organic ciders and other rarer beverages. Others, particularly the gastropubs, have invested in a good wine list.

In winter, some pubs offer mulled wine; in summer the must-have drink is Pimms and lemonade (if it's properly done it should have fresh mint leaves, citrus, strawberries and cucumber).

The City

Sky Pod — Bar

(Map p250; 0333-772 0020; http://skygarden.london/sky-pod-bar; 20 Fenchurch St, EC3; 7am-2am Mon-Fri, 8am-2am Sat, 9am-9pm Sun; Monument) One of the best places in the City to get high is the Sky Pod in the **Sky Garden** on level 35 of the so-called **Walkie Talkie**, the city's fifth-tallest building. The views are nothing short of phenomenal (especially from the open-air South Terrace) the gardens are lush and it's the only place where this obstructive building won't be in your face.

You can enjoy a cocktail or a drink. The only drawback is that without a restaurant reservation, entry is ticketed (see website) from 10am to 6pm weekdays and 11am to 9pm on Saturday and Sunday. Outside those hours, be prepared to queue (and perhaps be disappointed).

Jamaica Wine House — Pub

(Map p250; www.shepherdneame.co.uk/pubs/london/jamaica-wine-house; 12 St Michael's Alley, EC3; 11am-11pm Mon-Fri; Bank) Not a wine bar at all, but a historic Victorian pub, the 'Jam Pot' stands on the site of what was London's first coffee house (1652), places that were often just fronts for brothels. At the end of a narrow alley, this is a difficult place to find but well worth it.

Counting House — Pub

(Map p250; www.the-counting-house.com; 50 Cornhill, EC3; 11am-11pm Mon-Fri; ; Bank or Monument) With its counters and basement vaults, this award-winning pub certainly looks and feels comfortable in the former headquarters of NatWest Bank (1893) with its domed skylight and beautifully appointed main bar. This is a favourite of City boys and girls, who come for the good range of real ales and the speciality pies (from £11.25).

The Counting House

this award-winning pub is a favourite of City boys and girls

The South Bank

Waterloo

Skylon Bar

(Map p250; www.skylon-restaurant.co.uk; Royal Festival Hall, Southbank Centre, Belvedere Rd, SE1; noon-1am Mon-Sat, to 10.30pm Sun; Waterloo) With its ravishing 1950s decor and show-stopping views, Skylon is a memorable place to come for a drink or meal (p143). You'll have to come early to bag the tables at the front with plunging views of the river however. Drinks-wise, just ask: from superb seasonal cocktails to infusions and a staggering choice of whiskys (and whiskeys!).

London Bridge

Wine Pantry Wine Bar

(Map p250; www.winepantry.co.uk; 1 Stoney St, SE1; tasting session £5; noon-8pm Thu-Fri, 11am-7pm Sat; London Bridge) British and proud, the Wine Pantry supports domestic winemakers with an exciting range of vintages, including Nyetimber, Bolney and Ridgeview. You can buy by the glass (£5 to £7) and sit at one of the handful of tables on the edge of Borough Market (p88). You're welcome to provide your own nibbles or grab a bottle to take away.

Oblix Bar

(Map p250; www.oblixrestaurant.com; Level 32, The Shard, 31 St Thomas St, SE1; noon-11pm; London Bridge) On the 32nd floor of the Shard, Oblix offers mesmerising vistas of London. You can come for anything from a coffee (£3.50) to a couple of cocktails (from £10) and enjoy virtually the same views as the official viewing galleries of the Shard (but at a reduced cost and with the added bonus of a drink!). Live music every night from 7pm.

Rake Pub

(Map p250; ☎020-7407 0557; www.utobeer.co.uk; 14 Winchester Walk, SE1; ⏰noon-11pm Mon-Sat, to 10pm Sun; ⊖London Bridge) The Rake offers more than 130 beers – many of them international craft brews – at any one time. There are 10 taps and the selection of craft beers, real ales, lagers and ciders (with one-third pint measures) changes constantly. It's a tiny place yet always busy; the bamboo-decorated decking outside is especially popular.

Clerkenwell, Shoreditch & Spitalfields

Clerkenwell

Fabric Club

(Map p255; www.fabriclondon.com; 77a Charterhouse St, EC1M; £14-26; ⏰from 11pm Fri-Sun; ⊖Farringdon) London's second-most-famous club (after Ministry of Sound), Fabric is comprised of three separate dance floors in a huge converted cold store opposite Smithfield meat market. Friday's FabricLive rumbles with drum and bass and dubstep, while Saturday's Fabric at Fabric and Sunday's WetYourSelf! deliver house, techno and electronica.

Jerusalem Tavern Pub

(Map p255; www.stpetersbrewery.co.uk; 55 Britton St, EC1M; ⏰11am-11pm Mon-Fri; 📶; ⊖Farringdon) Pick a wood-panelled cubicle to park yourself in at this tiny and highly atmospheric 1720 pub, and select from the fantastic beverages brewed by St Peter's Brewery in North Suffolk. Be warned, it's hugely popular and often very crowded.

Ye Olde Mitre Pub

(Map p255; www.yeoldemitreholborn.co.uk; 1 Ely Ct, EC1N; ⏰11am-11pm Mon-Fri; 📶; ⊖Farringdon) A delightfully cosy historic pub with an extensive beer selection, tucked away in a backstreet off Hatton Garden (look for a Fullers sign above a low archway on the left), Ye Olde Mitre was built in 1546 for the servants of Ely Palace. There's no music, so the rooms only echo with the sound of amiable chit-chat.

Zetter Townhouse Cocktail Lounge Cocktail Bar

(Map p255; ☎020-7324 4545; www.thezettertownhouse.com; 49-50 St John's Sq, EC1V; ⏰7.30am-12.45am; ⊖Farringdon) Tucked away behind an unassuming door on St John's Sq, this ground-floor bar is quirkily decorated with plush armchairs, stuffed animal heads and a legion of lamps. The cocktail list takes its theme from the area's distilling history – recipes of yesteryear and homemade tinctures and cordials are used to create interesting and unusual tipples.

Hoxton & Shoreditch

Worship St Whistling Shop Cocktail Bar

(Map p255; ☎020-7247 0015; www.whistlingshop.com; 63 Worship St, EC2A; ⏰5pm-midnight Mon-Thu, to 2am Fri & Sat; ⊖Old St) While the name is Victorian slang for a place selling illicit booze, this subterranean drinking den's master mixologists explore the futuristic outer limits of cocktail chemistry and aromatic science. Many ingredients are made with the rotary evaporators in the on-site lab.

XOYO Club

(Map p255; www.xoyo.co.uk; 32-37 Cowper St, EC2A; ⏰hours vary; ⊖Old St) This excellent Shoreditch warehouse club throws together a pulsingly popular mix of gigs, club nights and art events. The varied line-up – expect indie bands, hip hop, electro, dubstep and much in between – attracts a mix of clubbers, from skinny-jeaned hipsters to more mature hedonists.

Old Blue Last Pub

(Map p255; www.theoldbluelast.com; 38 Great Eastern St, EC2A; ⏰9am-12.30am Mon-Fri, 12.30pm-12.30am Sat & Sun; 📶; ⊖Old St) Frequently crammed with a hip teenage-and-up crowd, this scuffed corner pub's edgy credentials are courtesy of *Vice* magazine, the bad-boy rag that owns the place. It hosts some of the best Shoreditch parties and lots of live music.

★London's Pubs

London without pubs would be like Paris *sans* cafes or New York shorn of its bars. Pub culture is part of London's DNA, and pubs are the place to be if you want to see locals in their hops-infused element. Longer opening hours have only cemented the pub's reputation as the cornerstone for a great night out.

Clockwise from top: Beers on tap; Exterior pub signage; Ye Olde Mitre

Clubbing

When it comes to clubbing, London is up there with the best of them. You'll probably know what you want to experience – it might be big clubs or sweaty shoebox clubs with the freshest DJ talent – but there's plenty to tempt you to branch out from your usual tastes and try something new.

Thursdays are loved by those who want to have their fun before the office workers mob the streets on Friday. Saturdays are the busiest and best if you're a serious clubber, and Sundays often see surprisingly good events throughout London, popular with hospitality workers who tradionally have Mondays off.

There are clubs across town. The East End is the top area for cutting-edge clubs, especially Shoreditch. Dalston and Hackney are popular for makeshift clubs in restaurant basements and former shops. Camden Town still favours the indie crowd. The gay party crowd mainly gravitates to the south of the river, especially Vauxhall, although they still maintain a toehold in the West and East End.

BrewDog Bar

(Map p255; www.brewdog.com; 51-55 Bethnal Green Rd, E1; noon-midnight; ; Shoreditch High St) BrewDog is an ale aficionado's paradise, with about 20 different brews on tap, hundreds by the bottle and Dirty Burgers to soak it all up with. Its own crowd-funded eco-brewery sits up in Scotland, near Aberdeen, but the bar stocks plenty of other microbrewery beers, too.

Spitalfields

93 Feet East Bar, Club

(Map p255; www.93feeteast.co.uk; 150 Brick Lane, E1; 5-11pm Thu, to 1am Fri & Sat, 2-10.30pm Sun; Shoreditch High St) Part of the Old Truman Brewery complex, this venue has a courtyard, three big rooms and an outdoor terrace that gets crowded with a cool East End crowd on sunny afternoons. As well as DJs, there's plenty of live music on offer.

East London

Bethnal Green

Carpenter's Arms Pub

(www.carpentersarmsfreehouse.com; 73 Cheshire St, E2; 4-11.30pm Mon-Wed, noon-11.30pm Thu-Sun; ; Shoreditch High St) Once owned by infamous gangsters the Kray brothers (who bought it for their old ma to run), this chic yet cosy pub has been beautifully restored and its many wooden surfaces positively gleam. A back room and small yard provide a little more space for the convivial drinkers. There's a great range of beers and ciders.

Bethnal Green Working Men's Club Club

(www.workersplaytime.net; 42-44 Pollard Row, E2; vary; Bethnal Green) As it says on the tin, this is a true working men's club. Except that this one has opened its doors and let in all kinds of off-the-wall club nights, including trashy burlesque, gay and lesbian shindigs, retro nights, beach parties and bake-offs. Expect sticky carpets, a shimmery stage set and a space akin to a school-hall disco.

Dalston

Dalston Superstore Gay

(www.dalstonsuperstore.com; 117 Kingsland High St, E8; 10am-12.30am Sun-Tue, to 2am Wed-Fri, to 4am Sat; Dalston Kingsland) Bar, club or diner? Gay or straight? Dalston Superstore is hard to pigeonhole, which we suspect is the point. This two-level industrial space is open all day but really comes into its own after dark when there are club nights in the basement. Lesbians should check out Clam Jam on Thursday.

London in a Glass

Garnishes include a slice or wedge of lime
Pour over a few or as many ice cubes (on the rocks) as you'd like
Use a classic, traditional London gin such as Sipsmith, Sacred or Beefeater 24
Top up with tonic water
Use a rocks glass (pictured) or a highball glass
Classic Gin & Tonic

P JOHNSON1/GETTY IMAGES ©

History of Gin & Tonic

Gin was imported from Holland in the 17th century, but Londoners quickly adopted the drink as their own. In the 1850s, Britons in the colonies had the enlightened idea of mixing their daily quinine dose (for malaria prevention) with gin – and the gin & tonic was born. There are many types of gins to try, but a typical London gin is one that draws all its flavours from the distillation process.

PAUL JOHNSON/GETTY IMAGES ©

★Top Five Spots for a Gin & Tonic

Little Bird Gin (www.littlebirdgin.com; Maltby St, SE1; 10am-4pm Sat, from 11am Sunday; London Bridge)

Dukes Bar (Map p252; 020-7491 4840; www.dukeshotel.com; 35 St James's Pl, SW1; 2-11pm Mon-Sat, 4-10.30pm Sun; ; Green Park)

Jensen (www.jensengin.com; 55 Stanworth St, SE1; 10am-4pm Sat; London Bridge)

Phene (www.thephene.com; 9 Phene St, SW3; noon-11pm Mon-Fri, from 11am Sat & Sun; ; Sloane Sq)

Portobello Star (020-3540 7781; www.portobellostarbar.co.uk; 171 Portobello Rd, W11; cocktails from £6; 11am-11.30pm Sun-Thu, to 12.30am Fri & Sat; ; Ladbroke Grove)

Bermondsey Beer Mile

Craft beer is having its moment in London, and Bermondsey is at the epicentre of this revival. There are seven microbreweries within a mile. They all produce a full range of beers – pale ales, porters, stouts, IPAs etc – and welcome discerning drinkers on Saturdays, generally from 11am to 4pm or 5pm.

Try **Southwark Brewing Company** (www.southwarkbrewing.co.uk; 46 Druid St, SE1; 11am-5pm Sat; London Bridge), the newest kid on the block, located in a hangarlike space kitted out with big tables and sofas; you're welcome to bring goodies from nearby Borough Market (p88) or **Maltby Street** (www.maltby.st; Maltby St, SE1; 9am-4pm Sat, 11am-4pm Sun; London Bridge) markets to accompany your beer. The London Pale Ale has a nice zing. Also good is **Anspach & Hobday** (www.anspachand-hobday.com; 118 Druid St, SE1; 5-9.30pm Fri, 11am-6pm Sat, noon-5pm Sun; London Bridge). Porter (a dark, roasted beer) is the name of the game here. There is a nice outdoor seating area.

CHRIS RATCLIFFE/GETTY IMAGES ©

Hackney

Cat & Mutton Pub

(www.catandmutton.com; 76 Broadway Market, E8; noon-midnight; 394) At this fabulous Georgian pub, Hackney hipsters sup pints under the watchful eyes of hunting trophies, black-and-white photos of old-time boxers and a large portrait of Karl Marx. If it's crammed downstairs, as it often is, head up the spiral staircase to the comfy couches. DJs spin funk, disco and soul on the weekends.

Dove Freehouse Pub

(020-7275 7617; www.dovepubs.com; 24-28 Broadway Market, E8; noon-11pm; 394) Alluring at any time, the Dove has a rambling series of rooms and a wide range of Belgian Trappist, wheat and fruit-flavoured beers. Drinkers spill onto the street in warmer weather, or hunker down in the low-lit back room with board games when it's chilly.

Netil360 Bar

(www.netil360.com; 1 Westgate St, E8; 10am-10pm Mon-Fri, noon-11pm Sat & Sun; 55) Perched atop Netil House, this uber hip rooftop cafe/bar offers incredible views over London, with brass telescopes enabling you to get better acquainted with workers in the Gherkin. In between drinks you can knock out a game of croquet on the AstroTurf, or perhaps book a hot tub for you and your mates to stew in.

Camden & North London

King's Cross & Euston

Drink, Shop & Do Bar

(Map p256; 020-7278 4335; www.drinkshopdo.com; 9 Caledonian Rd, N1; 10.30am-midnight Mon-Thu, to 2am Fri, 9am-2am Sat, 10.30am-10pm Sun; King's Cross St Pancras) This kooky little outlet will not be pigeonholed. As its name suggests, it is many things to many people: a bar, a cafe, an activities centre, a gift store, a disco even. But the idea is that there will always be drinking (be it tea or gin), music and activities – anything from dancing to building Lego robots.

Euston Tap Bar

(Map p256; 020-3137 8837; www.eustontap.com; 190 Euston Rd, NW1; noon-11pm; Euston) Part of a twinset with the Cider Tap, this specialist boozery inhabits a monumental stone structure on the approach to Euston Station. Craft-beer devotees can choose between eight cask ales, 20 keg beers and 150 by the bottle. Cider rules over the road. Grab a seat on the pavement, or take the tight spiral staircase upstairs.

Bar Pepito Wine Bar
(Map p256; www.barpepito.co.uk; 3 Varnishers Yard, The Regent's Quarter, N1; 5pm-midnight Mon-Sat; King's Cross St Pancras) This tiny, intimate Andalusian bodega specialises in sherry and tapas. Novices fear not: the staff are on hand to advise. They're also experts at food pairings (top-notch ham and cheese selections). To go the whole hog, try a tasting flight of three selected sherries with snacks to match.

Camden Town

Proud Camden Bar
(Map p256; www.proudcamden.com; Stables Market, Chalk Farm Rd, NW1; free-£15; 10.30am-1.30am Mon-Sat, noon-midnight Sun; Chalk Farm) Proud occupies a former horse hospital within Stables Market, with private booths in the stalls, ice-cool rock photography on the walls and a kooky garden terrace complete with a hot tub. It's also one of Camden's best music venues, with live bands and DJs most nights.

Edinboro Castle Pub
(Map p256; www.edinborocastlepub.co.uk; 57 Mornington Tce, NW1; noon-11pm; ; Camden Town) The large and relaxed Edinboro has a refined atmosphere, gorgeous furniture designed for slumping, a fine bar and a full menu. The highlight, however, is the huge beer garden, complete with a BBQ and foosball table and adorned with coloured lights on long summer evenings.

Notting Hill & West London

Kensington Roof Gardens Club
(Map p249; www.roofgardens.virgin.com; 99 Kensington High St, W8; club 10pm-3am Fri & Sat, garden 9am-5pm; ; High St Kensington) Atop the former Derry and Toms building high above Kensington High St is this enchanting venue – a nightclub with

Dove Freehouse

Beer

Beer comes in a multitude of flavours and guises: English pubs generally serve a good selection of lager (highly carbonated and drunk cool or cold) and a smaller selection of real ales or 'bitter' (still or only slightly gassy, drunk at room temperature, with strong flavours). The best-known British lager brand is Carling, although you'll find everything from Fosters to San Miguel. Stout, the best known of which is Irish Guinness, will also be on offer. This is a slightly sweet, dark beer with a distinct flavour that comes from malt that is roasted before fermentation.

Among the multitude of ales on offer in London pubs, London Pride, Courage Best, Burton Ale, Adnam's, Theakston (in particular Old Peculiar) and Old Speckled Hen are among the best. Once considered something of an old man's drink, real ale is enjoying a renaissance among young Londoners. Staff at bars serving good selections of real ales and craft beers are often hugely knowledgable, just like a sommelier in a restaurant with a good cellar, so ask them for recommendations if you're not sure what to order.

Numerous microbreweries have sprouted throughout London in recent years. Names to look out for include Meantime, Sambrooks, Camden Town Brewery, London Fields Brewery or Beavertown.

On draught (drawn from the cask), beer is served by the pint (570mL) or half-pint (285mL).

0.6 hectares of gardens and resident flamingos. The wow-factor comes at a premium: entry is £20 (£25 from May to September), you must register on the guest list (http://gls.roofgardens.com) before going and drinks are £10 a pop. Dress to impress.

Windsor Castle Pub

(www.thewindsorcastlekensington.co.uk; 114 Campden Hill Rd, W11; noon-11pm Mon-Sat, to 10.30pm Sun; ; Notting Hill Gate) A classic tavern on the brow of Campden Hill Rd, this place has history, nooks and charm on tap. It's worth the search for its historic compartmentalised interior, roaring fire (in winter), delightful beer garden (in summer) and affable regulars (most always). According to legend, the bones of Thomas Paine (author of *Rights of Man*) are in the cellar.

In the old days, Windsor Castle was visible from the pub, hence the name.

Greenwich & South London

Greenwich

Cutty Sark Tavern Pub

(www.cuttysarktavern.co.uk; 4-6 Ballast Quay, SE10; 11am-11pm Mon-Sat, noon-10.30pm Sun; DLR Cutty Sark) Housed in a delightful bow-windowed, wood-beamed Georgian building directly on the Thames, the Cutty Sark is one of the few independent pubs left in Greenwich. Half a dozen cask-conditioned ales on tap line the bar, with an inviting riverside sitting-out area opposite. It's a 10-minute walk from the DLR station.

Trafalgar Tavern Pub

(020-8858 2909; www.trafalgartavern.co.uk; 6 Park Row, SE10; noon-11pm Mon-Sat, to 10.30pm Sun; DLR Cutty Sark) This elegant tavern with big windows overlooking the Thames is steeped in history. Dickens apparently knocked back a few here – and used it as the setting for the wedding breakfast scene in *Our Mutual Friend* – and prime ministers Gladstone and Disraeli used to dine on the pub's celebrated whitebait.

Windsor Castle

Elephant & Castle

Corsica Studios Club

(www.corsicastudios.com; 4/5 Elephant Rd, SE17; £6-17.50; hours vary; Elephant & Castle) It's places like Corsica Studios that have given the once-rough Elephant & Castle area an edge. This not-for-profit, underground club is a well-known venue for electronic music. It's a small, intimate space with excellent sound and a mix of gigs and club nights till 3am weekdays and 6am weekends.

Ministry of Sound Club

(www.ministryofsound.com; 103 Gaunt St, SE1; £16-22; 10pm-6.30am Fri-Sun; Elephant & Castle) This legendary club-cum-enormous-global-brand (four bars, four dance floors) lost some 'edge' in the early noughties but, after pumping in top DJs, the Ministry has firmly rejoined the top club ranks. Fridays is the Gallery trance night, while Saturday sessions offer the crème de la crème of house, electro and techno DJs.

SHOWTIME

From a night out at the theatre to live-music venues

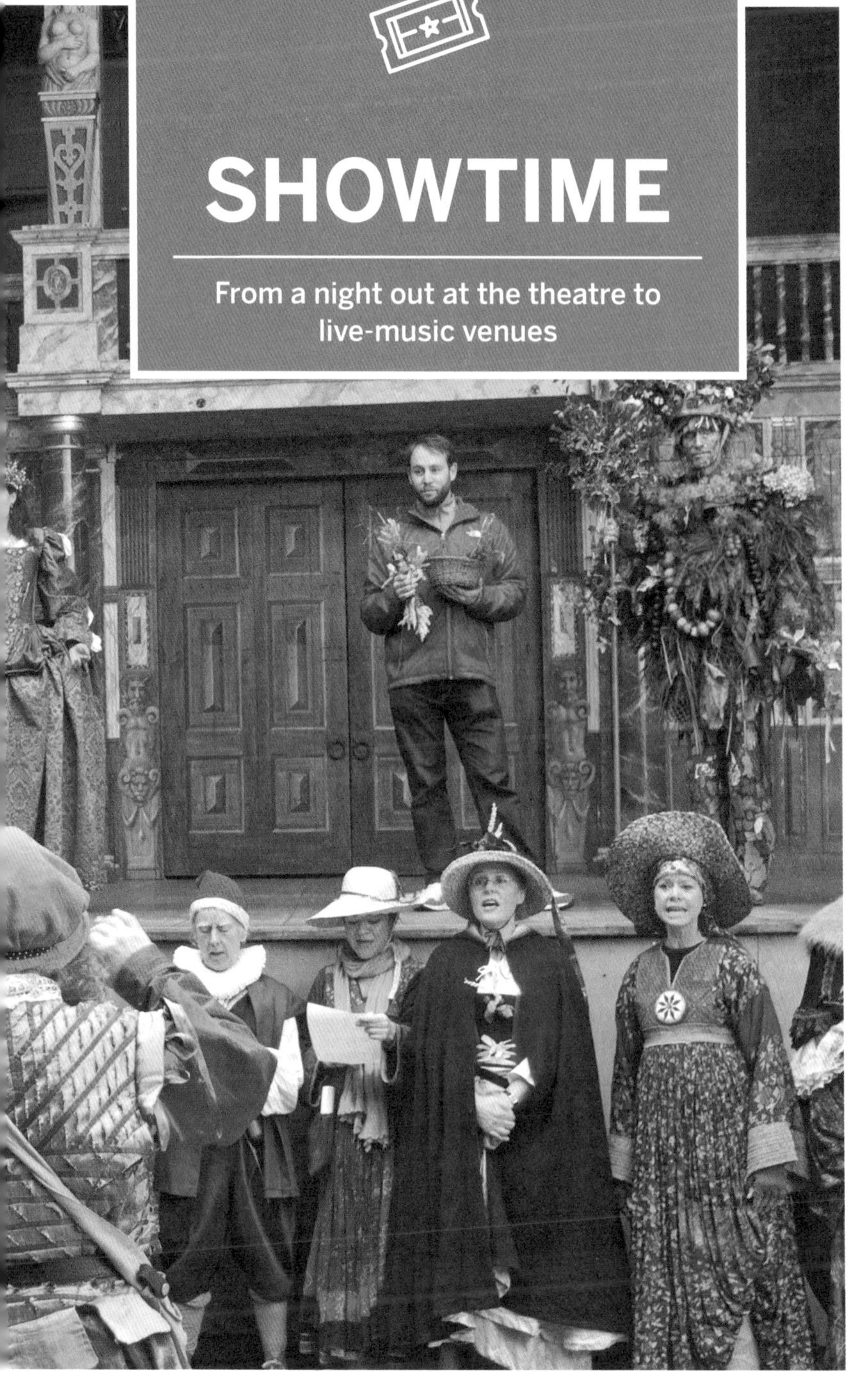

Showtime

Whatever it is that sets your spirits soaring or your booty shaking, you'll find it in London. The city has been a world leader in theatre ever since a young man from Stratford-upon-Avon set up shop here in the 16th century. And if London started swinging in the 1960s, its live rock and pop scene has barely let up since.

The trick to bag tickets to high-profile events and performances is to book ahead – or hope there will be standby tickets on the day. And don't worry if you miss out: there are literally hundreds of smaller gigs and performances every night, and the joy is to stumble upon them.

In This Section

Tickets

Book well ahead for performances – or buy standby tickets on the day directly from the venue.

Websites

Tkts Leicester Sq (www.tkts.co.uk/leicester-square) sells discounted tickets for the day's performances across various West End venues, sometimes up to 50% off.

Royal Albert Hall (p196)

The Best...

Theatre

Shakespeare's Globe (p195) Shakespeare, as it would have been 400 years ago.

National Theatre (p194) Contemporary theatre on the South Bank.

Wilton's (p196) The Victorian music-hall tradition lives on in the East End.

Live Music

Royal Albert Hall (p196) Gorgeous, grand and spacious.

KOKO (p198) Fabulously glitzy venue showcasing indie rock.

Royal Opera House (p192) One of the world's great opera venues.

O2 Academy Brixton (p199) Legendary concert hall.

☆ The West End

Soho & Chinatown

Soho Theatre Comedy

(Map p252; 020-7478 0100; www.sohotheatre.com; 21 Dean St, W1; admission £10-25; Tottenham Court Rd) The Soho Theatre has developed a superb reputation for showcasing new comedy-writing talent and comedians. It's also hosted some top-notch stand-up or sketch-based comedians, including Alexei Sayle and Doctor Brown, plus cabaret.

Covent Garden & Leicester Square

Royal Opera House Opera

(Map p252; 020-7304 4000; www.roh.org.uk; Bow St, WC2; tickets £7-250; Covent Garden) The £210-million redevelopment for the millennium gave classic opera a fantastic setting in London, and coming here for a night is a sumptuous – if pricey – affair. Although the program has been fluffed up by modern influences, the main attractions are still the opera and classical ballet – all are wonderful productions and feature world-class performers.

Midweek matinées are usually cheaper than evening performances, and restricted-view seats cost as little as £7. There are same-day tickets (one per customer available to the first 67 people in the queue) from 10am for £8 to £44, and student standby tickets for £10. Half-price standby tickets four hours before the performance are only occasionally available.

The Comedy Store Comedy

(Map p252; 0844 871 7699; www.thecomedystore.co.uk; 1a Oxendon St, SW1; £8-23.50; Piccadilly Circus) One of the first (and still one of the best) comedy clubs in London. Wednesday and Sunday night's Comedy Store Players is the most famous improvisation outfit in town, with the wonderful Josie Lawrence; on Thursdays, Fridays and Saturdays Best in Stand Up features the best on London's comedy circuit.

★ London's Theatre Scene

A trip to London is incomplete without seeing a West End show. Whether it's world-class drama or smash-hit musicals, you'll find it in this glitzy theatreland. There's always something new drawing accolades from critics and an enthusiastic public alike, alongside the filler of long-run hits.

Clockwise from top: London's Theatreland (p198); Interior of Hackney Empire theatre (p197); Paul Hamlyn Hall, Royal Opera House

Classical Music, Ballet & Opera

With multiple world-class orchestras and ensembles, quality venues, reasonable ticket prices and performances covering the whole musical gamut from traditional crowd-pleasers to innovative compositions, London will satisfy even the fussiest classical-music buff. The Southbank Centre (p195), Barbican (p194) and Royal Albert Hall (p196) all maintain an alluring program of performances, further gilding London's outstanding reputation as a cosmopolitan centre for classical music. The Proms (p12) is the festival calendar's biggest event.

Opera and ballet lovers should make an evening at the Royal Opera House (p192) a priority – the setting and quality of the programming are truly world-class.

BBC Proms Concert

Prince Charles Cinema

(Map p252; www.princecharlescinema.com; 7 Leicester Pl, WC2; tickets £8-16; ⊖Leicester Sq) Leicester Sq cinema ticket prices are brutal, so wait until the new releases have moved to the Prince Charles, central London's cheapest cinema, where non-members pay only £8 to £10. Also on the cards are mini festivals, Q&As with film directors, classics, sleepover movie marathons and exuberant sing-along screenings of *Frozen*, *The Sound of Music* and *Rocky Horror Picture Show*.

Mayfair

Wigmore Hall Classical Music

(www.wigmore-hall.org.uk; 36 Wigmore St, W1; ⊖Bond St) This is one of the best and most active (400 events a year) classical-music venues in town, not only because of its fantastic acoustics, beautiful art nouveau hall and great variety of concerts and recitals, but also because of the sheer standard of the performances. Built in 1901, it has remained one of the world's top places for chamber music.

The Sunday coffee concerts at 11.30am and the lunchtime ones at 1pm on Monday (both adult/concession £13/11) are excellent value. Evening concerts cost between £15 and £35.

☆ The City

Barbican Performing Arts

(Map p255; ☎0845 121 6823, box office 10am-8pm Mon-Sat, from 11am Sun ☎020-7638 8891; www.barbican.org.uk; Silk St, EC2; ⊖Barbican) Home to the wonderful London Symphony Orchestra and its associate orchestra, the lesser-known BBC Symphony Orchestra, the arts centre also hosts scores of other leading musicians, focusing in particular on jazz, folk, world and soul artists. Dance is another strong point here.

☆ The South Bank

Waterloo

National Theatre Theatre

(Map p250; ☎020-7452 3000; www.nationaltheatre.org.uk; South Bank, SE1; ⊖Waterloo) England's flagship theatre showcases a mix of classic and contemporary plays performed by excellent casts in three theatres (Olivier, Lyttelton and Dorfman). Outstanding artistic director Nicholas Hytner oversaw a golden decade at the theatre, with landmark productions such as *War Horse*. His replacement, Rufus Norris, started in April 2015.

Travelex tickets costing just £15 are available to certain performances during the peak period; same-day tickets also cost £15. Under-18s pay half-price.

Southbank Centre Concert Venue
(Map p250; 0844 875 0073; www.southbankcentre.co.uk; Belvedere Rd, SE1; Waterloo) The Southbank Centre's Royal Festival Hall (p102) seats 3000 in its amphitheatre and is one of the best places for catching world- and classical-music artists. The sound is fantastic, the programming impeccable and there are frequent free gigs in the wonderfully expansive foyer.

The centre organises fantastic festivals, including London Wonderground (dedicated to circus and cabaret), Udderbelly (a festival of comedy in all its guises – stand up, music, mime etc) and Meltdown (a music event curated by the best and most eclectic names in music – Guys Garvey in 2016, Yoko Ono in 2013, Massive Attack in 2008 etc).

London Bridge

Shakespeare's Globe Theatre
(Map p250; 020-7401 9919; www.shakespearesglobe.com; 21 New Globe Walk, SE1; seats £10-43, standing £5; Blackfriars or London Bridge) If you love Shakespeare and the theatre, the Globe will knock you off your feet. This authentic Shakespearean theatre is a wooden O without a roof over the central stage area, and although there are covered wooden bench seats in tiers around the stage, many people (there's room for 700) do as 17th-century 'groundlings' did, standing in front of the stage.

The theatre season runs from late April to mid-October and includes works by Shakespeare and his contemporaries such as Christopher Marlowe.

Because the building is quite open to the elements, you may have to wrap up. No umbrellas are allowed, but cheap raincoats are on sale. A warning: two pillars holding up the stage canopy (the so-called Heavens) obscure much of the view in section D; you'd almost do better to stand.

National Theatre

CLAUDIO DIVIZIA/SHUTTERSTOCK ©

If you don't like the idea of standing in the rain or sitting in the cold, opt for a indoor candlelit play in the Sam Wanamaker Playhouse (p93), a Jacobean theatre similar to the one Shakespeare would have used in winter. The programming also includes opera.

☆ Kensington & Hyde Park

Royal Albert Hall Concert Venue

(Map p249; ☎0845 401 5034; www.royalalberthall.com; Kensington Gore, SW7; ⊖South Kensington) This splendid Victorian concert hall hosts classical-music, rock and other performances, but is most famously the venue for the BBC-sponsored Proms. Booking is possible, but from mid-July to mid-September Proms punters also queue for £5 standing (or 'promenading') tickets that go on sale one hour before curtain-up. Otherwise, the box office and prepaid ticket collection counter are both through door 12 (south side of the hall).

☆ Clerkenwell, Shoreditch & Spitalfields

Sadler's Wells Dance

(Map p255; ☎0844 412 4300; www.sadlerswells.com; Rosebery Ave, EC1R; ⊖Angel) A glittering modern venue that was, in fact, first established in 1683, Sadler's Wells is the most eclectic modern-dance and ballet venue in town, with experimental dance shows of all genres and from all corners of the globe. The Lilian Baylis Studio stages smaller productions.

☆ East London

Wapping

Wilton's Theatre

(☎020-7702 2789; www.wiltons.org.uk; 1 Graces Alley, E1; tour £6; ⏲tours 6pm most Mon, bar 5-11pm Mon-Sat; ⊖Tower Hill) A gloriously atmospheric example of one of London's Victorian public-house music halls, Wilton's hosts a variety of shows, from comedy

A ballet performance at Sadler's Wells

and classical music to theatre and opera. One-hour guided tours offer an insight into its fascinating history. The Mahogany Bar is a great way to get a taste of the place if you're not attending a performance.

Hackney

Hackney Empire Theatre

(020-8985 2424; www.hackneyempire.co.uk; 291 Mare St, E8; Hackney Central) One of London's most beautiful theatres, this renovated Edwardian music hall (1901) offers an extremely diverse range of performances, from hard-edged political theatre to musicals, opera and comedy. It's one of the very best places to catch a pantomime at Christmas.

Dalston

Passing Clouds Club

(www.passingclouds.org; 1 Richmond Rd, E8; 7pm-12.30am Mon-Thu, to 3.30am Fri & Sat, 2pm-12.30am Sun; Dalston Junction) Decked out with colourful lanterns and tropical titbits, Passing Clouds throws legendary parties that go until the early hours of the morning, with DJs, live music and a multicultural crowd that makes you feel you're really in London. The music is predominantly world oriented, with regular Afrobeat bands and a reputable Sunday-night jam session (from 8.30pm).

Vortex Jazz Club Jazz

(www.vortexjazz.co.uk; 11 Gillet Sq, N16; Dalston Kingsland) The Vortex hosts an outstanding line-up of jazz musicians, singers and songwriters from the UK, US, Europe, Africa and beyond. It's a small venue so make sure you book if there's an act you particularly fancy.

Live Music

Musically diverse and defiantly different, London is a hot spot of musical innovation and talent. It leads the world in articulate indie rock, in particular, and tomorrow's guitar heroes are right this minute paying their dues on sticky-floored stages in Camden Town, Shoreditch and Dalston.

Monster international acts see London as an essential stop on their transglobal stomps, but be prepared for tickets selling out faster than you can find your credit card. The city's beautiful old theatres and music halls play host to a constant roster of well-known names in more intimate settings. In summer, giant festivals take over the city's parks, while smaller, more localised events such as the Dalston Music Festival (www.dalstonmusicfestival.com) showcase up-and-comers in multiple spaces.

If jazz or blues are your thing, London has some truly excellent clubs and pubs where you can catch classics and contemporary tunes. The city's major jazz event is the London Jazz Festival (p16) in November.

Lee Hogans performing at the London Jazz Festival
ANDY SHEPPARD/REDFERNS/GETTY IMAGES ©

☆ Camden & North London

King's Cross & Euston

Scala Live Music

(Map p256; 020-7833 2022; www.scala-london.co.uk; 275 Pentonville Rd, N1; King's Cross St Pancras) Opened in 1920 as a salubrious golden-age cinema, Scala slipped into porn-movie hell in the 1970s only to be reborn as a club and live-music venue in the noughties. It's one of the best places in London to catch an intimate gig and is a great dance space too, hosting a diverse range of club nights.

Theatre

A night out at the theatre is as much a must-do London experience as a trip on the top deck of a double-decker bus. London's Theatreland in the dazzling West End – from Aldwych in the east, past Shaftesbury Ave to Regent St in the west – has a concentration of theatres only rivalled by New York's Broadway. It's a thrillingly diverse scene, encompassing Shakespeare's classics performed with old-school precision, edgy new works, raise-the-roof musicals and some of the world's longest-running shows.

There are around 40 theatres in the West End alone, but Theatreland is just the brightest facet of London's sparkling theatre world, where venues range from highbrow theatrical institutions to tiny fringe stages tucked away above pubs.

Garrick Theatre in London's Theatreland

MAREMAGNUM/GETTY IMAGES ©

Camden

Cecil Sharp House Traditional Music

(Map p256; www.cecilsharphouse.org; 2 Regent's Park Rd, NW1; ⊖Camden Town) If you've ever fancied clog stamping, hanky waving or bell jingling, this is the place for you. Home to the English Folk Dance and Song Society, this institute keeps all manner of wacky folk traditions alive, with performances and classes held in its gorgeous mural-covered Kennedy Hall. The dance classes are oodles of fun; no experience necessary.

KOKO Live Music

(Map p256; www.koko.uk.com; 1a Camden High St, NW1; ⊖Mornington Cres) Once the legendary Camden Palace, where Charlie Chaplin, the Goons and the Sex Pistols all performed, KOKO is maintaining its reputation as one of London's better gig venues. The theatre has a dance floor and decadent balconies and attracts an indie crowd with Club NME on Friday. There are live bands almost every night of the week.

Jazz Cafe Live Music

(Map p256; ☎0844 847 2514; www.thejazzcafelondon.com; 5 Parkway, NW1; ⊖Camden Town) Although its name would have you think that jazz is this venue's main staple, it's only a small part of what's on the menu. The intimate clublike space also serves up funk, hip hop, R&B and soul, with big-name acts regularly dropping in. The Saturday club night, 'I love the 80s v I love the 90s', is a long-standing favourite.

Barfly Live Music

(Map p256; www.thebarflylondon.com; 49 Chalk Farm Rd, NW1; ⊖Chalk Farm) This typically grungy indie-rock venue is well known for hosting small-time artists looking for their big break. The venue is small, so you'll feel like the band is playing just for you and your mates. There are club nights most nights of the week. Jubilee on Fridays is probably the best, with a mix of live bands and DJs.

☆ Notting Hill & West London

Electric Cinema Cinema

(☎020-7908 9696; www.electriccinema.co.uk; 191 Portobello Rd, W11; tickets £8-22.50; ⊖Ladbroke Grove) Having notched up its first centenary a few years back, the Electric is one of the UK's oldest cinemas, updated. Avail yourself of the luxurious leather armchairs, sofas, footstools and tables for food and drink in the auditorium, or select one of the six front-row double beds! Tickets are cheapest on Mondays.

Tory Lanez performs at KOKO

Opera Holland Park Opera

(www.operahollandpark.com; Holland Park, W8; High St Kensington or Holland Park) Sit under the 800-seat canopy, temporarily erected every summer for a nine-week season in the middle of **Holland Park** (Ilchester Pl; 7.30am-dusk) for a mix of crowd-pleasers and rare (even obscure) works. Six operas are generally performed each year.

☆ Greenwich & South London

Greenwich

Up the Creek Comedy

(www.up-the-creek.com; 302 Creek Rd, SE10; admission £5-15; 7-11pm Thu & Sun, to 2am Fri & Sat; DLR Cutty Sark) Bizarrely enough, the hecklers can be funnier than the acts at this great club. Mischief, rowdiness and excellent comedy are the norm, with the Blackout open-mic night on Thursdays (www.the-blackout.co.uk, £5) and Sunday specials (www.sundayspecial.co.uk, £7). There's an after-party disco on Fridays and Saturdays.

Brixton

O2 Academy Brixton Live Music

(www.o2academybrixton.co.uk; 211 Stockwell Rd, SW9; doors open 7pm most nights; Brixton) It's hard to have a bad night at the Brixton Academy, even if you leave with your soles sticky with beer, as this cavernous former-5000-capacity art deco theatre always thrums with bonhomie. There's a properly raked floor for good views, as well as plenty of bars and an excellent mixed bill of established and emerging talent.

O2 Arena Live Music

(www.theo2.co.uk; Peninsula Sq, SE10; North Greenwich) One of the city's major concert venues, hosting all the biggies – the Rolling Stones, Paul Simon and Sting, Barbra Streisand and many others – inside the 20,000-capacity arena. It's also a popular venue for sporting events. The smaller Indigo at the O2 seats 2350.

ACTIVE LONDON

Exploring the city on two wheels and more

Active London

The 2012 Olympic Games put a spring in London's step and left the city with a sudden embarrassment of world-class sports facilities in the east of town, some of which are now open to the public. The rest of London boasts a well-developed infrastructure for participatory and spectator sports to get your heart racing and the endorphins flowing.

Many events are free to watch; and if you've missed out on expensive ones, you can always watch in a pub or on a big screen somewhere. Active types will love the Santander Cycle Hire Scheme, which allows you to explore the city easily (and cheaply!) on two wheels.

In This Section

Sports Seasons

Football The football season runs from mid-August to May.

Rugby The Six Nations (www.rbssixnations.com) is rugby's big annual tournament, spread over five weekends in February and March.

Tennis London is gripped by tennis fever during Wimbledon (July).

IZABELA HABUR/GETTY IMAGES ©

Where to Watch

Being generally sports mad, London has a long tradition of erecting big outdoor screens showing major sporting events in the summer such as the Football World Cup, Wimbledon, the Rugby World Cup or the Athletics World Championships. Locations vary, but Trafalgar Square (p58) is usually a good bet, as is the Queen Elizabeth Olympic Park in East London.

The Best...

Free Spectator Sports

London Marathon (April) Watch runners pound the pavement from Greenwich to Buckingham Palace.

Oxford & Cambridge Boat Race (early April) Features the arch-rival universities on a course from Putney to Mortlake.

Head of the River Race (late March) Held along the same course as the Boat Race, but in reverse and with international crews.

Tennis

Wimbledon (www.wimbledon.com; Wimbledon) becomes the centre of the sporting universe for a fortnight in June/July when the thrilling grass tennis tournament gets underway, but obtaining tickets is far from straightforward. To look out onto or visit Centre Court at other times of the year, head to the **Wimbledon Lawn Tennis Museum** (020-8946 6131; www.wimbledon.com/museum; Gate 4, Church Rd, SW19; adult/child £13/8, museum & tour £24/15; 10am-5pm; Wimbledon, then bus 93, Wimbledon). Numerous parks around London have tennis courts, many free.

Cricket

On a long summer's day, you could do a lot worse than packing up a picnic and enjoying the thwack of leather on willow. The **English Cricket Board** (020-7432 1200; www.ecb.co.uk) has complete details of match schedules and tickets. Test matches are regularly played at **Lord's** (tour info 020-7616 8595; www.lords.org; St John's Wood Rd, NW8; St John's Wood) and the **Oval** (0844 375 1845; www.kiaoval.com; Kennington, SE11; international match £20-350, county £20-35; Oval).

Boat Tours

Thames River Services Boat Tour
(www.thamesriverservices.co.uk; adult/child one-way £12.25/6.13, return £16/8) These cruise boats leave Westminster Pier for Greenwich, stopping at the Tower of London. Every second service continues on from Greenwich to the Thames Barrier (one way adult/child £14/7, return £17/8.50, hourly 11.30am to 3.30pm) but does not land there, passing the O2 along the way.

London Waterbus Company Cruise
(020-7482 2550; www.londonwaterbus.co.uk; 58 Camden Lock Pl, NW1; adult/child one-way £8.30/6.80, return £12/9.80; hourly 10am-5pm Apr-Sep; Warwick Ave or Camden Town) This enclosed barge runs enjoyable 50-minute trips on Regent's Canal between Little Venice and Camden Lock, passing by Regent's Park and stopping at London Zoo. There are fewer departures outside of high season; check the website for schedules.

London RIB Voyages Boat Tour
(Map p250; 020-7928 8933; www.londonribvoyages.com; Boarding Gate 1, London Eye, Waterloo Millennium Pier, Westminster Bridge Rd, SE1; adult/child £42/22.95; hourly 10am-6pm) Feel like James Bond – or David Beckham en route to the 2012 Olympic Games – on this high-speed inflatable boat that flies down the Thames at 30 to 35 knots. RIB also does a Captain Kidd–themed trip between the London Eye and Canary Wharf for the same price.

Santander Cycles

Like Paris and other European cities, London has its own bicycle-hire scheme called **Santander Cycles** (0343 222 6666; ww), also variously referred to as 'Barclays Bikes' after their former sponsor, or 'Boris Bikes' after Boris Johnson (the city's mayor from 2008 to 2016), who launched the initiative. The bikes have proved as popular with visitors as with Londoners.

The idea is simple: pick up a bike from one of the 700 docking stations dotted around the capital. Cycle. Drop it off at another docking station.

The access fee is £2 for 24 hours. All you need is a credit or debit card. The first 30 minutes are free. It's then £2 for any additional period of 30 minutes. You can take as many bikes as you like during your access period (24 hours), leaving five minutes between each trip.

The pricing structure is designed to encourage short journeys rather than longer rentals; for those, go to a hire company. You'll also find that although easy to ride, the bikes only have three gears and are quite heavy. You must be 18 years of age to buy access and at least 14 to ride a bike.

★ Sporting London

You may not land tickets to the FA Cup Final at Wembley Stadium or front-row seats for the men's and women's finals at Wimbledon, but there are plenty of ways to enjoy sports and activities in London.

Clockwise from top: Boat tour along the River Thames; Bike hire near the Houses of Parliament; Bus tour across Tower Bridge

Football

Football is at the very heart of English culture, with about a dozen league teams in London and usually around five or six in the Premier League. Tickets for Premier League fixtures (August to mid-May) can be impossible to secure for visitors. Stadiums where you can watch matches (or, more realistically, take tours) include the city's landmark national stadium, **Wembley** (☎0844 980 8001; www.wembleystadium.com; tours adult/child £19/11; ⊖Wembley Park); **Arsenal Emirates Stadium** (☎020-7619 5000; www.arsenal.com/tours; Hornsey Rd, N5; self-guided tour adult/child £20/10, guided tour £40; ⏰10am-6pm Mon-Sat, to 4pm Sun; ⊖Holloway Rd); **Chelsea** (☎0871 984 1955; www.chelseafc.com; Stamford Bridge, Fulham Rd, SW6; tours adult/child £20/13; ⏰museum 9.30am-5pm; ⊖Fulham Broadway); and West Ham United (www.whufc.com), who are making the Olympic Stadium their new ground from 2016.

Numerous pubs across the capital show Premier League games (as well as fixtures from other European championships), and watching a football game in a pub is an experience in itself.

PAUL ELLIS/AFP/GETTY IMAGES ©

Bus Tours

Big Bus Tours Bus Tour

(www.bigbustours.com; adult/child £32/13; ⏰every 20min 8.30am-6pm Apr-Sep, to 5pm Oct & Mar, to 4.30pm Nov-Feb) Informative commentaries in eight languages. The ticket includes a free river cruise with City Cruises and three thematic walking tours (Royal London, film locations, mysteries). Good online booking discounts available.

Original Tour Bus Tour

(www.theoriginaltour.com; adult/child £30/15; ⏰8.30am-8.30pm) A hop-on-hop-off bus service with a river cruise thrown in as well as three themed walks: Changing of the Guard, Rock 'n' Roll and Jack the Ripper. Buses run every five to 20 minutes; you can buy tickets on the bus or online.

Specialist Tours

Guide London Tour

(Association of Professional Tourist Guides; ☎020-7611 2545; www.guidelondon.org.uk; half-/full day £150/240) Hire a prestigious Blue Badge Tourist Guide, know-it-all guides who have studied for two years and passed a dozen written and practical exams to do their job. They can tell you stories behind the sights that you'd only hear from them or take you on a themed tour, from royalty and the Beatles to parks and shopping. Go by car, public transport, bike or on foot.

London Walks Walking Tour

(☎020-7624 3978; www.walks.com; adult/child £10/free) A huge choice of themed walks, including Jack the Ripper, the Beatles, Sherlock Holmes and Harry Potter. Check the website for schedule; there are walks every day.

Pools & Spas

Serpentine Lido Swimming

(Map p249; ☎020-7706 3422; Hyde Park, W2; adult/child £4.60/1.60; ⏰10am-6pm daily Jun-Aug, 10am-6pm Sat & Sun May; ⊖Hyde Park Corner or Knightsbridge) Perhaps the ultimate London pool inside the Serpentine lake, this fabulous lido is open May to August.

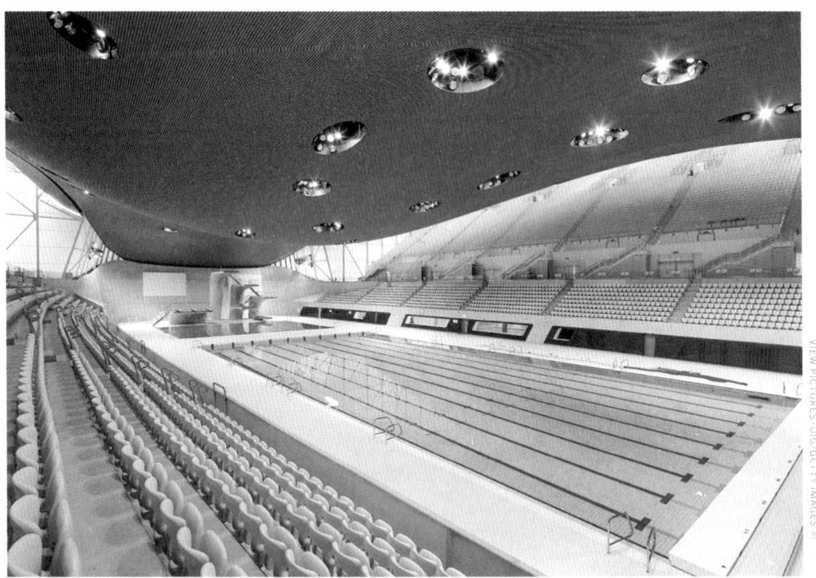

Competition pools at the London Aquatics Centre

Porchester Spa Spa

(Porchester Centre, Queensway, W2; admission £28; 10am-10pm; Bayswater or Royal Oak) Housed in a gorgeous, art deco building, the Porchester is a no-frills spa run by Westminster Council. With a 30m swimming pool, a large Finnish log sauna, two steam rooms, three Turkish hot rooms and a massive plunge pool, there are plenty of affordable treatments on offer, including massages and male and female pampering/grooming sessions.

It's women only on Tuesdays, Thursdays and Fridays all day and between 10am and 2pm on Sundays; men only on Mondays, Wednesdays and Saturdays. Couples are welcome from 4pm to 10pm on Sundays.

London Aquatics Centre Swimming

(www.londonaquaticscentre.org; Queen Elizabeth Olympic Park, E20; adult/child £4.50/2.50; 6am-10.30pm; Stratford) The sweeping lines and wavelike movement of Zaha Hadid's award-winning Aquatics Centre make it the architectural highlight of Olympic Park. Bathed in natural light, the 50m competition pool beneath the huge undulating roof (which sits on just three supports) is an extraordinary place to swim. There's also a second 50m pool, a diving area, gym, créche and cafe.

Adventure Sports

Up at the O2 Adventure Sports

(www.theo2.co.uk/upattheo2; O2, Greenwich Peninsula, SE10; weekdays/weekends from £28/35; hours vary; North Greenwich) London isn't exactly your thrill-seeking destination, but this ascent of the O2 dome is definitely not for the faint-hearted. Equipped with climbing suit and a harness, you'll scale the famous white dome to arrive at a viewing platform perched 52m above the Thames with sweeping views of Canary Wharf, the river, Greenwich and beyond.

Not suitable for children under 10 (also check height and weight restrictions).

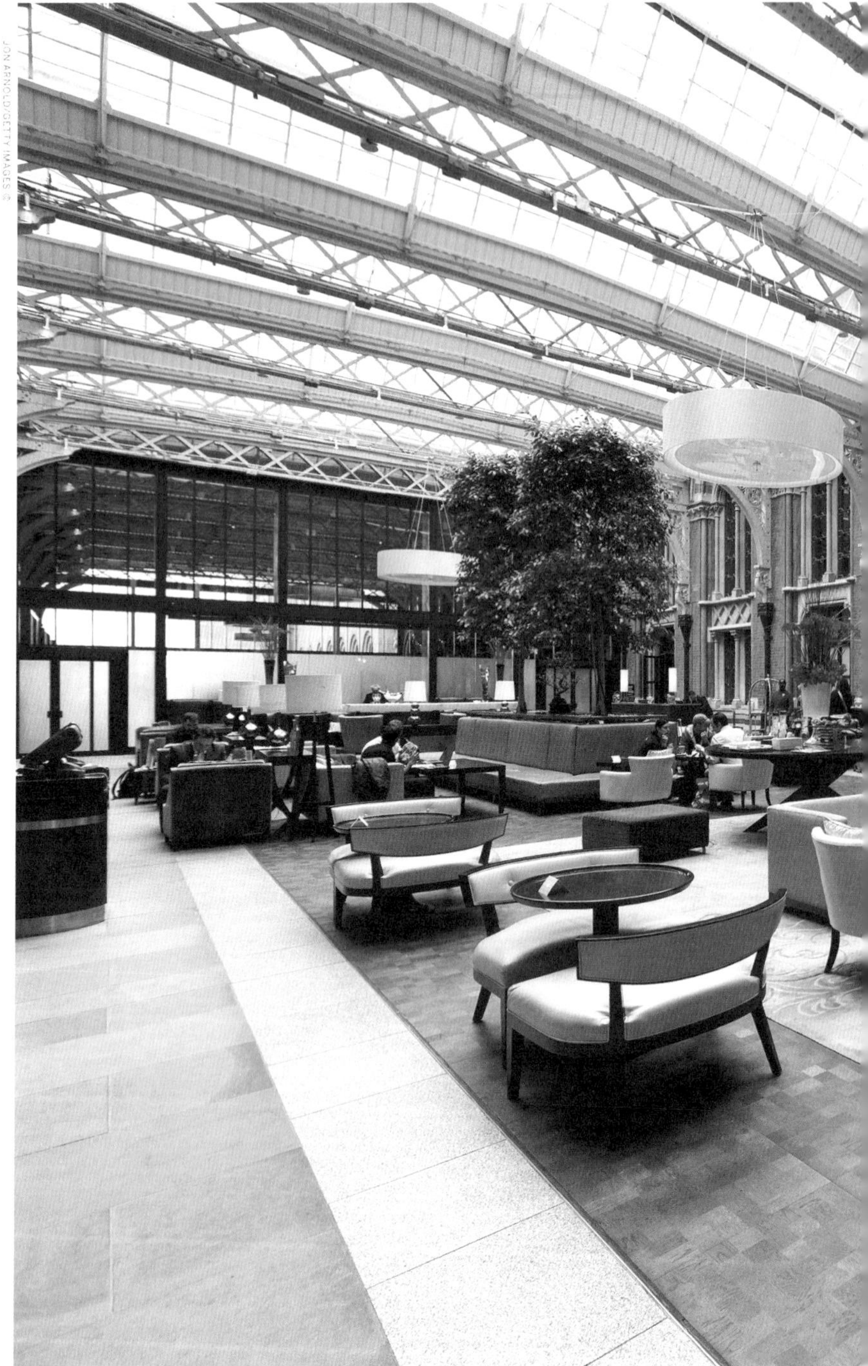

JON ARNOLD/GETTY IMAGES ©

REST YOUR HEAD

Top tips for the best accommodation

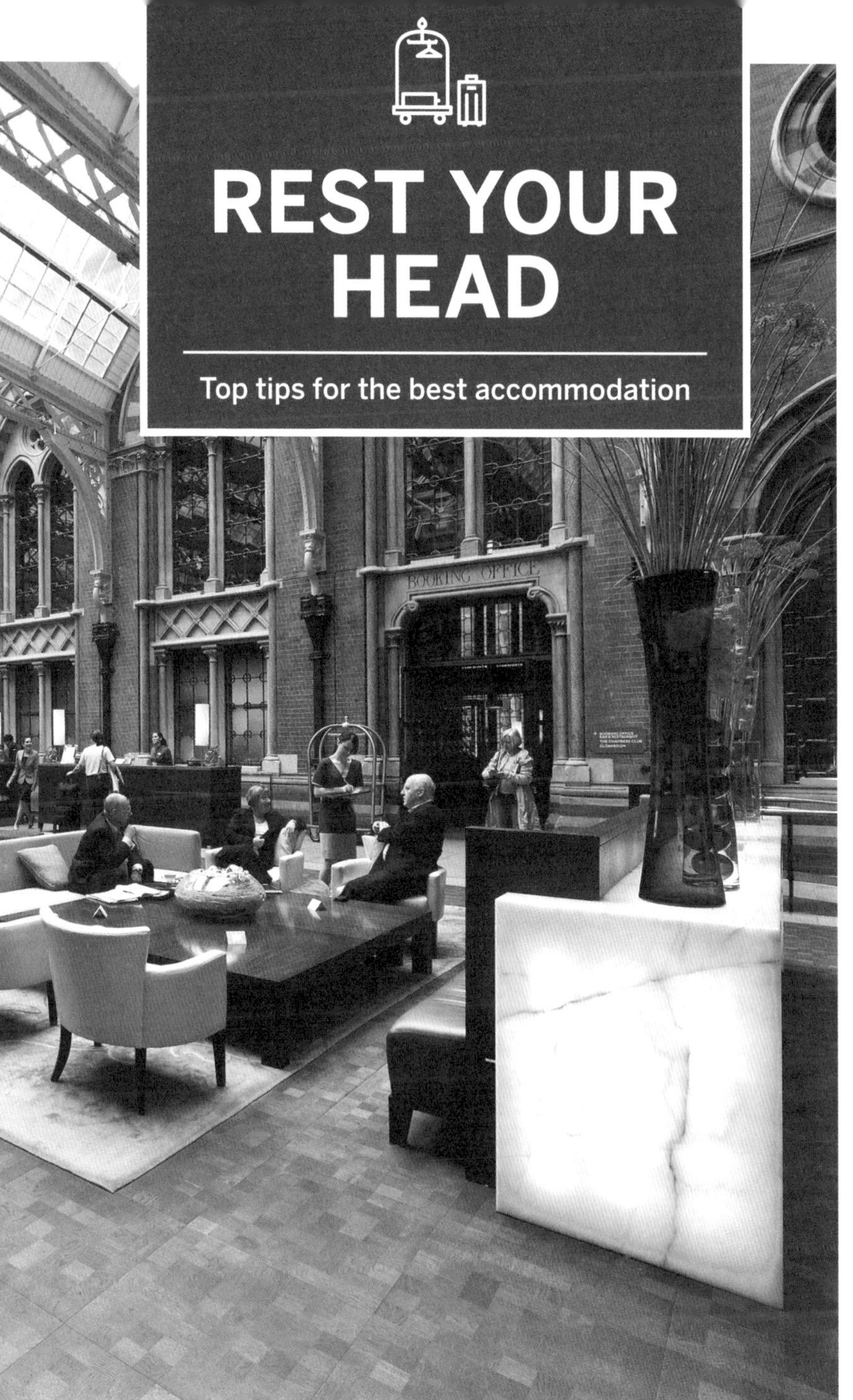

Rest Your Head

Landing the right accommodation is integral to your London experience, and there's no shortage of choice. There's some fantastic accommodation about – from party-oriented hostels to stately top-end hotels – so it's worth spending a little time ahead of your trip researching your options.

Budget is likely to be your number one consideration, given how pricey accommodation is in London, but you should also think about the neighbourhood you'd like to stay in. Are you a culture vulture? Would you like to be able to walk (or hop a quick cab ride) home after a night out? Are you after village charm or cool cachet? Make sure you think your options through and book ahead: London is busy year-round.

In This Section

Prices

A 'budget hotel' in London generally costs up to £100 for a standard double room with bathroom. For a midrange option, plan on spending £100 to £200. Luxury options run £200 and higher.

Tipping

Tipping isn't expected in hotels in London, except perhaps for porters in top-end hotels (although it remains discretionary).

VISITBRITAIN/ANDREW PICKETT/GETTY IMAGES ©

Mandarin Oriental Hyde Park

Reservations

Book rooms as far in advance as possible, especially for weekends and holiday periods.

The British Hotel Reservation Centre (www.bhrconline.com) has desks at airports and major train stations.

Visit London (www.visitlondonoffers.com) offers a free accommodation booking service and has a list of gay-friendly accommodation.

Useful Websites

Lonely Planet (www.lonelyplanet.com/london) Hundreds of properties, from budget hostels to luxury apartments.

London Town (www.londontown.com) Excellent last-minute offers on boutique hotels and B&Bs.

Alastair Sawdays (www.sawdays.co.uk) Hand-picked selection of bolt-holes in the capital.

There are various accommodation options in London, which cater to all budgets and needs.

Hotels

London has a grand roll-call of stately hotels and many are experiences in their own right. Standards across the top end and much of the boutique bracket are high, but so are prices. Quirkiness and individuality can be found in abundance, alongside dyed-in-the-wool traditionalism. A wealth of budget boutique hotels has exploited a lucrative niche, while a rung or two down in overall quality and charm, midrange chain hotels generally offer good locations and dependable comfort. Demand can often outstrip supply – especially on the bottom step of the market – so book ahead, particularly during holiday periods and in summer.

B&Bs

Housed in good-looking old properties, bed and breakfasts come in a tier below hotels, often promising boutique-style charm and a more personal level of service. Handy B&B clusters appear in Paddington, South Kensington, Victoria and Bloomsbury.

Hostels

After B&Bs the cheapest form of accommodation is hostels, both the official Youth Hostel Association (YHA) ones and the usually hipper, more party-orientated independent ones. Hostels vary in quality so select carefully; most offer twins as well as dorms.

Rates & Booking

Deluxe hotel rooms will cost from around £350 per double but there's good variety at the top end, so you should find a room from about £200 offering superior comfort without the prestige. Some boutique hotels also occupy this bracket. There's a noticeable dip in quality below this price. Under £100 and you're at the more serviceable, budget end of the market. Look out for weekend deals that can put a better class of hotel within reach. Rates often slide in winter. Book through the hotels' websites for the best online deals or promotional rates.

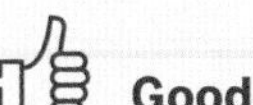

Good to Know

Value-added tax (VAT; 20%) is added to hotel rooms. Some hotels include this in their advertised rates, some don't.

Breakfast may be included in the room rate. Sometimes this is a continental breakfast; full English breakfast might cost extra.

Room & Apartment Rentals

If you're in London for a week or more, a short-term or serviced apartment may make sense: rates at the bottom end are comparable to a B&B, you can manage your budget more carefully by eating in, and you'll get to feel like a local.

Great neighbourhoods to consider for their vibe include Notting Hill, Hackney, Bermondsey, Pimlico and Camden, where you'll find plenty of food markets, great local pubs and lots of boutiques. Airbnb (www.airbnb.co.uk/london) is the go-to source for finding a London pad, but you can also try Holiday Lettings (www.holidaylettings.co.uk/london).

For something a little more hotel-like, serviced apartments are a great option. Try the following, which are all in the centre: **196 Bishopsgate** (020-7621 8788; www.196bishopsgate.com; 196 Bishopsgate, EC2; apt from £175; ; Liverpool St), **Number 5 Maddox Street** (020-7647 0200; www.living-rooms.co.uk/hotel/no5maddoxstreet; 5 Maddox St, W1; ste £250-925; ; Oxford Circus), and **Beaufort House** (020-7584 2600; www.beauforthouse.co.uk; 45 Beaufort Gardens, SW3; 1- to 4-bed apt £440-1346; ; Knightsbridge).

Where to Stay

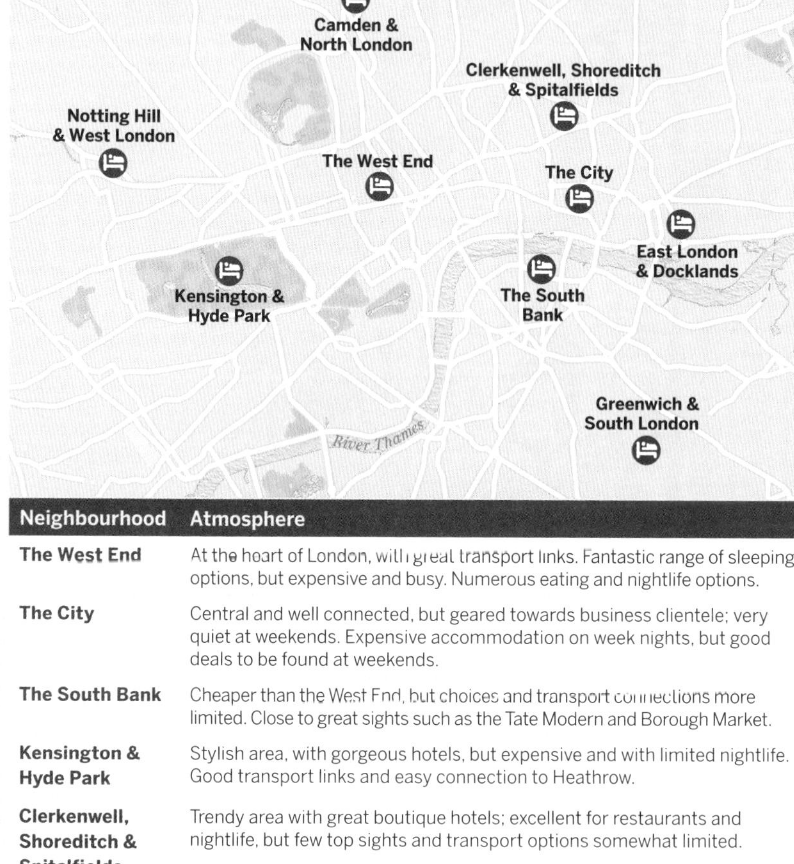

Neighbourhood	Atmosphere
The West End	At the heart of London, with great transport links. Fantastic range of sleeping options, but expensive and busy. Numerous eating and nightlife options.
The City	Central and well connected, but geared towards business clientele; very quiet at weekends. Expensive accommodation on week nights, but good deals to be found at weekends.
The South Bank	Cheaper than the West End, but choices and transport connections more limited. Close to great sights such as the Tate Modern and Borough Market.
Kensington & Hyde Park	Stylish area, with gorgeous hotels, but expensive and with limited nightlife. Good transport links and easy connection to Heathrow.
Clerkenwell, Shoreditch & Spitalfields	Trendy area with great boutique hotels; excellent for restaurants and nightlife, but few top sights and transport options somewhat limited.
East London & Docklands	Limited sleeping options, but great multicultural local feel; some areas less safe at night.
Camden & North London	Leafy area, with great sleeping options and a vibrant nightlife, but further from main sights and with fewer transport options.
Notting Hill & West London	Lovely neighbourhood with village charm, great vibe at weekends; plenty of cheap but average hotels. Light on top sights.
Greenwich & South London	Villagelike feel, but limited sleeping and transport options; great for Greenwich sights, but inconvenient for everything else.
Richmond, Kew & Hampton Court	Smart riverside hotels, semirural pockets, but sights spread out and far from central London.

Trafalgar Square's (p58) bronze lion and Big Ben (p50)

In Focus

London Today

The 2012 Olympic legacy bequeathed a feel-good factor to London that just seems to go on and on. Tourism has increased by leaps and bounds in the past few years – aided and abetted not just by the Games but by one royal wedding and two royal births. But it's more than all that. London has reaffirmed itself over and over as a capital of new ideas, cultural dynamism and change.

Above: Millennium Bridge (p85) and St Paul's Cathedral (p80)

London vs the Rest?

London is the world's leading financial centre for international business and commerce and the fifth-largest city economy in the world. As the economic downturn of the last decade fades into memory, the UK is increasingly a nation of two halves: London (and the southeast) and the rest of the country. The capital generates more than 20% of Britain's income, a percentage that has been rising over the decade The price of property is double the national average; and incomes are 30% higher in London than elsewhere in the country. But there's a flip side: 28% of Londoners are living in poverty, compared with just 21% in the rest of England.

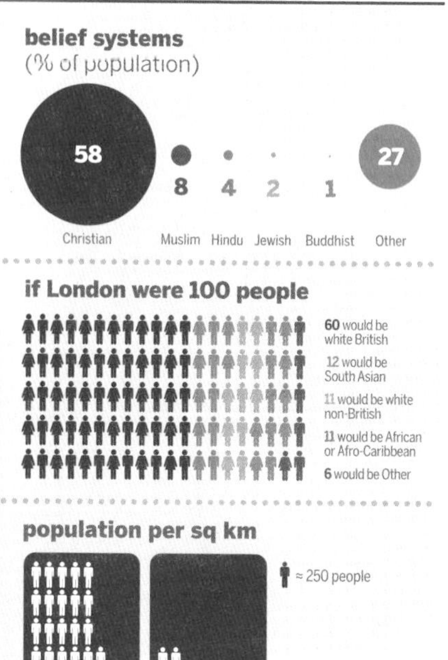

Ethnicity & Multiculturalism

What has become the world's most cosmopolitan place in which to live continues to lure immigrants from around the globe. Rich investors from Russia, the Middle East and China seeking a stable place to invest capital jostle for space with others looking for opportunities that are in short supply back home. According to the last census (2011), almost 37% of London's population is foreign born – with almost a quarter born outside Europe. Today, an estimated 270 different ethnic groups speak 300 different languages and, despite some tensions, most get along well.

Building Boom

The huge rise in population – London is expected have nine million inhabitants by 2020, up from 8.3 million today – has led to a building boom not seen since the end of WWII. More than 50,000 new homes are needed annually over the next 20 years to keep up with demand. Church spires are now dwarfed by a forest of construction cranes working to build more than 230 high-rise condos and office buildings. New landmark skyscrapers in the City include the 37-storey Walkie Talkie (20 Fenchurch St) and the 225m-tall Cheesegrater (Leadenhall Building), with many more on the cards or under construction south of the river.

Austerity & Change

Virtually no one foresaw the outcome of the 2015 national elections, in which the Conservative Party soundly beat Labour, gaining 28 seats and a narrow majority in Parliament. What that all means to the London mayoral race in May 2016 is anyone's guess. London tends to vote on personality, often bucking the national trend (it voted Labour in the national elections). Whether any of the candidates can fill the sizeable gap left by the bouncy and often Teflon-coated outgoing mayor, Conservative Boris Johnson, remains to be seen.

Moving Forward

With London's underground trains, its buses and its roads packed to bursting point, an ambitious redesign of London's transport options is under way. To help cope with demand, the city is building miles of new lanes for cyclists, including those on Santander Cycles (more commonly known as 'Boris Bikes'). Crossrail, a 73-mile railway line running east–west across Greater London, will begin operations in 2018. And even the crusty old tube has begun 24-hour operations at the weekend on certain lines.

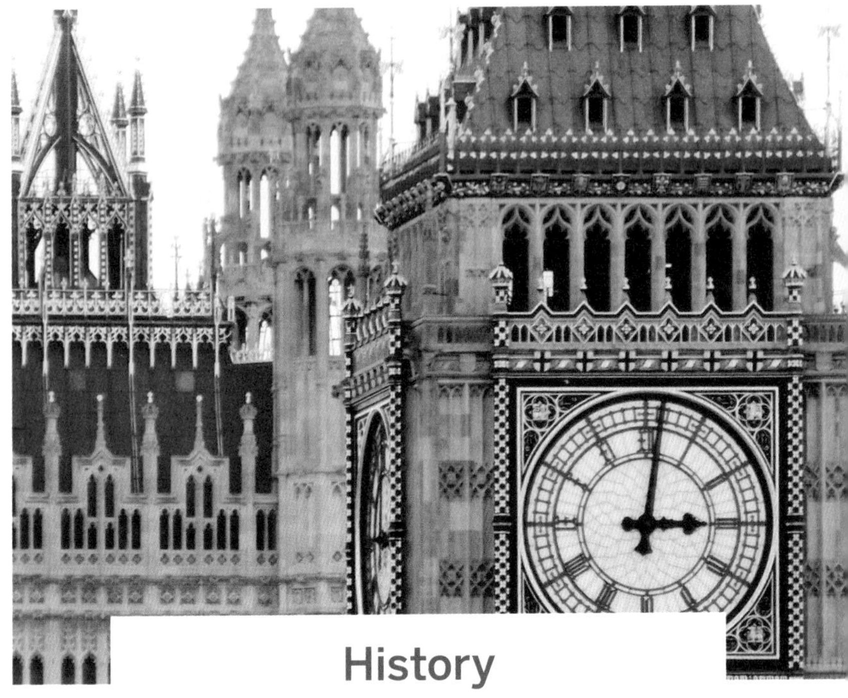

History

London's history is a long and turbulent narrative spanning more than two millennia. Over those years there have been good times of strength and economic prosperity and horrific times of plague, fire and war. But even when down on its knees, London has always been able to get up, dust itself off and move on, constantly re-inventing itself along the way.

Above: Close-up of Big Ben (p50) SARA LYNCH/EYEEM/GETTY IMAGES ©
Above right: Henry VII's Lady Chapel, Westminster Abbey (p36) DE AGOSTINI/S. VANNINI/ GETTY IMAGES ©

AD 43
The Romans invade Britain, led by Emperor Claudius; they mix with the local Celtic tribespeople and stay for almost four centuries.

852
Vikings settle in London; a period of great struggle between the kingdoms of Wessex and Denmark begins.

1066
Following his decisive victory at the Battle of Hastings, William, Duke of Normandy, is crowned in Westminster Abbey.

Londinium

The Celts were the first to arrive in the area that is now London, some time around the 4th century BC. It was the Romans, however, who established a real settlement in AD 43, the port of Londinium. They slung a wooden bridge over the Thames (near the site of today's London Bridge) and created a thriving colonial outpost before abandoning British soil for good in 410.

Saxon & Norman London

Saxon settlers, who colonised the southeast of England from the 5th century onwards, established themselves outside the city walls due west of Londinium in Lundenwic. This infant trading community grew in importance and attracted the attention of the Vikings in Denmark. They attacked in 842 and again nine years later, burning Lundenwic to the ground. Under the leadership of King Alfred the Great of Wessex, the Saxon population fought back, driving the Danes out in 886.

1215
King John signs the Magna Carta, an agreement forming the basis of constitutional law in England.

1348
Rats on ships from Europe bring the Black Death, a plague that eventually wipes out almost two-thirds of the city's residents.

1605
A Catholic plot to blow up James I is foiled; Guy Fawkes, one of the alleged plotters, is executed the following year.

★ **Best for Royal History**

Hampton Court Palace (p120)
Westminster Abbey (p36)
Buckingham Palace (p46)
Tower of London (p74)
Kensington Palace (p106)

Kensington Gardens (p107) at Kensington Palace

EURASIA PRESS/GETTY IMAGES ©

Saxon London grew into a prosperous and well-organised town segmented into 20 wards, each with its own alderman and resident colonies of German merchants and French vintners. But attacks by the Danes continued apace, and the Saxon leadership was weakening; in 1016 Londoners were forced to accept the Danish leader Canute as king of England. With the death of Canute's brutal son Harthacanute in 1042, the throne passed to the Saxon Edward the Confessor, who went on to found a palace and an abbey at Westminster.

On his deathbed in 1066, Edward anointed Harold Godwinson, the Earl of Wessex, as his successor. This enraged William, Duke of Normandy, who claimed that Edward had promised him the throne. William mounted a massive invasion from France, and on 14 October defeated (and killed) Harold at the Battle of Hastings, before marching on London to claim his prize. William, now dubbed 'the Conqueror', was crowned king of England in Westminster Abbey on 25 December 1066, ensuring the Norman conquest was complete.

Medieval & Tudor London

Successive medieval kings were happy to let the City of London keep its independence as long as its merchants continued to finance their wars and building projects. During the Tudor dynasty, which coincided with the discovery of the Americas and thriving world trade, London became one of the largest and most important cities in Europe. Henry VIII reigned from 1509 to 1547, built palaces at Whitehall and St James's, and bullied his lord chancellor, Cardinal Thomas Wolsey, into giving him the one at Hampton Court.

The most momentous event of his reign, however, was his split with the Catholic Church in 1534 after the Pope refused to annul his marriage to Catherine of Aragon, who had borne him only one surviving daughter after 24 years of marriage.

The 45-year reign (1558–1603) of Henry's daughter Elizabeth I is still regarded as one of the most extraordinary periods in English history. During these four decades English literature reached new heights, and religious tolerance gradually grew. With the defeat of the Spanish Armada in 1588, England became a naval superpower, and London established itself as the premier world trade market with the opening of the Royal Exchange in 1570.

1666
The Great Fire of London burns for five days, leaving four-fifths of the metropolis in smoking ruins.

1708
The last stone of Sir Christopher Wren's masterpiece, St Paul's Cathedral, is laid by his son and the son of his master mason.

1838
The coronation of Queen Victoria ushers in a new era for London; the British capital becomes the economic centre of the world.

Civil Wars, Plague & Fire

Elizabeth was succeeded by her second cousin James I, and then his son Charles I. The latter's belief in the 'divine right of kings' set him on a collision course with an increasingly confident parliament at Westminster and a powerful City of London. The latter two rallied behind Oliver Cromwell against Royalist troops. Charles was defeated in 1646 and executed in 1649.

Cromwell ruled the country as a republic for the next 11 years. Under the Commonwealth of England, as the English republic was known, Cromwell banned theatre, dancing, Christmas and just about anything remotely fun.

After Cromwell's death, parliament restored the exiled Charles II to the throne in 1660. Charles II's reign witnessed two great tragedies in London: the Great Plague of 1665, which decimated the population, and the Great Fire of London, which swept ferociously through the city's densely packed streets the following year. The wreckage of the inferno at least allowed master architect Christopher Wren to build his 51 magnificent churches. The crowning glory of the 'Great Rebuilding' was his St Paul's Cathedral, completed in 1708. A masterpiece of English baroque architecture, it remains one of the city's most prominent and iconic landmarks.

The Blitz

The Blitz (from the German Blitzkrieg, meaning 'lightning war') struck England between September 1940 and May 1941, when London and other parts of Britain were heavily bombed by the German Luftwaffe. Londoners responded with legendary resilience and stoicism. Underground stations were converted into giant bomb shelters, although this was not always safe – one bomb rolled down the escalator at Bank station and exploded on the platform, killing more than 100 people. Buckingham Palace took a direct hit during a bombing raid early in the campaign, famously prompting Queen Elizabeth (the present monarch's late mother) to announce that 'now we can look the East End in the face'.

Georgian & Victorian London

While the achievements of the 18th-century Georgian kings were impressive (though 'mad' George III will forever be remembered as the king who lost the American colonies), they were overshadowed by those of the dazzling Victorian era, dating from Queen Victoria's ascension to the throne in 1837.

During the Industrial Revolution, London became the nerve centre of the largest and richest empire the world had ever witnessed, in an imperial expansion that covered a quarter of the earth's surface area and ruled over more than 500 million people. Queen Victoria lived to celebrate her Diamond Jubilee in 1897, but died four years later aged 81 and was laid to rest beside her beloved consort, Prince Albert, at Windsor. Her reign is seen as the climax of Britain's world supremacy, when London was the de facto capital of the world.

1851
The Great Exhibition, the brainchild of Victoria's consort, Albert, opens to great fanfare in the Crystal Palace in Hyde Park.

1901
Queen Victoria dies after reigning for 63 years and 217 days – a record stint only broken by Elizabeth II in September 2015.

1940–41
London is devastated by the Blitz, although St Paul's Cathedral and the Tower of London escape largely unscathed.

★ Best for London History

Museum of London (p84)
London Dungeon (p103)
Monument (p78)
Houses of Parliament (p50)

'Witch Weighing' at the London Dungeon

SHAUN CURRY/AFP//GETTY IMAGES ©

The World Wars

What became known as the Great War, WWI broke out in August 1914, and the first German bombs fell from zeppelins near the Guildhall a year later, killing 39 people. Planes were soon dropping bombs on the capital, killing in all some 670 Londoners (half the national total of civilian deaths).

In the 1930s, Prime Minister Neville Chamberlain's policy of appeasing Adolf Hitler eventually proved misguided, as the German Führer's lust for expansion appeared insatiable. When Nazi Germany invaded Poland on 1 September 1939, Britain declared war, having signed a mutual-assistance pact with that country only a few days before. World War II (1939–45), which would prove to be Europe's darkest hour, had begun.

Winston Churchill, prime minister from 1940, orchestrated much of the nation's war strategy from the Cabinet War Rooms deep below Whitehall, lifting the nation's spirit from here with his stirring wartime speeches. By the time Nazi Germany capitulated in May 1945, up to a third of the East End and the City of London had been flattened, almost 30,000 Londoners had been killed and a further 50,000 seriously wounded.

Postwar London

Once the celebrations of Victory in Europe (VE) day had died down, the nation began to confront the war's appalling toll and to rebuild. The years of austerity had begun, with rationing of essential items and high-rise residences sprouting up from bomb sites. Rationing of most goods ended in 1953, the year Elizabeth II was crowned following the death the year before of her father King George VI.

Immigrants from around the world – particularly the former colonies – flocked to postwar London, where a dwindling population had generated labour shortages, and the city's character changed forever. The place to be during the 1960s, 'Swinging London' became the epicentre of cool in fashion and music, its streets awash with colour and vitality.

1953
Queen Elizabeth II's coronation is broadcast live around the world on television; many English families buy their first TV.

1981
Brixton sees the worst race riots in London's history.

2000
Ken Livingstone is elected mayor of London as an independent.

The ensuing 1970s brought glam rock, punk, economic depression and the country's first female prime minister in 1979. In power for the entire 1980s and pushing an unprecedented program of privatisation, the late Margaret Thatcher is easily the most significant of Britain's postwar leaders. Opinions about 'Maggie' still polarise the Brits today.

While poorer Londoners suffered under Thatcher's significant trimming back of the welfare state, things had rarely looked better for the wealthy, as London underwent explosive economic growth. In 1992, much to the astonishment of most Londoners, the Conservative Party was elected for their fourth successive term in government, despite Mrs Thatcher being jettisoned by her party a year and a half before. By 1995, the writing was on the wall for the Conservative Party, as the Labour Party, apparently unelectable for a decade, came back with a new face.

Great Fire of London

The Great Fire of London broke out in Thomas Farriner's bakery in Pudding Lane on the evening of 2 September 1666. Initially dismissed by London's lord mayor as 'something a woman might pisse out', the fire spread uncontrollably and destroyed 89 churches and more than 13,000 houses, raging for days. Amazingly, fewer than a dozen people died. The fire destroyed medieval London, changing the city forever. Many Londoners left for the countryside or to seek their fortunes in the New World, while the city itself rebuilt its medieval heart with grand buildings such as Sir Christopher Wren's St Paul's Cathedral. Wren's magnificent Monument (1677) near London Bridge stands as a memorial to the fire and its victims.

London in the New Century

Invigorated by its sheer desperation to return to power, the Labour Party elected the thoroughly telegenic Tony Blair as its leader, who in turn managed to ditch some of the more socialist-sounding clauses in its party credo and reinvent it as New Labour, leading to a huge landslide win in the May 1997 general election. The Conservatives atomised nationwide; the Blair era had begun in earnest.

Most importantly for London, Labour recognised the demand the city had for local government, and created the London Assembly and the post of mayor. In Ken Livingstone, London elected a mayor who introduced a congestion charge and sought to update the ageing public transport network. In 2008, he was defeated by his arch-rival, Conservative Boris Johnson.

Johnson won his second term in 2012, the year of the Olympic Games (overwhelmingly judged an unqualified success) and the Queen's Diamond Jubilee (the 60th anniversary of her ascension to the throne).

2005

A day after London is awarded the 2012 Olympics, 52 people are killed in a series of suicide bombings on London's transport network.

2012

Boris Johnson narrowly beats Ken Livingstone to win his second mayoral election; London hosts the 2012 Olympics and Paralympics.

2013

The Shard, the tallest building in the EU at 310m, opens to the public; MPs vote in favour of legalising gay marriage.

Architecture

Unlike many other world-class cities, London has never been methodically planned. Rather, it has developed in an organic fashion. London retains architectural reminders from every period of its long history. This is a city for explorers; seek out part of a Roman wall enclosed in the lobby of a modern building, for example, or a coaching inn dating to the Restoration tucked away in a courtyard.

Above: Tower Bridge (p86) and the Shard (p91) ALAN COPSON/GETTY IMAGES ©

Ancient London Architecture

Traces of medieval London are hard to find thanks to the devastating Great Fire of 1666, but several works by the architect Inigo Jones (1573–1652) have endured, including Covent Garden Piazza in the West End.

There are a few even older treasures scattered around – including the mighty Tower of London in the City, parts of which date back to the late 11th century. Westminster Abbey and Temple Church are 12th- to 13th-century creations. Few Roman traces survive outside museums, though the Temple of Mithras, built in AD 240, was relocated to the eastern end of Queen Victoria St in the City when the Bloomberg headquarters were completed at Walbrook Sq in 2016. Stretches of the Roman wall remain as foundations to a medieval wall outside Tower Hill tube station and in a few sections below Bastion high walk, next to the Museum of London, all in the City.

The Saxons, who moved into the area after the decline of the Roman Empire, found Londinium too small, ignored what the Romans had left behind and built their communities farther up the Thames. The best place to see in situ what the Saxons left behind is the church of All Hallows by the Tower, northwest of the Tower of London, which boasts an important archway, the walls of a 7th-century Saxon church and fragments from a Roman pavement.

Noteworthy medieval secular structures include the 1365 Jewel Tower, opposite the Houses of Parliament, and Westminster Hall, both surviving chunks of the Medieval Palace of Westminster.

After the Great Fire

After the 1666 fire, Sir Christopher Wren was commissioned to oversee reconstruction, but his vision of a new city layout of broad, symmetrical avenues never made it past the planners. His legacy lives on, however, in St Paul's Cathedral (1708), in the maritime precincts at Greenwich and in numerous City churches.

Nicholas Hawksmoor joined contemporary James Gibb in taking Wren's English baroque style even further; one great example is St Martin-in-the-Fields in Trafalgar Sq.

Like Wren before him, Georgian architect John Nash aimed to impose some symmetry on unruly London and was slightly more successful in achieving this, through grand creations such as Trafalgar Sq and the elegantly curving arcade of Regent St. Built in similar style, the surrounding squares of St James's remain some of the finest public spaces in London – little wonder then that Queen Victoria decided to move into the recently vacated Buckingham Palace in 1837.

Toward Modernity

Pragmatism replaced grand vision with the Victorians, who desired ornate civic buildings that reflected the glory of empire but were open to the masses, too. The style's turrets, towers and arches are best exemplified by the flamboyant Natural History Museum (Alfred Waterhouse), St Pancras Chambers (George Gilbert Scott) and the Houses of Parliament (Augustus Pugin and Charles Barry), the latter replacing the Palace of Westminster that had largely burned down in 1834.

The Victorians and Edwardians were also ardent builders of functional and cheap terraced houses, many of which became slums, but today house London's urban middle classes.

A flirtation with art deco and the great suburban residential building boom of the 1930s was followed by a utilitarian modernism after WWII, as the city rushed to build new housing to replace terraces lost in the Blitz. Low-cost developments and unattractive high-rise housing were thrown up on bomb sites; many of these blocks still fragment the London horizon today.

Brutalism – a hard-edged and uncompromising architectural style that flourished from the 1950s to the 1970s, favouring concrete and reflecting socialist utopian principles – worked better on paper than in real life, but made significant contributions to London's architectural melange. Denys Lasdun's National Theatre, begun in 1966, is representative of the style.

★ **Best Modern Architecture**

Shard (p91)
Tate Modern (p94)
30 St Mary Axe (p79)
Millennium Bridge (p85)
London Aquatics Centre (p207)

London Aquatics Centre

RON ELLIS/SHUTTERSTOCK ©

Postmodernism & Beyond

The next big wave of development arrived in the derelict wasteland of the former London docks, which were emptied of their terraces and warehouses and rebuilt as towering skyscrapers and 'loft' apartments. Taking pride of place in the Docklands was Cesar Pelli's 244m-high 1 Canada Square (1991), commonly known as Canary Wharf and easily visible from central London. The City was also the site of architectural innovation, including the centrepiece 1986 Lloyd's of London, Sir Richard Rogers' 'inside-out' masterpiece of ducts, pipes, glass and stainless steel.

Contemporary Architecture

There followed a lull in new construction until around 2000, when a glut of millennium projects unveiled new structures and rejuvenated others: the London Eye, Tate Modern and the Millennium Bridge all spiced up the South Bank, while Norman Foster's iconic 30 St Mary Axe, better known as the Gherkin, started a new wave of skyscraper construction in the City. Even the once-mocked Millennium Dome won a new lease of life as the 02 concert and sports hall.

By the middle of the decade, London's biggest urban development project ever was under way, the 200-hectare Queen Elizabeth Olympic Park in the Lea River Valley near Stratford in East London, where most of the events of the 2012 Summer Olympics and Paralympics took place. But the park would offer few architectural surprises – except for Zaha Hadid's stunning Aquatics Centre, a breathtaking structure suitably inspired by the fluid geometry of water, and the ArcelorMittal Orbit, a zany public work of art with viewing platforms designed by the sculptor Anish Kapoor.

The spotlight may have been shining on East London, but the City and South London have also undergone energetic developments, too. Most notable is the so-called Shard, at 310m the EU's tallest building, completed in 2012. In the City, the Walkie Talkie has divided opinions, but its jungle-like Sky Garden on levels 35 to 37 are universally loved.

Literary London

For over six centuries, London has been the setting for works of prose. Indeed, the capital has been the inspiration for the masterful imaginations of such eminent wordsmiths as Shakespeare, Defoe, Dickens, Orwell, Conrad, Eliot, Greene and Woolf (even though not all were native to the city, or even British).

Above: Portrait of London writer, Charles Dickens NEIL HOLMES/GETTY IMAGES ©

It's hard to reconcile the bawdy portrayal of London in Geoffrey Chaucer's *Canterbury Tales* with Charles Dickens' bleak hellhole in *Oliver Twist*, let alone Daniel Defoe's plague-ravaged metropolis in *Journal of the Plague Year* with Zadie Smith's multi-ethnic romp *White Teeth*. Ever-changing, yet somehow eerily consistent, London has left its mark on some of the most influential writing in the English language.

Chaucerian London

The first literary reference to London appears in Chaucer's *Canterbury Tales*, written between 1387 and 1400: the 29 pilgrims of the tale gather for their trip to Canterbury at the

★ Best Literary Sites

Interior of the British Library

GABRIELE GELSI/SHUTTERSTOCK ©

Tabard Inn in Talbot Yard, Southwark, and agree to share stories on the way there and back. The inn burned down in 1676; a blue plaque marks the site of the building today.

Shakespearian London

Born in Warwickshire, William Shakespeare spent most of his life as an actor and playwright in London around the turn of the 17th century. He trod the boards of several theatres in Shoreditch and Southwark and wrote his greatest tragedies, among them *Hamlet, Othello, Macbeth* and *King Lear,* for the original Globe theatre on the South Bank. Although London was his home for most of his life, Shakespeare set nearly all his plays in foreign or imaginary lands. Only *Henry IV: Parts I & II* include a London setting – a tavern called the Boar's Head in Eastcheap.

18th-Century London

Daniel Defoe was perhaps the first true London writer, both living in and writing about the city during the early 18th century. He is most famous for his novels *Robinson Crusoe* (1719–20) and *Moll Flanders* (1722), which he wrote while living in Church St in Stoke Newington. Defoe's *Journal of the Plague Year* is his most absorbing account of London life, documenting the horrors of the Great Plague during the summer and autumn of 1665, when the author was a young child.

Dickensian & 19th-Century London

Two early 19th-century Romantic poets drew inspiration from London. John Keats, born above a Moorgate public house in 1795, wrote 'Ode to a Nightingale' while living near Hampstead Heath in 1819 and 'Ode on a Grecian Urn' reportedly after viewing the Parthenon frieze in the British Museum the same year. William Wordsworth discovered inspiration for the poem 'Upon Westminster Bridge' while visiting London in 1802.

Charles Dickens was the definitive London author. When his father and family were interned at Marshalsea Prison in Southwark for not paying their debts, the 12-year-old Charles was forced to fend for himself on the streets. That grim period provided a font of experiences on which to draw. His novels most closely associated with London are *Oliver Twist,* with its gang of thieves led by Fagin in Clerkenwell, and *Little Dorrit,* whose hero was born in the Marshalsea. The house in Bloomsbury where he wrote *Oliver Twist* and two other novels now houses the expanded Charles Dickens Museum.

Sir Arthur Conan Doyle (1858–1930) portrayed a very different London, his pipe-smoking, cocaine-snorting sleuth, Sherlock Holmes, coming to exemplify a cool and unflappable Englishness. Letters to the mythical hero and his admiring friend, Dr Watson, still arrive at 221b Baker St, where there's a museum to everyone's favourite Victorian detective.

London at the end of the 19th century appears in many books, but especially those of Somerset Maugham. His first novel, *Liza of Lambeth,* was based on his experiences as an intern in the slums of South London, while *Of Human Bondage* provides a portrait of late-Victorian London.

American Writers & London in the 20th Century

Of Americans who wrote about London at the turn of the century, Henry James, who settled here, stands supreme with his *Daisy Miller* and *The Europeans.* St Louis–born TS Eliot moved to London in 1915, where he published his poems 'The Love Song of J Alfred Prufrock' and 'The Waste Land', in which London is portrayed as an 'unreal city'.

Interwar Developments

Between the world wars, PG Wodehouse depicted London high life with his hilarious lampooning of the English upper classes in the Jeeves stories. George Orwell's experience of living as a beggar in London's East End coloured his book *Down and Out in Paris and London* (1933).

The Modern Age

This period is marked by the emergence of multicultural voices. Hanif Kureishi explored London from the perspective of young Pakistanis in his best-known novels *The Black Album* and *The Buddha of Suburbia,* while Timothy Mo's *Sour Sweet* is a poignant and funny account of a Chinese family in the 1960s trying to adjust to English life.

The decades leading up to the turn of the millennium were great ones for British literature, bringing a dazzling new generation of writers to the fore, such as Martin Amis *(Money, London Fields)*, Julian Barnes *(Metroland, Talking it Over)*, Ian McEwan *(Enduring Love, Atonement)* and Salman Rushdie *(Midnight's Children, The Satanic Verses)*.

Millennium London

Helen Fielding's *Bridget Jones's Diary* and its sequel, *Bridget Jones: The Edge of Reason,* launched the 'chick lit' genre, one that transcended the travails of a young single Londoner to become a worldwide phenomenon.

Peter Ackroyd named the city as the love of his life; *London: The Biography* was his inexhaustible paean to the capital.

The Current Scene

Home to most of the UK's major publishers and its best bookshops, London remains a vibrant place for writers and readers alike. New London writers in recent years include Monica Ali *(Brick Lane)*, Zadie Smith *(NW)*, Jake Arnott *(The Long Firm)* and Gautam Malkani *(Londonstani)*.

Every bookshop in town has a London section, where you will find many of these titles and lots more.

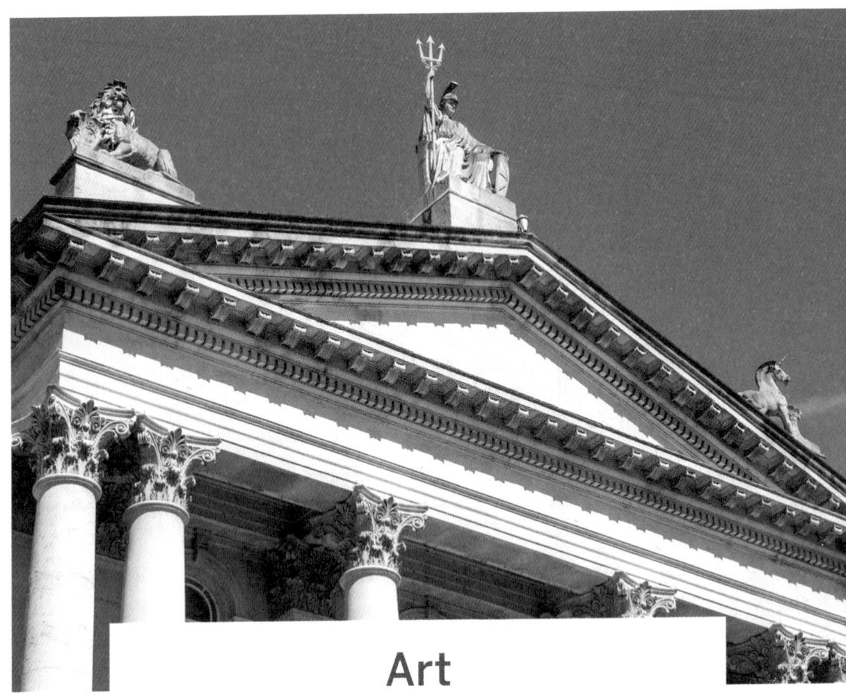

Art

When it comes to art, London has traditionally been overshadowed by other European capitals. Yet many of history's greatest artists have spent time in London, including the likes of Monet and Van Gogh, and in terms of contemporary art, there's a compelling argument for putting London at the very top of the European pack.

Above: Tate Britain (p53) CHRISDORNEY/SHUTTERSTOCK ©

Holbein to Turner

It wasn't until the rule of the Tudors that art began to take off in London. The German Hans Holbein the Younger (1497–1543) was court painter to Henry VIII, and one of his finest works, *The Ambassadors* (1533), hangs in the National Gallery. A batch of great portrait artists worked at court during the 17th century, the best being Anthony Van Dyck (1599–1641), who painted *Charles I on Horseback* (1638), also in the National Gallery.

Local artists began to emerge in the 18th century, including landscapists Thomas Gainsborough (1727–88) and John Constable (1776–1837).

JMW Turner (1775–1851), equally at home with oils and watercolours, represented the pinnacle of 19th-century British art. His later works, including *Snow Storm – Steam-boat off a Harbour's Mouth* (1842) and *Rain, Steam and Speed – the Great Western Railway* (1844), now in the Tate Britain and the National Gallery, later inspired the Impressionist works of Claude Monet.

★ Best for British Art

Tate Britain (p53)

Tate Modern (p94)

National Gallery (p54)

National Portrait Gallery (p56)

Fourth Plinth Project (p61)

The Pre-Raphaelites to Hockney

The brief but splendid flowering of the Pre-Raphaelite Brotherhood (1848–54) with the likes of William Holman Hunt and John Everett Millais took its inspiration from the Romantic poets. The Tate Britain has the best selection of works from this period.

Sculptors Henry Moore (1898–1986) and Barbara Hepworth (1903–75) both typified the modernist movement in British sculpture (you can see examples of their work in Kensington Gardens).

After WWII, art transformed yet again. In 1945, the tortured, Irish-born painter Francis Bacon (1909–92) caused a stir when he exhibited his *Three Studies for Figures at the Base of a Crucifixion* – now on display at the Tate Britain – and afterwards continued to spook the art world with his repulsive yet mesmerising visions.

Australian art critic Robert Hughes once eulogised Bacon's contemporary, Lucian Freud (1922–2011), as 'the greatest living realist painter'. Freud's early work was often surrealist, but from the 1950s the bohemian Freud exclusively focused on pale, muted portraits.

London in the swinging 1960s was perfectly encapsulated by pop art, its vocabulary best articulated by the brilliant David Hockney (b 1937). Two of his most famous works, *Mr and Mrs Clark and Percy* (1971) and *A Bigger Splash* (1974), are displayed at the Tate Britain.

Brit Art & Beyond

Brit Art sprang from a show called *Freeze,* which was staged in a Docklands warehouse in 1988, organised by artist and showman Damien Hirst and largely featuring his fellow graduates from Goldsmiths' College. Influenced by pop culture and punk, Brit Art was brash, decadent, ironic, easy to grasp and eminently marketable. Hirst's *Mother & Child (Divided),* a cow and her calf sliced into sections and preserved in formaldehyde, and Tracey Emin's *My Bed,* the artist's unmade bed and the mess next to it, are seminal works from this era.

The best way to take the pulse of the British contemporary art scene is to attend the annual Summer Exhibition at the Royal Academy of Arts, which features works by established as well as unknown artists.

Survival Guide

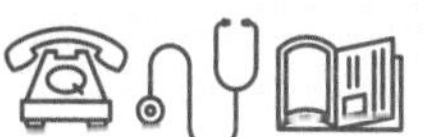

Directory A–Z

Customs Regulations

The UK distinguishes between goods bought duty-free outside the EU and those bought in another EU country, where taxes and duties will have already been paid.

If you exceed your duty-free allowance, you will have to pay tax on the items. For European goods, there is officially no limit to how much you can bring, but customs use certain guidelines to distinguish between personal and commercial use.

For details on limits and restrictions, see www.gov.uk/duty-free-goods.

Discount Cards

Of interest to visitors who want to take in lots of paid sights in a short time is the **London Pass** (www.londonpass.com; 1/2/3/6 days £52/71/85/116). The pass offers free entry and queue-jumping to all major attractions and can be altered to include use of the Underground and buses. Check the website for details.

Electricity

230V/50Hz

Emergency

Dial ☎999 to call the police, fire brigade or ambulance in the event of an emergency.

Gay & Lesbian Travellers

London has a thriving gay and lesbian community. Protection from discrimination is enshrined in law, but that's not to say that homophobia doesn't exist. Always report homophobic crimes to the police (☎999).

Soho and the East End (Shoreditch, Bethnal Green & Dalston) are London's most vibrant gay neighbourhoods. Vauxhall is where serious clubbing happens.

Useful Websites

60by80 (www.60by80.com/london)

Ginger Beer (www.gingerbeer.co.uk)

Jake (www.jaketm.com)

Time Out London LGBT (www.timeout.com/london/lgbt)

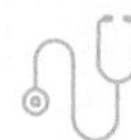

Health

Nationals of the EU can obtain free emergency treatment (and, in some cases, reduced-cost healthcare) on presentation of a **European Health Insurance Card** (www.ehic.org.uk).

Reciprocal arrangements with the UK allow Australians, New Zealanders and residents and nationals of several other countries to receive free emergency medical treatment and subsidised dental care through the **National Health Service** (NHS; ☎111; www.nhs.uk). They can use hospital emergency departments, GPs and dentists. For a full list, click on 'Services near you' on the NHS website.

Hospitals

A number of hospitals have 24-hour accident and emergency departments. However, in an emergency just call ☎999 and an ambulance will normally be dispatched from the hospital nearest to you.

University College London Hospital (☎020-3456 7890,

0845 155 5000; www.uclh.nhs.uk; 235 Euston Rd, NW1; ⊖Warren St, Euston) One of central London's busiest hospitals.

Guy's Hospital (☎020-7188 7188; www.guysandstthomas.nhs.uk; Great Maze Pond, SE1; ⊖London Bridge) Busy hospital near London Bridge.

Insurance

Travel insurance is advisable for non-EU residents as it offers greater flexibility over where and how you're treated and covers expenses for an ambulance and repatriation that will not be picked up by the NHS.

Pharmacies

The main pharmacy chains in London are Boots and Superdrug; a branch of either – or both – can be found on virtually every high street.

The Boots in **Piccadilly Circus** (☎020-7734 6126; www.boots.com; 44-46 Regent St, W1; ⏰8am-midnight Mon-Fri, 9am-midnight Sat, 12.30-6.30pm Sun; ⊖Piccadilly Circus) is one of the biggest and most centrally located and has extended opening times.

Internet Access

- Virtually every hotel in London now provides wi-fi free of charge (only a couple of budget places have it as an add-on). A number of hotels (and especially hostels) also provide guest computers and access to a printer.
- A huge number of cafes, and an increasing number of restaurants, offer free wi-fi to customers, including chains such as Starbucks, Costa and Pret a Manger, as well as McDonalds. Cultural venues such as the Barbican or the Southbank Centre also have free wi-fi.
- Most major train stations, airport terminals and even some Underground stations also have wi-fi, but access isn't always free.

Legal Matters

Should you face any legal difficulties while in London, visit a branch of the **Citizens Advice Bureau** (www.citizensadvice.org.uk) or contact your embassy.

Drugs

Illegal drugs of every type are widely available in London, especially in clubs. Nonetheless, all the usual drug warnings apply. Cannabis was downgraded to a Class C drug in 2004, but reclassified as a Class B drug in 2009 following a government rethink. If you're caught with pot today, you're likely to be arrested. Possession of harder drugs, including heroin and cocaine, is always treated seriously. Searches on entering clubs are common.

Fines

In general you rarely have to pay on the spot for an offence. The exceptions are trains, the tube and buses, where people who can't produce a valid ticket for the journey when asked to by an inspector can be fined then and there.

Money

Although it is a member of the EU, the UK has not adopted the euro and has retained the pound sterling (£) as its unit of currency. One pound sterling is made up of 100 pence (called 'pee', colloquially).

Notes come in denominations of £5, £10, £20 and £50, while coins are 1p ('penny'), 2p, 5p, 10p, 20p, 50p, £1 and £2.

ATMs

ATMs are everywhere and will generally accept Visa, MasterCard, Cirrus or Maestro cards, as well as more obscure ones. There is almost always a transaction surcharge for cash withdrawals with foreign cards.

Changing Money

- The best place to change money is in any local post office branch, where no commission is charged.
- You can also change money in most high-street banks and some travel agencies, as well as at the numerous bureaux de change throughout the city.

Practicalities

- **Smoking** Forbidden in all enclosed public places nationwide. Most pubs have some sort of smoking area outside.
- **Weights & Measures** The UK uses a confusing mix of metric and imperial systems.

Credit & Debit Cards

- Credit and debit cards are accepted almost universally in London, from restaurants and bars to shops and even by some taxis.
- American Express and Diners Club are far less widely used than Visa and MasterCard.
- Contactless cards and payments (which do not require a chip and pin or a signature) are increasingly widespread (watch for the wi-fi like symbol on cards and in shops). Contactless transactions are limited to a maximum of £30.

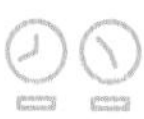

Opening Hours

Standard business hours are as follows:

Banks 9am to 5pm Monday to Friday

Bars & Pubs 11am to 11pm

Restaurants noon to 2.30pm and 6pm to 11pm

Sights 10am to 6pm

Shops 9am to 7pm Monday to Saturday, noon to 6pm Sunday

Public Holidays

Most attractions and businesses close for a couple of days over Christmas and sometimes over Easter. Places that normally shut on Sunday will probably close on bank holiday Mondays.

New Year's Day 1 January

Good Friday Late March/April

Easter Monday Late March/April

May Day Holiday First Monday in May

Spring Bank Holiday Last Monday in May

Summer Bank Holiday Last Monday in August

Christmas Day 25 December

Boxing Day 26 December

Safe Travel

London is a fairly safe city for its size, so exercising common sense should keep you secure.

If you're getting a cab after a night's clubbing, make sure you go for a black taxi or a licensed minicab firm. Many of the touts operating outside clubs and bars are unlicensed and can therefore be unsafe.

Pickpocketing does happen in London, so keep an eye on your handbag and wallet, especially in bars and nightclubs, and in crowded areas such as the Underground.

Telephone

British Telecom's famous red phone boxes survive in conservation areas only (notably Westminster).

Some BT phones still accept coins, but most take phonecards (available from retailers, including most post offices and some newsagents) or credit cards.

Mobile Phones

The UK uses the GSM 900 network, which covers Europe, Australia and New Zealand, but is not compatible with CDMA mobile technology used in the US and Japan (although some American and Japanese phones can work on both GSM and CDMA networks).

If you have a GSM phone, check with your service provider about using it in the UK and enquire about roaming charges.

It's usually better to buy a local SIM card from any mobile-phone shop, though in order to do that you must ensure your handset from home is unlocked.

Useful Numbers

Directory Enquiries (International)	☎118 505
Directory Enquiries (Local & National)	☎118 118, ☎118 500
International dialling code	☎00
Premium rate applies	☎09
Reverse charge/ collect calls	☎155
Special rates apply	☎084 and ☎087
Toll-free	☎0800

Time

London uses Greenwich Meridian Time (GMT) from late October to late March; it's British Summer Time (GMT +1) the rest of the year.

Toilets

It's an offence to urinate in the streets. Train stations, bus terminals and attractions generally have good facilities, providing also for people with disabilities and those with young children. You'll also find public toilets across the city, some operated by local councils, others automated and self-cleaning. Most now charge 50p.

Tourist Information

City of London Information Centre (www.visitthecity.co.uk; St Paul's Churchyard, EC4; ⌚9.30am-5.30pm Mon-Sat, 10am-4pm Sun; 📶; ⊖St Paul's) Tourist information, fast-track tickets to City attractions and guided walks (adult/child £7/6).

Greenwich Tourist Office (☎0870 608 2000; www.visitgreenwich.org.uk; Pepys House, 2 Cutty Sark Gardens, SE10; ⌚10am-5pm; 🚆DLR Cutty Sark) Has a wealth of information about Greenwich and the surrounding areas. Free daily guided walks leave at 12.15pm and 2.15pm.

Visit London (☎0870 156 6366; www.visitlondon.com) Visit London can fill you in on everything from tourist attractions and events (such as the Changing of the Guard and Chinese New Year parade) to river trips and tours, accommodation, eating, theatre, shopping, children's London, and gay and lesbian venues. There are helpful kiosks at the following:

Heathrow Airport (Terminal 1, 2 & 3 Underground station; ⌚7.30am-7.30pm)

King's Cross St Pancras Station (⌚8.15am-6.15pm)

Liverpool Street Station (⌚7.15am-7pm Sun-Thu, to 9pm Fri & Sat)

Piccadilly Circus Underground Station (⌚8am-7pm Mon-Fri, 9.15-6pm Sat & Sun)

Victoria Station (⌚7.15am-8pm Mon-Sat, 8.15am-7pm Sun).

Travellers with Disabilities

For travellers with disabilities, London is an odd mix of user-friendliness and downright disinterest. New hotels and modern tourist attractions are legally required to be accessible to people in wheelchairs, but many historic buildings, B&Bs and guesthouses are in older buildings, which are hard to adapt.

Transport is equally hit and miss, but slowly improving:

- Only 66 of London's 270 tube stations have step-free access; the rest have escalators or stairs.
- The above-ground DLR (Docklands Light Railway) is entirely accessible for wheelchairs.
- All buses can be lowered to street level when they stop; wheelchair users travel free.
- Guide dogs are universally welcome on public transport and in hotels, restaurants, attractions etc.

Transport for London (www.tfl.gov.uk) publishes the *Getting Around London* guide, which contains the latest information on accessibility for passengers with disabilities.

Visas

Visas are not required for US, Canadian, Australian or New Zealand visitors for stays of up to six months. European Union nationals can stay indefinitely. Check the website of the **UK Border Agency** (www.gov.uk/check-uk-visa) or with your local British embassy or consulate for the most up-to-date information.

Women Travellers

Female visitors to London are unlikely to have many problems, provided they take the usual big-city precautions. Don't get into an Underground carriage with no one else in it or with just one or two men. And if you feel unsafe, you should take a taxi or licensed minicab.

Apart from the occasional wolf whistle and unwelcome body contact on the tube, women will find male Londoners reasonably enlightened. Going into pubs alone may not always be a comfortable experience, though it is in no way out of the ordinary.

Transport

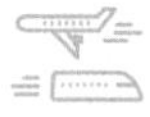

Arriving in London

Most people arrive in London by air, but an increasing number of visitors coming from Europe let the train take the strain, while buses from across the Continent are another option.

The city has five airports: Heathrow, Gatwick, Stansted, Luton and London City. Most trans-Atlantic flights land at Heathrow. Visitors from Europe are more likely to arrive at Gatwick, Stansted or Luton (the latter two are used exclusively by low-cost airlines such as easyJet and Ryanair).

Flights, cars and tours can be booked online at lonelyplanet.com.

Heathrow Airport

Some 15 miles west of central London, **Heathrow** (LHR; www.heathrowairport.com; 📶) is the world's busiest international airport and counts four terminals (numbered 2 to 5), including the totally revamped Terminal 2.

Train

Underground (www.tfl.gov.uk; one-way £5.10) Three Underground stations on the Piccadilly line serve Heathrow: one for Terminals 2 and 3, another for Terminal 4, and the terminus for Terminal 5. Commonly referred to as 'the tube', the Underground is the cheapest way of getting to Heathrow (one hour from central London, every three to nine minutes). It runs from just after 5am/5.45am from/to the airport to 11.45pm/12.30am (and all night Friday and Saturday, with reduced frequency). Buy tickets at the station.

Heathrow Express (www.heathrowexpress.com; one way/return £21.50/35) This high-speed train whisks passengers from Heathrow Central station (serving Terminals 2 and 3) and Terminal 5 to Paddington in just 15 minutes. Terminal 4 passengers should take the free inter-terminal shuttle train available to Heathrow Central and board there. Trains run every 15 minutes from just after 5am in both directions to around 11.30pm.

Heathrow Connect (www.heathrowconnect.com; adult £10.10) Travelling between Heathrow and Paddington station, this modern passenger train service departs every 30 minutes and makes five stops en route. The journey takes about 30 minutes. The first trains leave around 5am (7am Sunday) and the last service is just before midnight.

Bus

National Express (www.nationalexpress.com) Coaches link the Heathrow Central bus station with Victoria coach station (one-way from £5.50, 35 to 90 minutes, every 30 minutes to one hour).

Climate Change & Travel

Every form of transport that relies on carbon-based fuel generates CO_2, the main cause of human-induced climate change. Modern travel is dependent on aeroplanes, which might use less fuel per kilometre per person than most cars but travel much greater distances. The altitude at which aircraft emit gases (including CO_2) and particles also contributes to their climate change impact. Many websites offer 'carbon calculators' that allow people to estimate the carbon emissions generated by their journey and, for those who wish to do so, to offset the impact of the greenhouse gases emitted with contributions to portfolios of climate-friendly initiatives throughout the world. Lonely Planet offsets the carbon footprint of all staff and author travel.

Transport for London (www.tfl.gov.uk) At night, the N9 bus (£1.50, 1¼ hours, every 20 minutes) connects Heathrow with central London, teminating at Aldwych.

Taxi

A metered black cab trip to/from central London will cost between £45 and £85 and take 45 minutes to an hour, depending on traffic and your departure point.

Gatwick Airport

Located some 30 miles south of central London, **Gatwick** (LGW; www.gatwickairport.com; 📶) is smaller than Heathrow. The North and South Terminals are linked by a 24-hour shuttle train, with the journey time about three minutes.

Train

National Rail (www.nationalrail.co.uk) Has regular train services to/from London Bridge (30 minutes, every 15 to 30 minutes), London King's Cross (55 minutes, every 15 to 30 minutes) and London Victoria (30 minutes, every 10 to 15 minutes). Fares vary depending on the time of travel and the train company, but allow £10 to £20 for a single.

Gatwick Express (www.gatwickexpress.com; one-way/return £19.90/34.90) This dedicated train service links the station near the South Terminal with Victoria station in central London every 15 minutes. From the airport, there are services between 4.30am and 1.35am. From Victoria, they leave between 3.30am and just after 12.30am. The journey takes 30 minutes.

Bus

National Express (www.nationalexpress.com) Coaches (one-way from £5, 80 minutes to two hours) run throughout the day from Gatwick to Victoria coach station. Services leave hourly around the clock.

EasyBus (www.easybus.co.uk) Runs 19-seater minibuses to Gatwick every 15 to 20 minutes on two routes: one from Earl's Court/West Brompton and one from Waterloo (one-way from £4.95). The service runs from 3am to 11pm daily. Journey time averages 75 minutes.

Taxi

A metered black cab trip to/from central London costs around £100 and takes just over an hour. Minicabs are usually cheaper.

Stansted Airport

Stansted (STN; www.stanstedairport.com; 📶) is 35 miles northeast of central London in the direction of Cambridge.

Train

Stansted Express (☎0845 8500150; www.stanstedexpress.com; one-way/return £19/32) This rail service (45 minutes, every 15 to 30 minutes) links the airport and Liverpool St station. From the airport, the first train leaves at 5.30am, the last at 1.30am (12.30am on Saturday). Trains depart Liverpool St station from 4.10am to just before 11.30pm.

Bus

National Express (www.nationalexpress.com) Coaches run around the clock, offering well over 100 services per day. The A6 runs to Victoria coach station (one-way from £12, 85 minutes to more than two hours, every 20 minutes) via North London. The A9 runs to Liverpool St station (one-way from £10, 60 to 80 minutes, every 30 minutes).

EasyBus (www.easybus.co.uk) Runs services to Baker St and Old

St tube stations every 15 minutes. The journey (one-way from £4.95) takes one hour from Old St, 1¼ hours from Baker St.

Terravision (www.terravision.eu) Coaches link Stansted to both Liverpool St train station (bus A51, one-way/return from £8/14, 55 minutes) and Victoria coach station (bus A50, one-way/return from £9/15, 75 minutes) every 20 to 40 minutes between 6am and 1am.

Taxi

A metered black cab trip to/from central London costs around £130. Minicabs are cheaper.

Luton Airport

A smallish airport 32 miles northwest of London, **Luton** (LTN; www.london-luton.co.uk) generally caters for cheap charter flights and discount airlines.

Train

National Rail (www.nationalrail.co.uk) Services (one-way from £14, 35 to 50 minutes, every six to 30 minutes, from 7am to 10pm) run from London Bridge and London King's Cross stations to Luton Airport Parkway station, from where an airport shuttle bus (one-way £1.60) will take you to the airport in 10 minutes.

Bus

EasyBus (www.easybus.co.uk) Minibuses run between Victoria coach station and Luton (one-way from £4.95) every half-hour round the clock. Another route links the airport with Liverpool St station (every 15 to 30 minutes).

Green Line Bus 757 (www.greenline.co.uk; one-way/return £10/15) Buses from/to Luton (75 to 90 minutes) run to/from Victoria coach station, leaving approximately every half-hour round the clock.

Taxi

A metered black cab trip to/from central London costs about £110.

London City Airport

Its proximity to central London, which is just 6 miles to the east, as well as to the commercial district of the Docklands, means **London City Airport** (LCY; www.londoncityairport.com; wi-fi) is predominantly a gateway airport for business travellers. You can also now fly to New York from here.

Train

Docklands Light Railway (DLR; www.tfl.gov.uk/dlr) Stops at the London City Airport station (one-way £2.80 to £3.30). The journey to Bank takes just over 20 minutes, and trains go every eight to 10 minutes from just after 5.30am to 12.15am Monday to Saturday, and 7am to 11.15pm Sunday.

Taxi

A metered black cab trip to or from the City/Oxford St costs about £25/35.

St Pancras International Train Station

St Pancras, the arrival point for **Eurostar** (www.eurostar.com) trains from Europe, is

c
gro
of the

Getting Ar

Public transport in L is extensive, often exc and always pricey. It is managed by **Transport for London** (www.tfl.gov.uk), which has a user-friendly, multilingual website with a journey planner, maps, detailed information on every mode of transport in the capital and live updates on traffic.

The cheapest way to get around London is with an Oyster Card or a UK contactless card (foreign card holders should check for contactless charges first). Paper tickets still exist and, although day travel cards cost the same on paper as on Oyster or contactless card, using paper singles or returns is substantially more expensive than using an Oyster.

The tube, DLR and Overground network are ideal for zooming across different parts of the city; buses and the Santander Cycles are great for shorter journeys.

Left-luggage facility **Excess Baggage** (www.left-baggage.co.uk) operates at London's main train stations: St Pancras, Paddington, Euston, Victoria, Waterloo, King's Cross, Liverpool St and Charing Cross. Allow £10 per 24-hour slot.

… you can store … velcards valid … ds are valid … London. … touch … le with … touch … luct the … rd. For bus … once upon boarding. … bought (£5 refundable deposit … d topped up at any Underground station, … vel information centre or shop displaying the Oyster logo. To get your deposit back along with any remaining credit, simply return your Oyster Card at a ticket booth.

Contactless cards (which do not require chip and pin or a signature) can now be used directly on Oyster Card readers and are subject to the same Oyster fares. The advantage is that you don't have to bother with buying, topping up and then returning an Oyster Card, but foreign visitors should bear in mind the cost of card transactions.

London Underground

The London Underground ('the tube'; 11 colour-coded lines) is part of an integrated transport system that also includes the Docklands Light Railway (DLR; a driverless overhead train operating in the eastern part of the city) and Overground network (mostly outside of Zone 1 and sometimes underground). Despite the never-ending upgrades and 'engineering works' requiring weekend closures, it is overall the quickest and easiest way of getting around the city, if not the cheapest.

The first trains operate from around 5.30am Monday to Saturday and 6.45am Sunday. The last trains leave around 12.30am Monday to Saturday and 11.30pm Sunday.

Additionally, selected lines (the Victoria and Jubilee lines, plus most of the Piccadilly, Central and Northern lines) run all night on Fridays and Saturdays to get revellers home, with trains every 10 minutes or so.

During weekend closures, schedules, maps and alternative route suggestions are posted in every station, and staff are at hand to help redirect you.

Some stations, most famously Leicester Square and Covent Garden, are much closer in reality than they appear on the map.

Fares

- London is divided into nine concentric fare zones. A single/day pass in Zones 1-2 costs £2.30/£6.40.
- Children under the age of 11 travel free; those ages 11 to 15 are half-price if registered on an accompanying adult's Oyster Card (register at Zone 1 or Heathrow tube stations).

Bus

London's ubiquitous red double-decker buses afford great views of the city, but be aware that the going can be slow. Bus services normally operate from 5am to 11.30pm.

There are excellent bus maps at every stop detailing all routes and destinations served from that particular area.

Night Bus

More than 50 night bus routes (prefixed with the letter 'N') run from around 11.30pm to 5am.

There are also another 60 bus routes operating 24 hours; the frequency decreases between 11pm and 5am.

Fares

- Cash cannot be used on London's buses. Pay with an Oyster Card, Travelcard or a contactless payment card.
- Bus fares are a flat £1.50, no matter the distance travelled.

- Children under 11 travel free; those aged 11 to 15 years are half-price if registered on an accompanying adult's Oyster Card (register at Zone 1 or Heathrow tube stations).

Taxi

Black Cabs

The black cab is as much a feature of the London cityscape as the red double-decker bus.

- Cabs are available for hire when the yellow sign above the windscreen is lit; just stick your arm out to signal one.
- Fares are metered, with a flagfall charge of £2.40 (covering the first 310m during a weekday), rising by increments of 20p for each subsequent 168m.
- Fares are more expensive in the evenings and overnight.
- Apps such as **Hailo** (www.hailocab.com) or **Black Cabs App** (www.blackcabsapp.com) use your smartphone's GPS to locate the nearest black cab to you. You only pay the metered fare.

Minicabs

- Minicabs, which are licensed, are cheaper (usually) competitors of black cabs.
- Unlike black cabs, minicabs cannot legally be hailed on the street; they must be hired by phone or through a dispatcher.
- Minicabs don't have meters; there's usually a fare set by the dispatcher. Make sure you ask before setting off.
- Your hotel or host (or restaurant/nightclub) will be able to recommend a reputable minicab company, or phone a large 24-hour operator such as **Addison Lee** (☎020 7407 9000; www.addisonlee.com).
- Apps such as **Uber** (www uber.com) or **Kabbee** (www.kabbee.com) allow you to book a minicab in double-quick time.

Boat

Thames Clippers (www.thamesclippers.com; adult/child £6.50/3.25) is a fast and pleasant boat service. Boats run every 20 minutes from 6am to between 10pm and 11pm. The route goes from London Eye Millennium Pier to Woolwich Arsenal Pier, serving the London Eye, Tate Modern, Shakespeare's Globe, Borough Market, Tower Bridge, Canary Wharf, Greenwich and the O2.

Bicycle

The Santander Cycle Hire Scheme (p204) is a great and affordable way to get around London.

Behind the Scenes

Acknowledgements

Climate map data adapted from Peel MC, Finlayson BL & McMahon TA (2007) 'Updated World Map of the Koppen-Geiger Climate Classification', *Hydrology and Earth System Sciences*, 11, 163344.

This Book

This book was curated by Emilie Filou, who also researched and wrote for it along with Peter Dragicevich, Steve Fallon and Damian Harper.

This guidebook was commissioned in Lonely Planet's Melbourne office, and produced by the following:
Destination Editor James Smart
Series Designer Katherine Marsh
Cartographic Series Designer Wayne Murphy
Associate Product Director Liz Heynes
Senior Product Editor Catherine Naghten
Product Editor Jenna Myers
Book Designer Virginia Moreno
Cartographer Julie Dodkins
Assisting Editors Victoria Harrison, Charlotte Orr, Gabrielle Stefanos, Saralinda Turner
Cover Researchers Campbell McKenzie, Naomi Parker
Thanks to Indra Kilfoyle, Anne Mason, Kate Mathews, Susan Paterson, Kirsten Rawlings, Alison Ridgway, Kathryn Rowan, Dianne Schallmeiner, Luna Soo, Angela Tinson

Send Us Your Feedback

We love to hear from travellers – your comments keep us on our toes and help make our books better. Our well-travelled team reads every word on what you loved or loathed about this book. Although we cannot reply individually to postal submissions, we always guarantee that your feedback goes straight to the appropriate authors, in time for the next edition. Each person who sends us information is thanked in the next edition, the most useful submissions are rewarded with a selection of digital PDF chapters.

Visit lonelyplanet.com/contact to submit your updates and suggestions or to ask for help. Our award-winning website also features inspirational travel stories, news and discussions.

Note: We may edit, reproduce and incorporate your comments in Lonely Planet products such as guidebooks, websites and digital products, so let us know if you don't want your comments reproduced or your name acknowledged. For a copy of our privacy policy visit lonelyplanet.com/privacy.

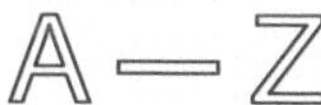

Index

000 Map pages

000 Map pages

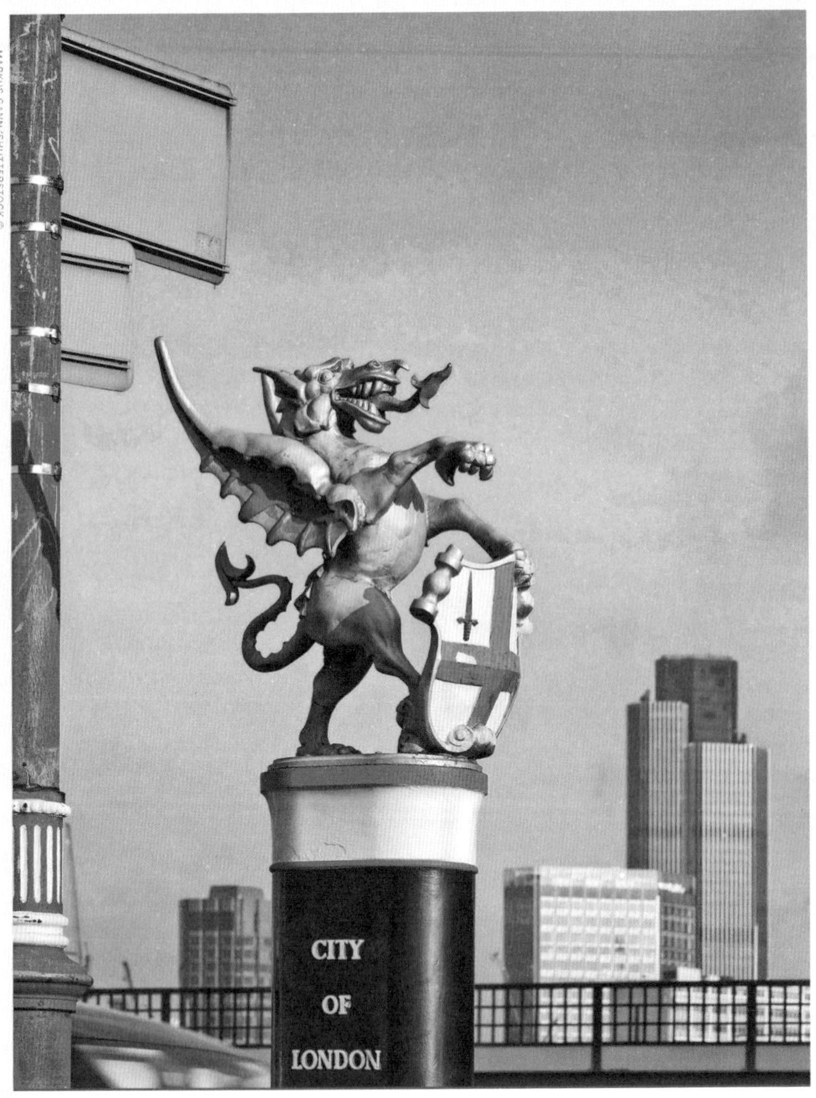

MARKUS GANN/SHUTTERSTOCK ©

London Maps

Kensington & Hyde Park

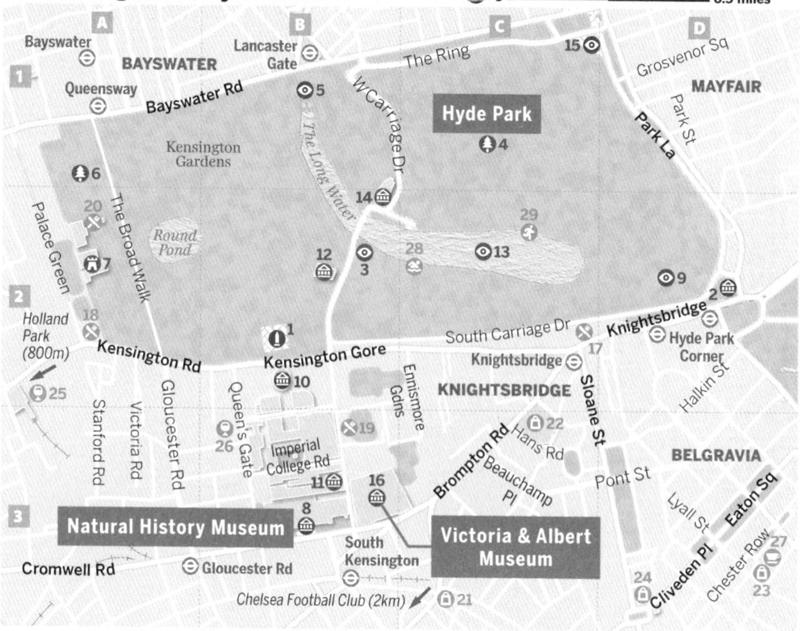

Sights
1 Albert Memorial B2
2 Apsley House D2
3 Diana, Princess of Wales Memorial Fountain B2
4 Hyde Park C1
5 Italian Gardens B1
6 Kensington Gardens A1
7 Kensington Palace A2
8 Natural History Museum B3
9 Rose Garden D2
10 Royal Albert Hall B2
11 Science Museum B3
12 Serpentine Galleries B2
13 Serpentine Lake C2
14 Serpentine Sackler Gallery B2
15 Speakers' Corner C1
16 Victoria & Albert Museum B3

Eating
17 Dinner by Heston Blumenthal C2
Magazine .... (see 14)
18 Min Jiang A2
19 Ognisko B3
20 Orangery A2

Shopping
21 Conran Shop C3
22 Harrods C3
23 Jo Loves D3
24 Pickett D3

Drinking & Nightlife
25 Kensington Roof Gardens A2
26 Queen's Arms B3
27 Tomtom Coffee House D3

Entertainment
Royal Albert Hall .... (see 10)

Activities, Courses & Tours
28 Serpentine Lido C2
29 Serpentine Solar Shuttle Boat C2

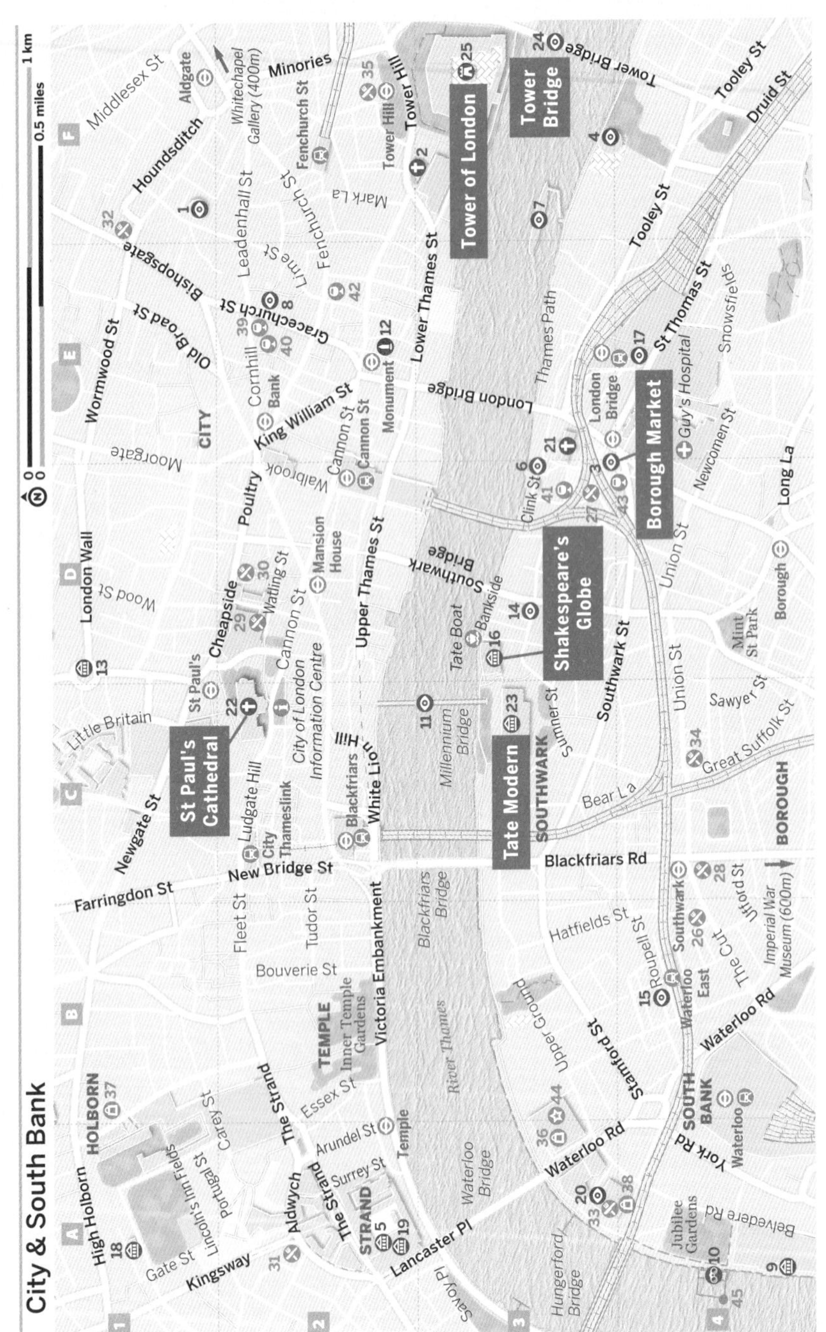
City & South Bank
0.5 miles
1 km
St Paul's Cathedral
Tate Modern
Shakespeare's Globe
Borough Market
Tower of London
Tower Bridge
HOLBORN
TEMPLE
STRAND
CITY
SOUTHWARK
SOUTH BANK
BOROUGH
High Holborn
Kingsway
Aldwych
The Strand
Lincoln's Inn Fields
Gate St
Portugal St
Carey St
Essex St
Arundel St
Surrey St
Temple
Inner Temple Gardens
Victoria Embankment
Lancaster Pl
Savoy Pl
Waterloo Bridge
Hungerford Bridge
River Thames
Blackfriars Bridge
Farringdon St
New Bridge St
Fleet St
Tudor St
Bouverie St
Newgate St
Little Britain
Ludgate Hill
City Thameslink
Blackfriars
White Lion Hill
City of London Information Centre
St Paul's
Cheapside
Cannon St
Watling St
Upper Thames St
London Wall
Wood St
Mansion House
Poultry
Walbrook
Moorgate
King William St
Cannon St
Monument
Bank
Cornhill
Wormwood St
Old Broad St
Bishopsgate
Gracechurch St
Lime St
Fenchurch St
Leadenhall St
Mark La
Lower Thames St
London Bridge
Houndsditch
Middlesex St
Aldgate
Whitechapel Gallery (400m)
Minories
Fenchurch St
Tower Hill
Millennium Bridge
Southwark Bridge
Tate Boat
Bankside
Thames Path
Clink St
Sumner St
Southwark St
Bear La
Blackfriars Rd
Hatfields St
Upper Ground
Stamford St
Roupell St
Waterloo
Waterloo East
Southwark
The Cut
Ufford St
Imperial War Museum (600m)
Waterloo Rd
York Rd
Belvedere Rd
Jubilee Gardens
Union St
Great Suffolk St
Sawyer St
Mint St Park
Borough
Long La
Newcomen St
Guy's Hospital
Snowsfields
St Thomas St
Tooley St
Druid St
Tower Bridge

City & South Bank

Sights

1 30 St Mary Axe F1
2 All Hallows by the Tower F3
3 Borough Market D3
4 City Hall F3
5 Courtauld Gallery A2
6 Golden Hinde D3
7 HMS Belfast F3
8 Leadenhall Market E2
9 London Dungeon A4
10 London Eye A4
11 Millennium Bridge C3
12 Monument E2
13 Museum of London D1
14 Rose Theatre D3
15 Roupell Street B4
16 Shakespeare's Globe D3
17 Shard E4
18 Sir John Soane's Museum A1
19 Somerset House A2
20 Southbank Centre A3
21 Southwark Cathedral E3
22 St Paul's Cathedral C2
23 Tate Modern C3
24 Tower Bridge F3
25 Tower of London F3

Eating

26 Anchor & Hope B4
27 Arabica Bar & Kitchen D3
28 Baltic C4
29 Bea's of Bloomsbury D2
30 Café Below D2
31 Counter A2
Crypt Café .... (see 22)
Delaunay .... (see 31)
32 Duck & Waffle F1
Restaurant at St Paul's .... (see 22)
33 Skylon A3
34 Union Street Cafe C4
35 Wine Library F2

Shopping

36 National Theatre Gift Shop A3
37 Silver Vaults B1
38 Southbank Centre Shop A4

Drinking & Nightlife

39 Counting House E2
40 Jamaica Wine House E2
Oblix .... (see 17)
41 Rake D3
42 Sky Pod E2
Skylon .... (see 33)
43 Wine Pantry D4

Entertainment

44 National Theatre B3
Royal Festival Hall .... (see 20)
Shakespeare's Globe .... (see 16)
Southbank Centre .... (see 20)

Activities, Courses & Tours

45 London RIB Voyages A4

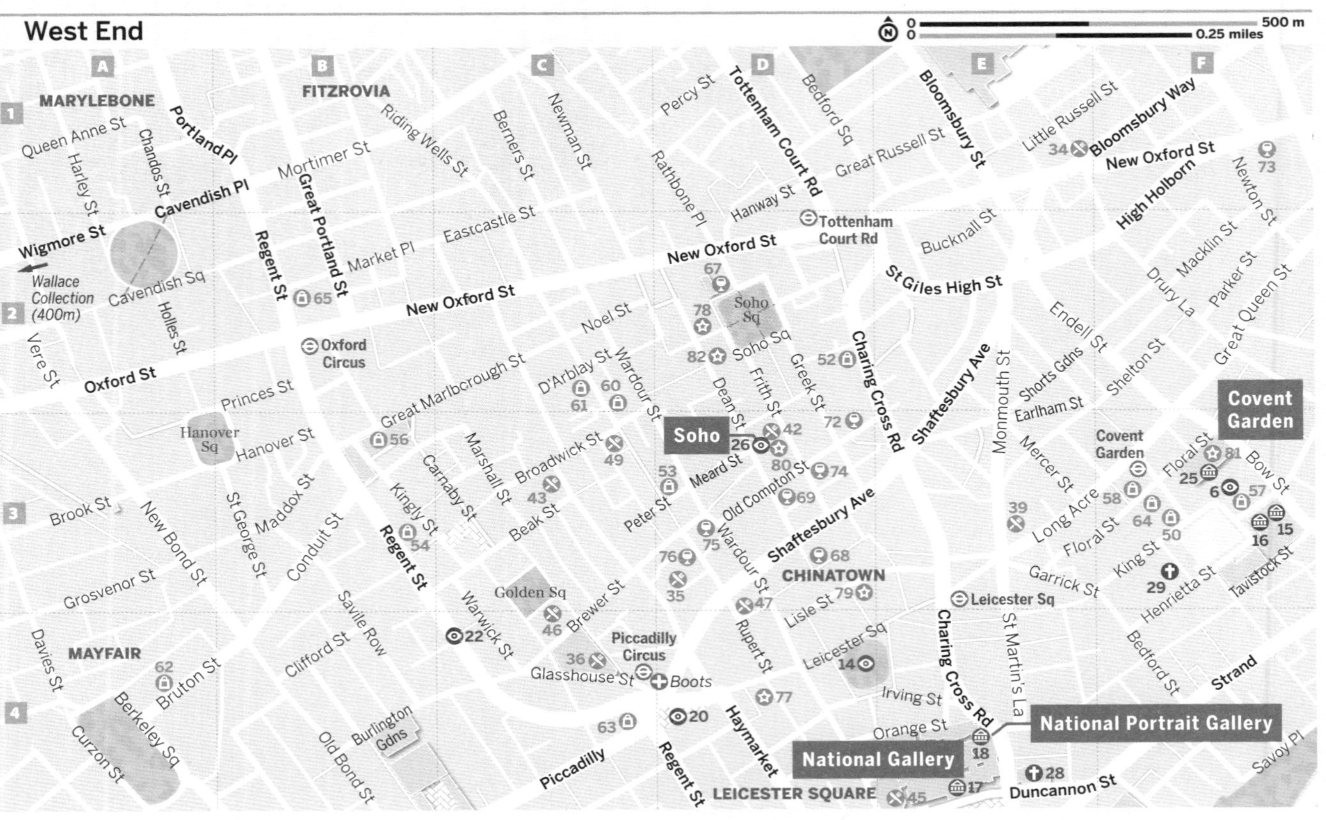
West End
500 m
0.25 miles
MARYLEBONE
FITZROVIA
Soho
CHINATOWN
MAYFAIR
LEICESTER SQUARE
Covent Garden
National Portrait Gallery
National Gallery
Wallace Collection (400m)
Oxford Circus
Tottenham Court Rd
Piccadilly Circus
Leicester Sq
Covent Garden
Boots
Queen Anne St
Harley St
Chandos St
Portland Pl
Cavendish Pl
Wigmore St
Cavendish Sq
Holles St
Vere St
Oxford St
Regent St
Great Portland St
Mortimer St
Riding Wells St
Berners St
Newman St
Market Pl
Eastcastle St
New Oxford St
Percy St
Rathbone Pl
Hanway St
Tottenham Court Rd
Bedford Sq
Great Russell St
Bloomsbury St
Little Russell St
Bloomsbury Way
New Oxford St
High Holborn
Newton St
Bucknall St
St Giles High St
Macklin St
Drury La
Parker St
Great Queen St
Endell St
Shelton St
Shorts Gdns
Earlham St
Monmouth St
Shaftesbury Ave
Charing Cross Rd
Soho Sq
Greek St
Frith St
Dean St
Noel St
Wardour St
D'Arblay St
Great Marlborough St
Princes St
Hanover Sq
Hanover St
Broadwick St
Marshall St
Carnaby St
Kingly St
Beak St
Meard St
Peter St
Old Compton St
Shaftesbury Ave
Wardour St
Lisle St
Rupert St
Leicester Sq
Irving St
Orange St
Charing Cross Rd
St Martin's La
Mercer St
Long Acre
Floral St
Bow St
King St
Garrick St
Henrietta St
Tavistock St
Bedford St
Strand
Savoy Pl
Duncannon St
Brook St
New Bond St
St George St
Maddox St
Conduit St
Grosvenor St
Savile Row
Golden Sq
Warwick St
Brewer St
Glasshouse St
Clifford St
Davies St
Bruton St
Berkeley Sq
Curzon St
Burlington Gdns
Old Bond St
Piccadilly
Haymarket

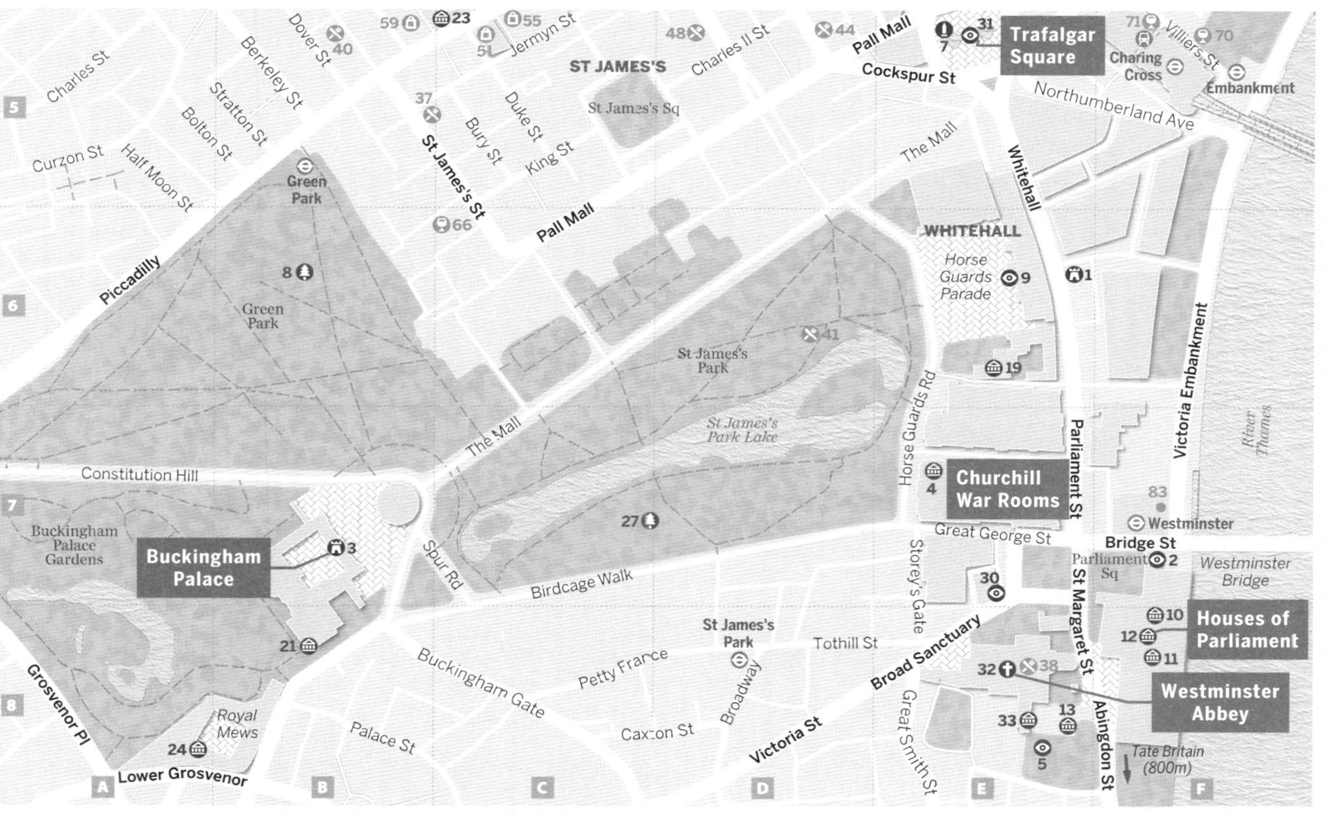

Trafalgar Square
Houses of Parliament
Westminster Abbey
Churchill War Rooms
Buckingham Palace
River Thames
Westminster Bridge
Victoria Embankment
Embankment
Villiers St
Charing Cross
Northumberland Ave
Whitehall
WHITEHALL
Horse Guards Parade
Horse Guards Rd
Parliament St
Bridge St
Westminster
Parliament Sq
St Margaret St
Abingdon St
Tate Britain (800m)
Great George St
Storey's Gate
Broad Sanctuary
Great Smith St
Tothill St
Victoria St
St James's Park
Broadway
Caxton St
Petty France
Birdcage Walk
St James's Park Lake
Buckingham Gate
Palace St
Spur Rd
The Mall
Pall Mall
Cockspur St
Charles II St
ST JAMES'S
St James's Sq
Jermyn St
Duke St
King St
Bury St
St James's St
Dover St
Berkeley St
Stratton St
Bolton St
Half Moon St
Curzon St
Charles St
Piccadilly
Green Park
Constitution Hill
Buckingham Palace Gardens
Royal Mews
Lower Grosvenor
Grosvenor Pl
A
B
C
D
E
F
5
6
7
8

West End

Sights
1 Banqueting House E6
2 Big Ben F7
3 Buckingham Palace B7
4 Churchill War Rooms E7
5 College Garden E8
6 Covent Garden Piazza F3
7 Fourth Plinth Project E5
8 Green Park B6
9 Horse Guards Parade E6
10 House of Commons F8
11 House of Lords F8
12 Houses of Parliament F8
13 Jewel Tower E8
14 Leicester Square D4
15 London Film Museum F3
16 London Transport Museum F3
17 National Gallery E4
18 National Portrait Gallery E4
19 No 10 Downing Street E6
20 Piccadilly Circus D4
21 Queen's Gallery B8
22 Regent Street C4
23 Royal Academy of Arts C5
24 Royal Mews A8
25 Royal Opera House F3
26 Soho D3
27 St James's Park C7
28 St Martin-in-the-Fields E4
29 St Paul's Church F3
30 Supreme Court E7
31 Trafalgar Square E5
32 Westminster Abbey E8
33 Westminster Abbey Museum E8

Eating
34 Abeno E1
35 Bocca di Lupo D3
36 Brasserie Zédel C4
37 Cafe Murano B5
38 Cellarium E8
39 Dishoom E3
40 Gymkhana B5
41 Inn the Park D6
42 Koya D3
43 Mildreds C3
44 Mint Leaf D5
45 National Dining Rooms E4
46 Nordic Bakery C4
47 Palomar D3
Portrait .... (see 18)
48 Shoryu D5
49 Yauatcha C3

Shopping
50 Cambridge Satchel Company F3
51 Fortnum & Mason C5
52 Foyles D2
53 Gosh! D3
54 Hamleys B3
55 Hatchards C5
56 Liberty B3
57 Molton Brown F3
58 Paul Smith F3
59 Penhaligon's B5
Ray's Jazz .... (see 52)
60 Reckless Records C2
61 Sister Ray C2
62 Stella McCartney A4
63 Sting C4
64 Ted Baker F3
65 Topshop B2

Drinking & Nightlife
66 Dukes Bar C6
67 Edge D2
68 Experimental Cocktail Club D3
69 French House D3
70 Gordon's Wine Bar F5
71 Heaven F5
72 LAB D3
73 Princess Louise F1
74 She Soho D3
75 Village D3
76 Yard D3

Entertainment
77 Comedy Store D4
78 Pizza Express Jazz Club D2
79 Prince Charles D3
80 Ronnie Scott's D3
81 Royal Opera House F3
82 Soho Theatre D2

Activities, Courses & Tours
83 Guided Tour F7

Shoreditch & Spitalfields

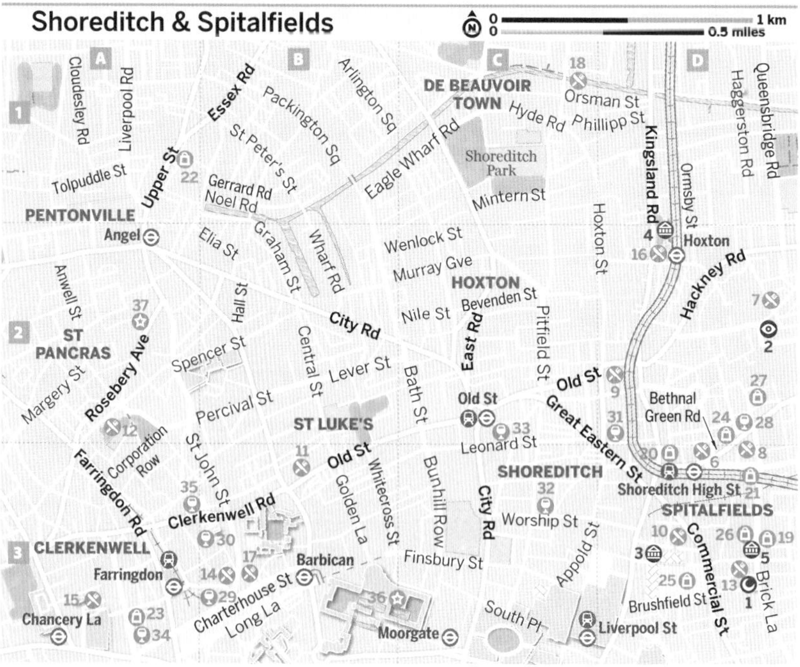

0 — 1 km
0 — 0.5 miles

Sights

1 Brick Lane Great Mosque........D3
2 Columbia Road Flower Market........D2
3 Dennis Severs' House........D3
4 Geffrye Museum........D2
5 Old Truman Brewery........D3

Eating

6 Allpress Espresso........D3
7 Brawn........D2
8 Brick Lane Beigel Bake........D3
9 Clove Club........D2
10 Hawksmoor........D3
11 Look Mum No Hands!........B3
12 Medcalf........A2
Morito........(see 12)
13 Nude Espresso........D3
14 Polpo........B3
15 Prufrock Coffee........A3
16 Sông Quê........D2
17 St John........B3
18 Towpath........C1

Shopping

19 Backyard Market........D3
20 Boxpark........D3
21 Brick Lane Market........D3
22 Camden Passage Market........A1
23 Hatton Garden........A3
24 Labour & Wait........D2
25 Old Spitalfields Market........D3
26 Rough Trade East........D3
Sunday UpMarket........(see 26)
27 Tatty Devine........D2

Drinking & Nightlife

93 Feet East........(see 19)
28 BrewDog........D2
29 Fabric........B3
30 Jerusalem Tavern........B3
31 Old Blue Last........D2
32 Worship St Whistling Shop........C3
33 XOYO........C2
34 Ye Olde Mitre........A3
35 Zetter Townhouse Cocktail Lounge........A3

Entertainment

36 Barbican........B3
37 Sadler's Wells........A2

North London

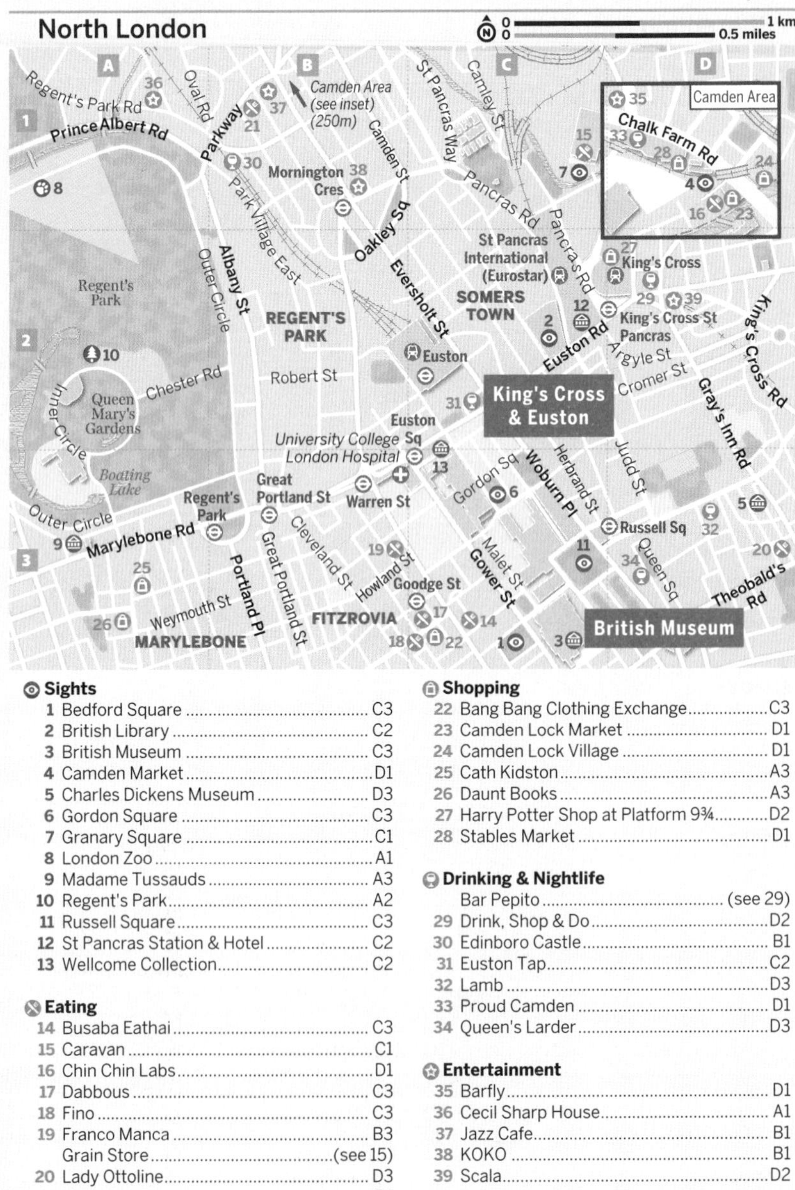

Sights
1 Bedford Square ... C3
2 British Library ... C2
3 British Museum ... C3
4 Camden Market ... D1
5 Charles Dickens Museum ... D3
6 Gordon Square ... C3
7 Granary Square ... C1
8 London Zoo ... A1
9 Madame Tussauds ... A3
10 Regent's Park ... A2
11 Russell Square ... C3
12 St Pancras Station & Hotel ... C2
13 Wellcome Collection ... C2

Eating
14 Busaba Eathai ... C3
15 Caravan ... C1
16 Chin Chin Labs ... D1
17 Dabbous ... C3
18 Fino ... C3
19 Franco Manca ... B3
Grain Store ... (see 15)
20 Lady Ottoline ... D3
21 Market ... B1

Shopping
22 Bang Bang Clothing Exchange ... C3
23 Camden Lock Market ... D1
24 Camden Lock Village ... D1
25 Cath Kidston ... A3
26 Daunt Books ... A3
27 Harry Potter Shop at Platform 9¾ ... D2
28 Stables Market ... D1

Drinking & Nightlife
Bar Pepito ... (see 29)
29 Drink, Shop & Do ... D2
30 Edinboro Castle ... B1
31 Euston Tap ... C2
32 Lamb ... D3
33 Proud Camden ... D1
34 Queen's Larder ... D3

Entertainment
35 Barfly ... D1
36 Cecil Sharp House ... A1
37 Jazz Cafe ... B1
38 KOKO ... B1
39 Scala ... D2

Symbols & Map Key

Look for these symbols to quickly identify listings:

- Sights
- Activities
- Courses
- Tours
- Festivals & Events
- Eating
- Drinking
- Entertainment
- Shopping
- Information & Transport

These symbols and abbreviations give vital information for each listing:

Sustainable or green recommendation

FREE No payment required

- Telephone number
- Opening hours
- Parking
- Nonsmoking
- Air-conditioning
- Internet access
- Wi-fi access
- Swimming pool
- Bus
- Ferry
- Tram
- Train
- English-language menu
- Vegetarian selection
- Family-friendly

Find your best experiences with these Great For... icons.

Budget

Short Trip

Food & Drink

Detour

Drinking

Walking

Cycling

Local Life

Shopping

History

Sport

Entertainment

Art & Culture

Beaches

Events

Winter Travel

Photo Op

Cafe/Coffee

Scenery

Nature & Wildlife

Family Travel

Sights

- Beach
- Bird Sanctuary
- Buddhist
- Castle/Palace
- Christian
- Confucian
- Hindu
- Islamic
- Jain
- Jewish
- Monument
- Museum/Gallery/Historic Building
- Ruin
- Shinto
- Sikh
- Taoist
- Winery/Vineyard
- Zoo/Wildlife Sanctuary
- Other Sight

Points of Interest

- Bodysurfing
- Camping
- Cafe
- Canoeing/Kayaking
- Course/Tour
- Diving
- Drinking & Nightlife
- Eating
- Entertainment
- Sento Hot Baths/Onsen
- Shopping
- Skiing
- Sleeping
- Snorkelling
- Surfing
- Swimming/Pool
- Walking
- Windsurfing
- Other Activity

Information

- Bank
- Embassy/Consulate
- Hospital/Medical
- Internet
- Police
- Post Office
- Telephone
- Toilet
- Tourist Information
- Other Information

Geographic

- Beach
- Gate
- Hut/Shelter
- Lighthouse
- Lookout
- Mountain/Volcano
- Oasis
- Park
- Pass
- Picnic Area
- Waterfall

Transport

- Airport
- BART station
- Border crossing
- Boston T station
- Bus
- Cable car/Funicular
- Cycling
- Ferry
- Metro/MRT station
- Monorail
- Parking
- Petrol station
- Subway/S-Bahn/Skytrain station
- Taxi
- Train station/Railway
- Tram
- Tube Station
- Underground/U-Bahn station
- Other Transport

Our Story

A beat-up old car, a few dollars in the pocket and a sense of adventure. In 1972 that's all Tony and Maureen Wheeler needed for the trip of a lifetime – across Europe and Asia overland to Australia. It took several months, and at the end – broke but inspired – they sat at their kitchen table writing and stapling together their first travel guide, *Across Asia on the Cheap*. Within a week they'd sold 1500 copies. Lonely Planet was born. Today, Lonely Planet has offices in Dublin, Melbourne, London, Oakland, Franklin, Delhi and Beijing, with more than 600 staff and writers. We share Tony's belief that 'a great guidebook should do three things: inform, educate and amuse'.

Our Writers

Emilie Filou

Emilie was born in Paris, where she lived until she was 18. Following her three-year degree and three gap years, she found herself in London, fell in love with the place and never really left. She now works as a journalist specialising in Africa and makes regular trips to the region from her home in northeast London. You can see her work on www.emiliefilou.com; she tweets at @EmilieFilou.

Peter Dragicevich

After a dozen years reviewing music and restaurants for publications in New Zealand and Australia, London's bright lights and loud guitars could no longer be resisted. Like all good Kiwis, Peter got to know the city while surfing his way between friends' flats all over London before finally putting down roots in North London.

Steve Fallon

After a full 15 years living in the centre of the known universe – East London – Steve cockney-rhymes in his sleep, eats jellied eel for brekkie, drinks lager by the bucketful and dances round the occasional handbag. As always, for his research he did everything the hard/fun way: walking the walks, seeing the sights, taking (some) advice from friends, colleagues and the odd taxi driver and digesting everything in sight.

Damian Harper

Born off the Strand within earshot of Bow Bells (favourable wind permitting), Damian grew up in Notting Hill way before it was discovered by Hollywood. A onetime Shakespeare and Company bookseller and radio presenter, Damian has been authoring guidebooks for Lonely Planet since the late 1990s. He lives in South London with his wife and two kids, frequently returning to China (his second home).

EUROPE Unit E, Digital Court, The Digital Hub, Rainsford St, Dublin 8, Ireland

AUSTRALIA Levels 2 & 3 551 Swanston St, Carlton, Victoria 3053 ☎ 03 8379 8000, fax 03 8379 8111

USA 150 Linden Street, Oakland, CA 94607 ☎ 510 250 6400, toll free 800 275 8555, fax 510 893 8572

UK 240 Blackfriars Road, London SE1 8NW ☎ 020 3771 5100, fax 020 3771 5101

 twitter.com/lonelyplanet
 facebook.com/lonelyplanet
 instagram.com/lonelyplanet
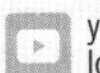 youtube.com/lonelyplanet
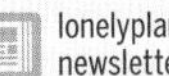 lonelyplanet.com/newsletter